URBAN GUERRILLA PROTEST

URBAN GUERRILLA PROTEST
[RECLAIM 95-05]

RECLAIM 9FIVE » 05

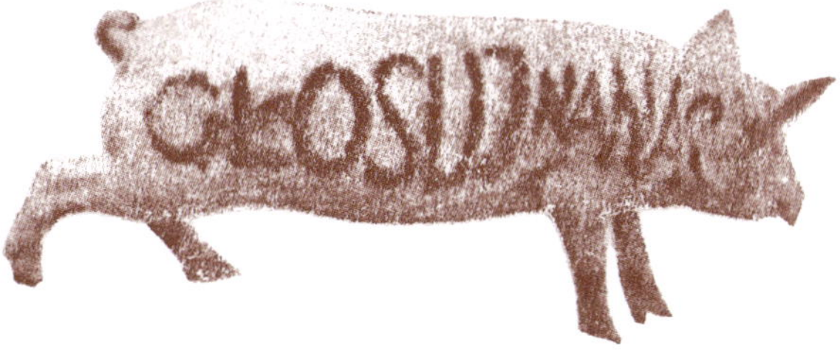

Researched, edited and designed by Ake Rudolf
(2003-2005). Reviewed and digitalised in 2007

Published by Mark Batty Publisher,
New York City (2008)

Designed in a hand-made layout using mixed media, printouts, photocopy enlargement and Letraset fonts. Originally printed on a 5-colour toner copy machine. Text font based on Interstate, adjusted to the original photocopy appearance.

My respect to all those featured in this book.

For Armida & Lina

«Vote For Us» Demonstration graphics (Poland, 1980s)

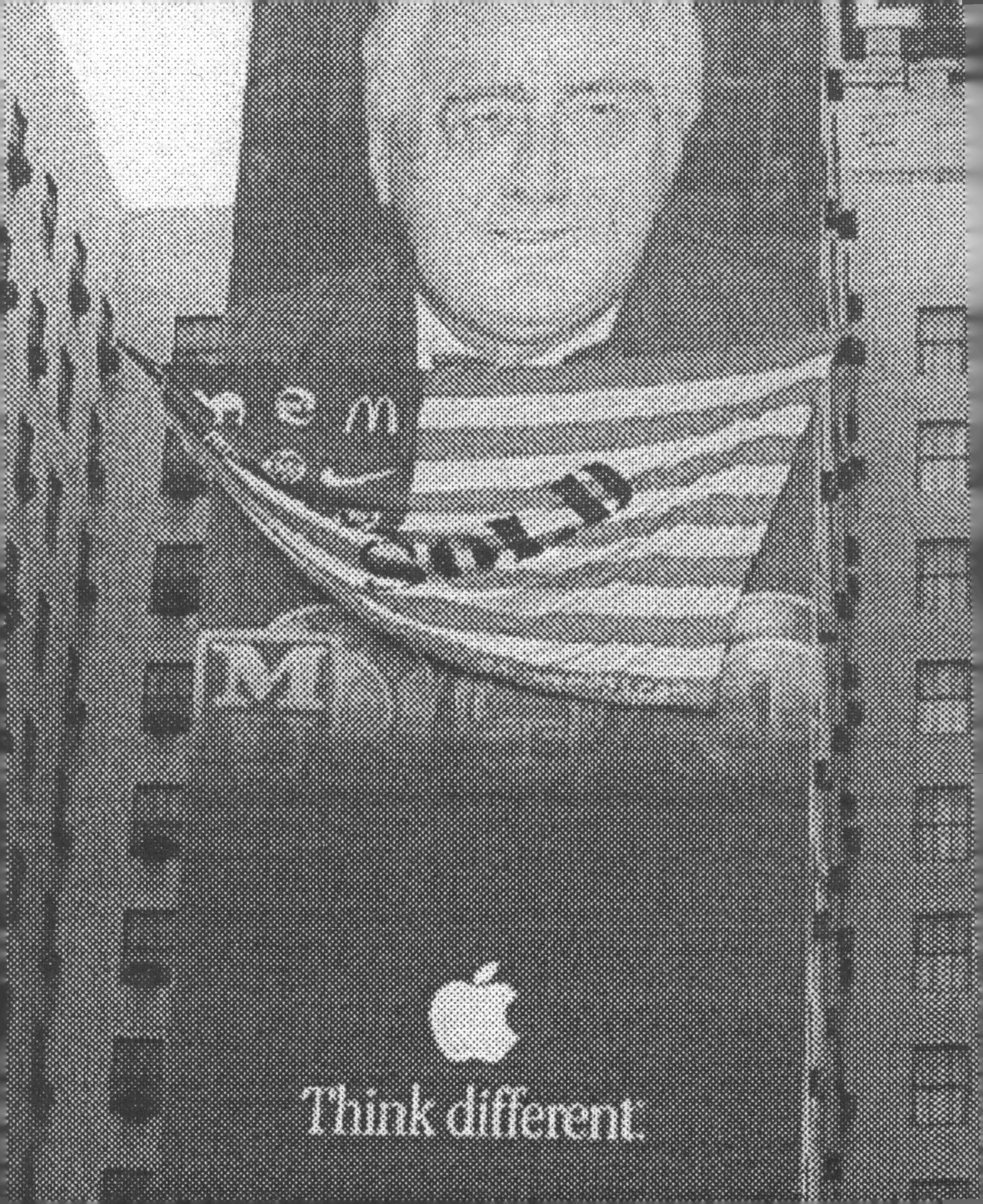
Think different.

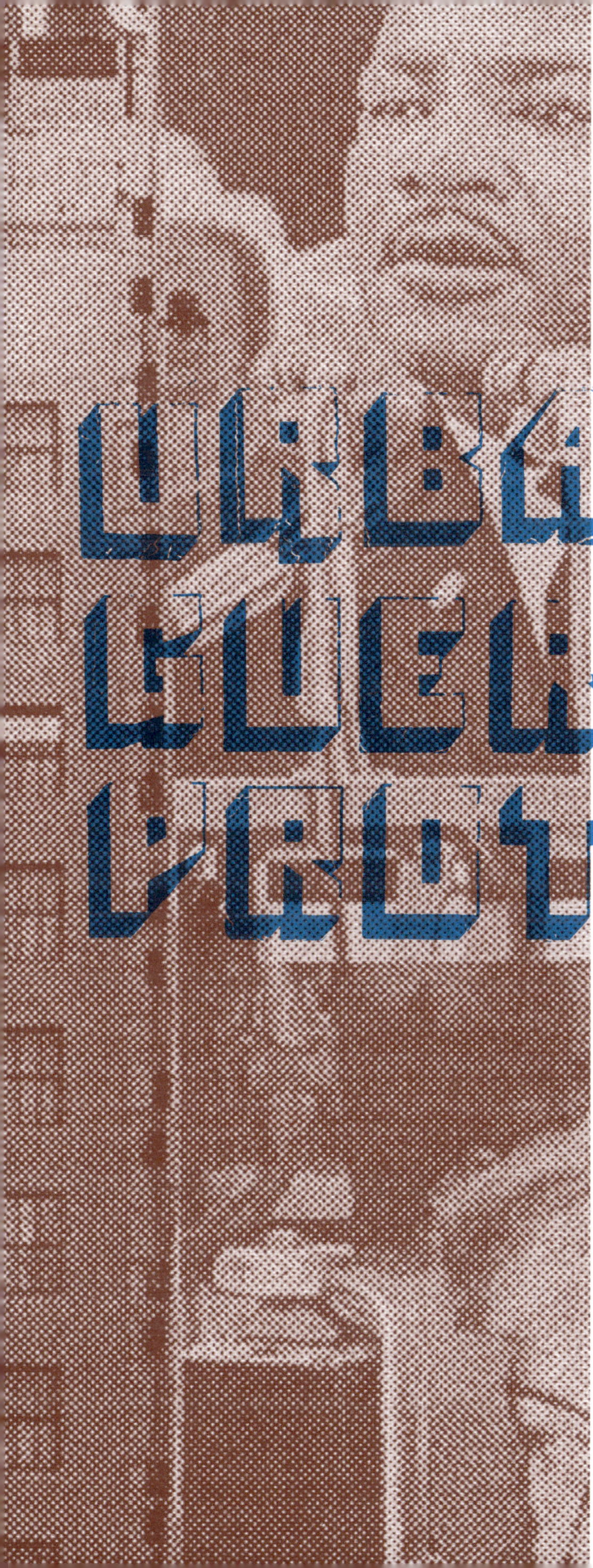

URBAN GUERRILLA PROTEST

The Ruckus Society > 55 / ruckus.org (USA / int.)

This book features the ways and means of individual, subversive protest actions; they are real initiatives that use accessible resources to place messages in the heart of the everyday – sometimes in very surprising ways.

They use infiltration tactics, performances, create confusion and moments of surprise. Existing codes and behavioural patterns get tangled up and estranged; fakes, pranks and satire unveil the hidden facets of society and its institutions.

Subversive communication practices mediate disobedience and visual insubordination. They create new meaning in consciously chosen situations.

This book covers the years between 1995 and 2005. This period saw the rise of many technical developments that benefited the «media-guerrilla». Communication had been revolutionised by the rise of the internet. The availability of modern production methods made and makes planning and executing deceptions easy.

This book is a purely theoretical documentation of unusual protest forms. By no means should it be used as an inspiration for future work of this kind. Enjoy the reading.

Dieses Buch stellt Wege und Mittel des individuellen, subversiven Protests vor – in einer Momentaufnahme realer Aktionen, die mit jedermann zugänglichen Mitteln es geschafft haben, ihre Positionen überraschend im Zentrum des Alltags zu plazieren.

Benutzt werden Taktiken der Infiltration, der Performance, Verwirrung und Überraschung. Existierende Codes und Verhaltenssysteme werden verändert und entfremdet, Fälschung und Satire legen die versteckten Facetten der Gesellschaft und ihrer Institutionen frei.

Subversive Kommunikation praktiziert mediales Ungehorsam und visuelle Insubordination. Sie setzt an ausgewählten Orten an und schafft neue Kontexte.

Das Buch umfasst die Jahre 1995 bis 2005; dieser Moment brachte technische Entwicklungen mit sich, die den «Medienguerrilleros» in die Hände spielen. Die Kommunikation wurde durch das Internet revolutioniert; allgemein zugängliche technische Arbeitsmittel machen die Planung und Realisierung von perfekten Täuschungen möglich.

Dieses Buch ist eine reine Dokumentation ungewöhnlicher Protestformen und sollte in keiner Weise als eine Inspiration für weitere Arbeiten dieser Art verstanden werden. Viel Vergnügen bei der Lektüre.

it's our playground

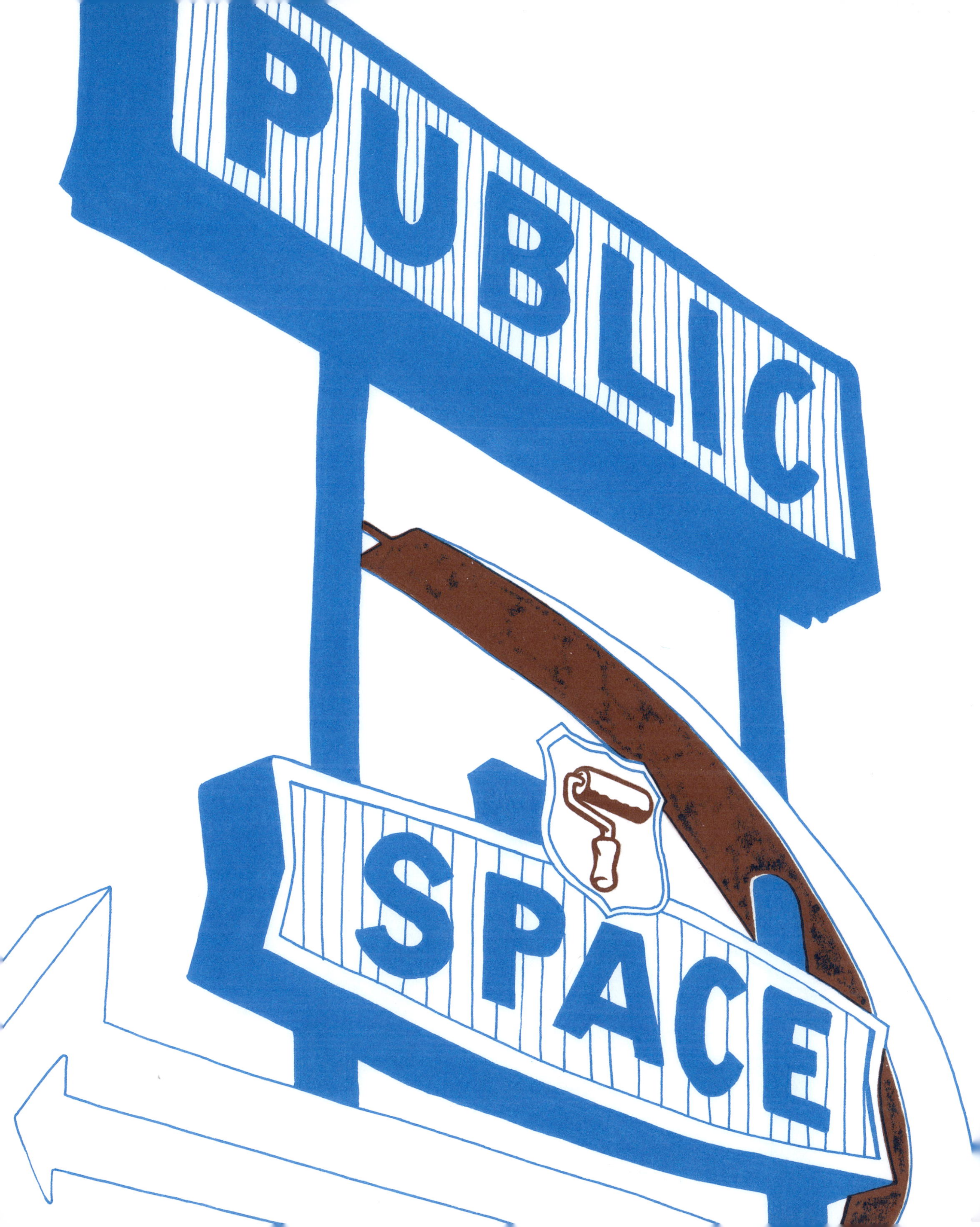
PUBLIC
SPACE

CONT

ENTS

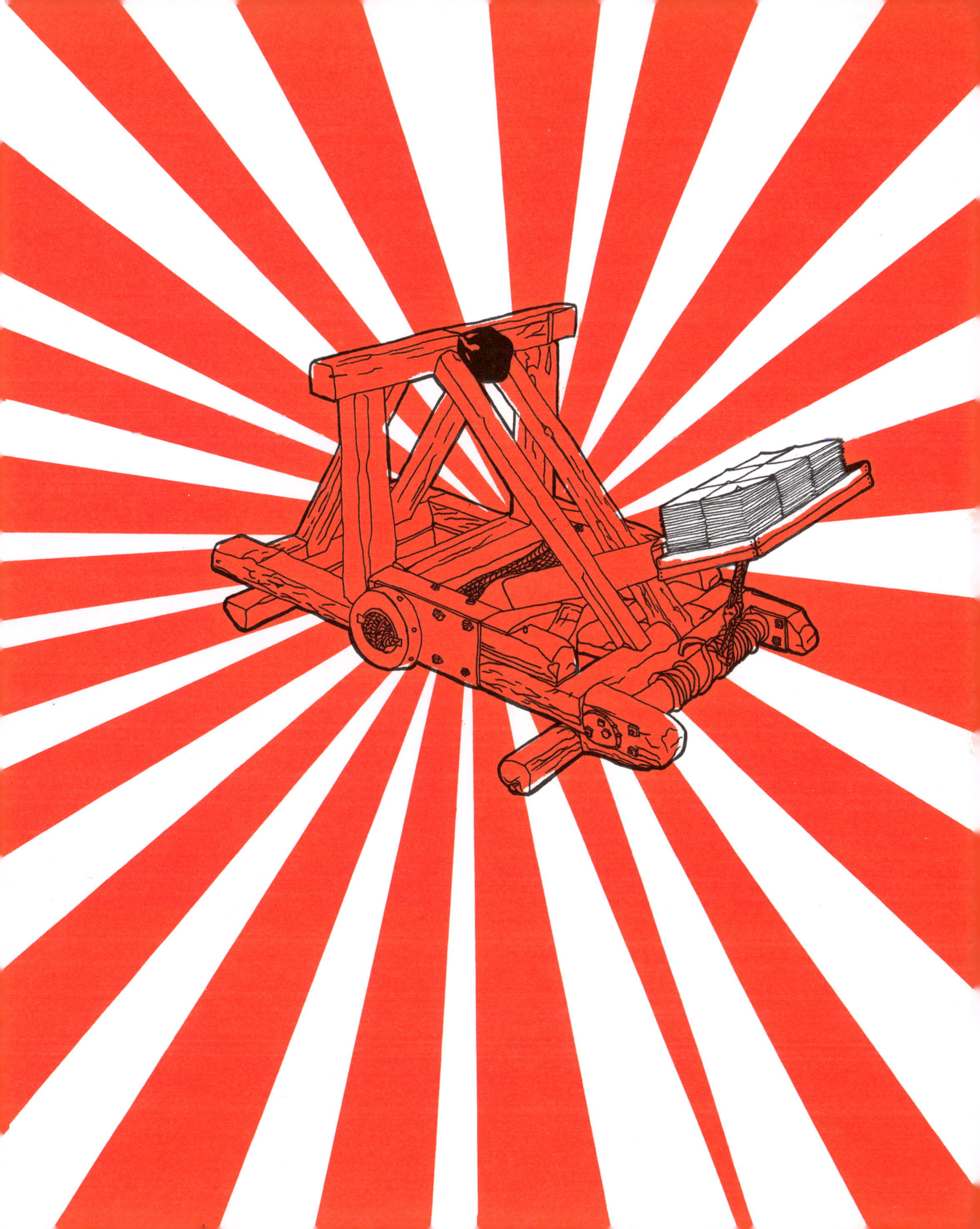

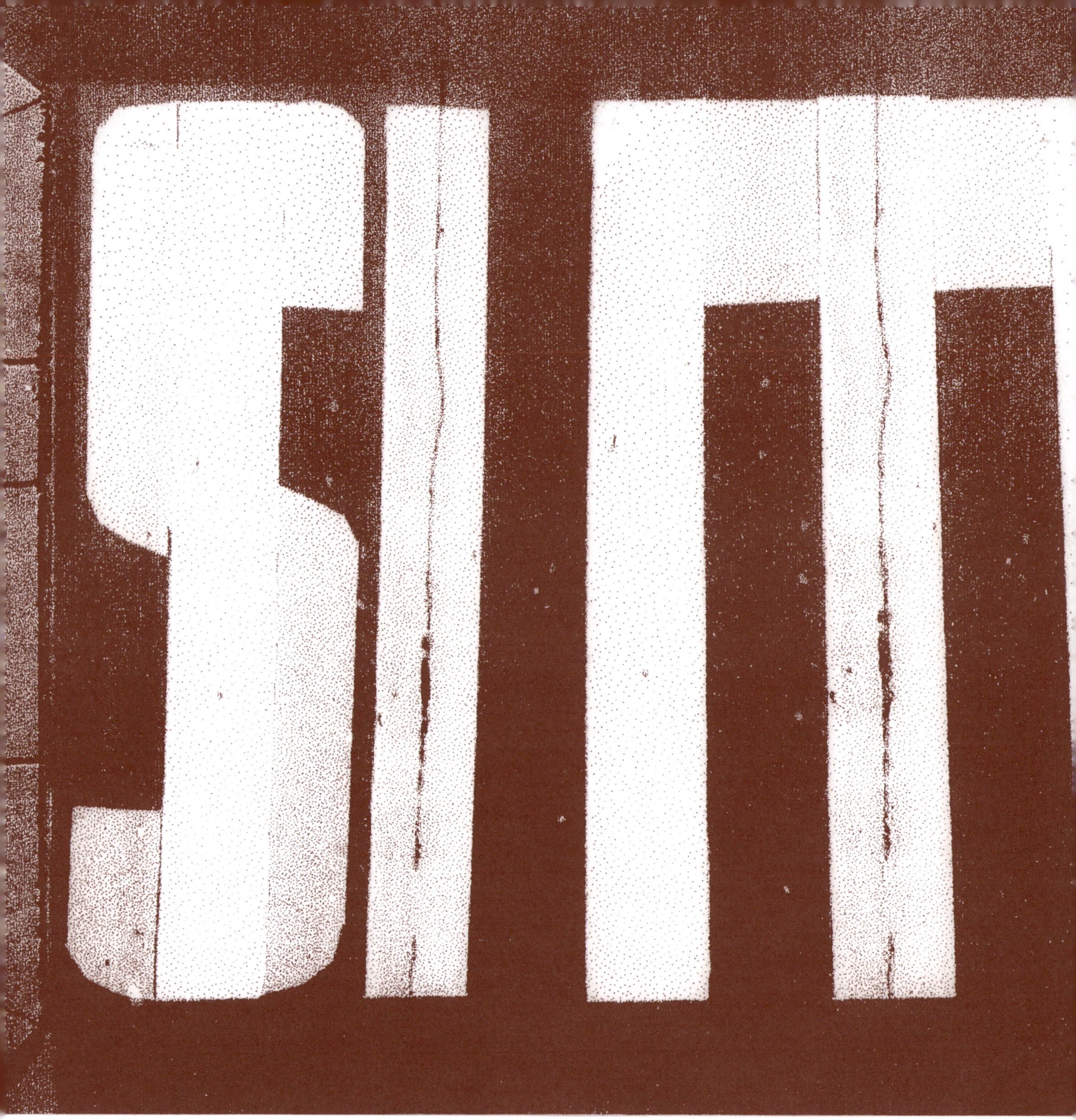

Simple Means. Ordinary, of daily use, already existing objects and situations - found and used to one's own goals. The immediate way to leave a message. Chance offers a medium, the gift is accepted and used. The plainness of the methods shouldn't be regarded as a limitation only. Interventions of this kind are open to anybody passing by, therefore giving an incentive to get involved within the mutual urban space. To some, re-arranging boards to form letters and changing adverisement texts may not seem to be outright protest but rather a simple prank. But behind these there is an unwillingness to put up with the given conditions and the will to change them. Without such intellectual autonomy there's no way for protest to exist. And if used well simple means can have great effects, too.

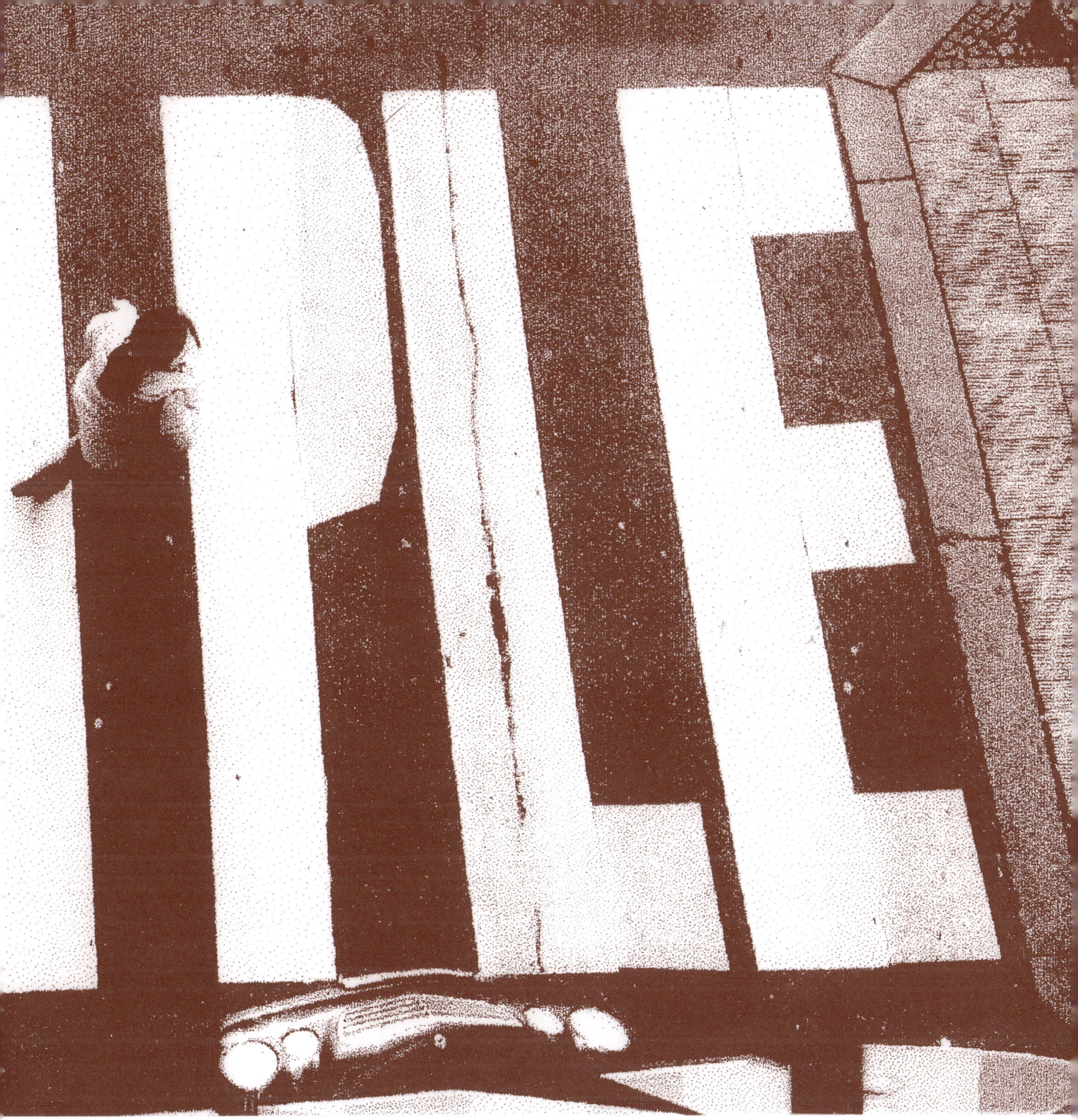

Einfache Mittel. Gewöhnlich, alltäglich; vorgefunden und für eigene Zwecke umgenutzt. Der direkteste Weg, um eine Botschaft zu hinterlassen. Der Zufall stellt ein Medium zur Verfügung und das Geschenk wird genutzt. Die Einfachheit der genutzten Mittel sollte nicht als Beschränkung missverstanden werden. Eingriffe dieser Art stehen jeden offen und sind so ein Anreiz zur Teilnahme innerhalb des gemeinsam genutzten Raumes. Das arrangieren von Brettern zu Worten oder das verdrehen von Werbeschriftzügen mag vielleicht nicht unmittelbar als ein Protest lesbar sein, eher als ein Streich. Doch hinter dem sich nicht abfinden wollen mit den gegebenen Verhältnissen und dem Willen zur Veränderung steckt eine geistige Autonomie, ohne der Protest nicht existieren kann.

 1 Jeroen Jongeleen > 23, 40-41

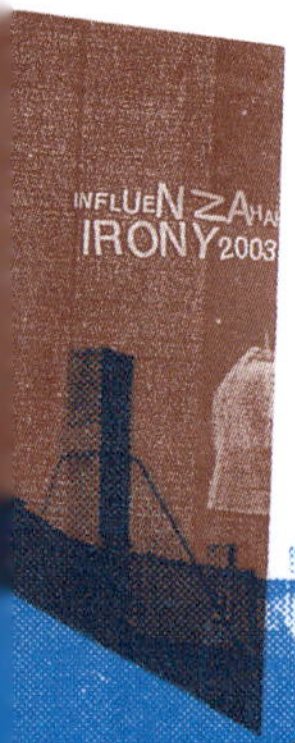

1

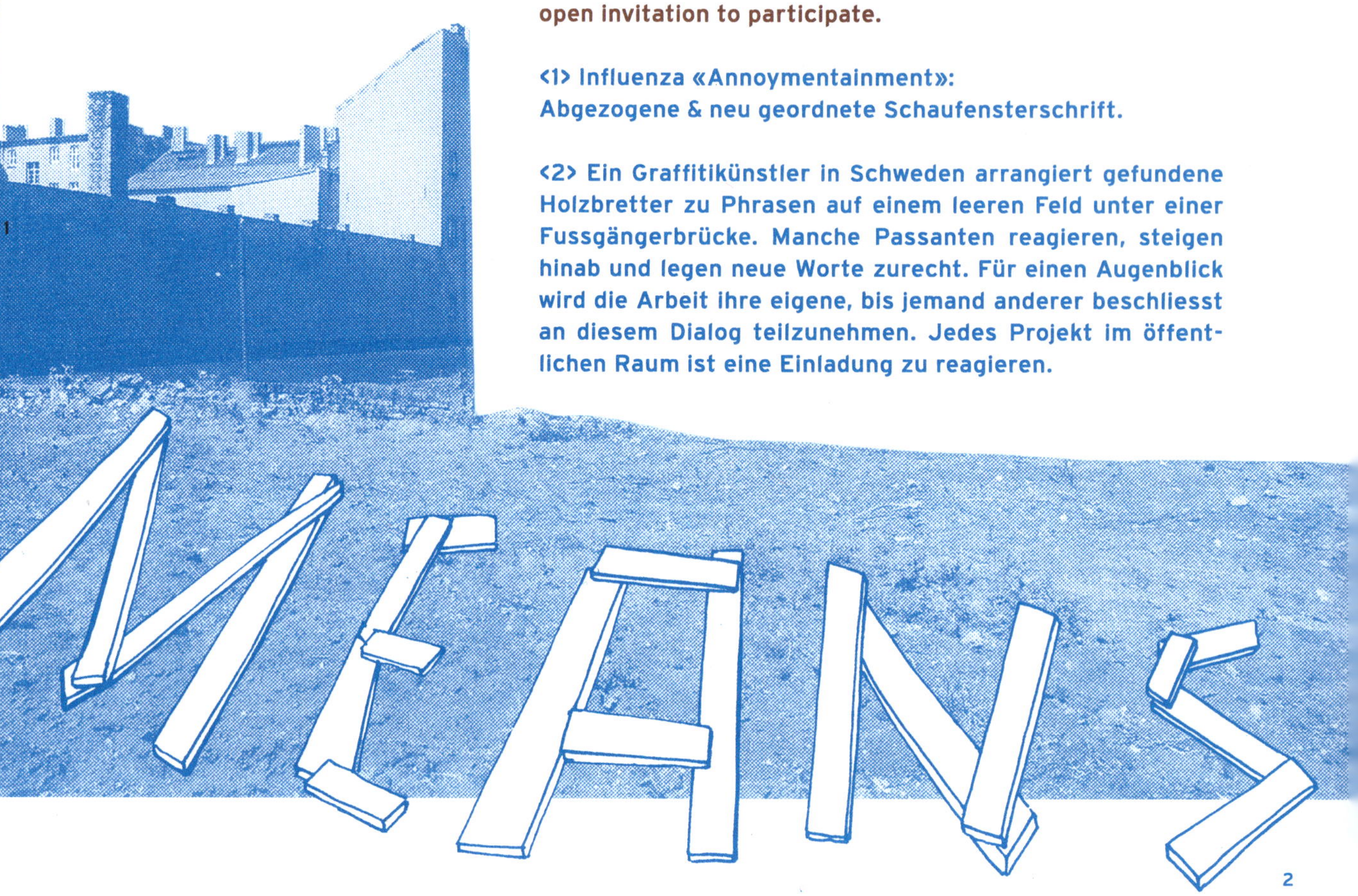

2

<1> Influenza «Annoymentainment»:
Peeled off & rearranged shop-window typography.

<2> An urban artist arranges white wooden boards to form catchphrases in an empty lot, overlooked by a pedestrian bridge in Sweden. People actually respond by climbing down and creating new words and phrases. For an instance the work becomes his or her own until someone else decides to take part in the dialogue. Just like any public project it's an open invitation to participate.

<1> Influenza «Annoymentainment»:
Abgezogene & neu geordnete Schaufensterschrift.

<2> Ein Graffitikünstler in Schweden arrangiert gefundene Holzbretter zu Phrasen auf einem leeren Feld unter einer Fussgängerbrücke. Manche Passanten reagieren, steigen hinab und legen neue Worte zurecht. Für einen Augenblick wird die Arbeit ihre eigene, bis jemand anderer beschliesst an diesem Dialog teilzunehmen. Jedes Projekt im öffentlichen Raum ist eine Einladung zu reagieren.

B

Busy Marquee «The idea behind BM is very simple: find signs that have interchangeable letters and rearrange omnipresent advertising to form Dadaist bits of landscape. Many of these signs require procuring a suction-cup pole to reach the letters. Look around if you can find an unlocked tool shed close to the target building; often the poles are kept there.» Quote: Busy Marquee

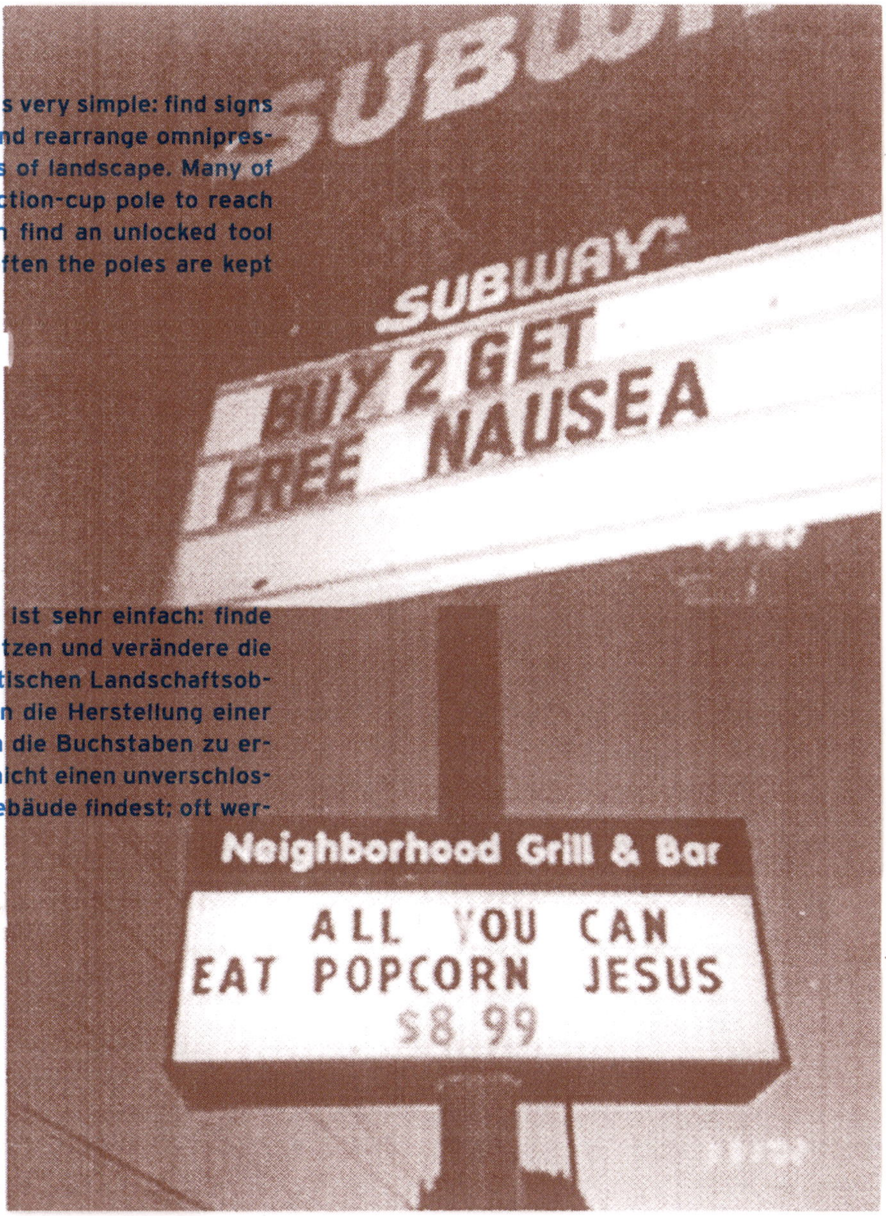

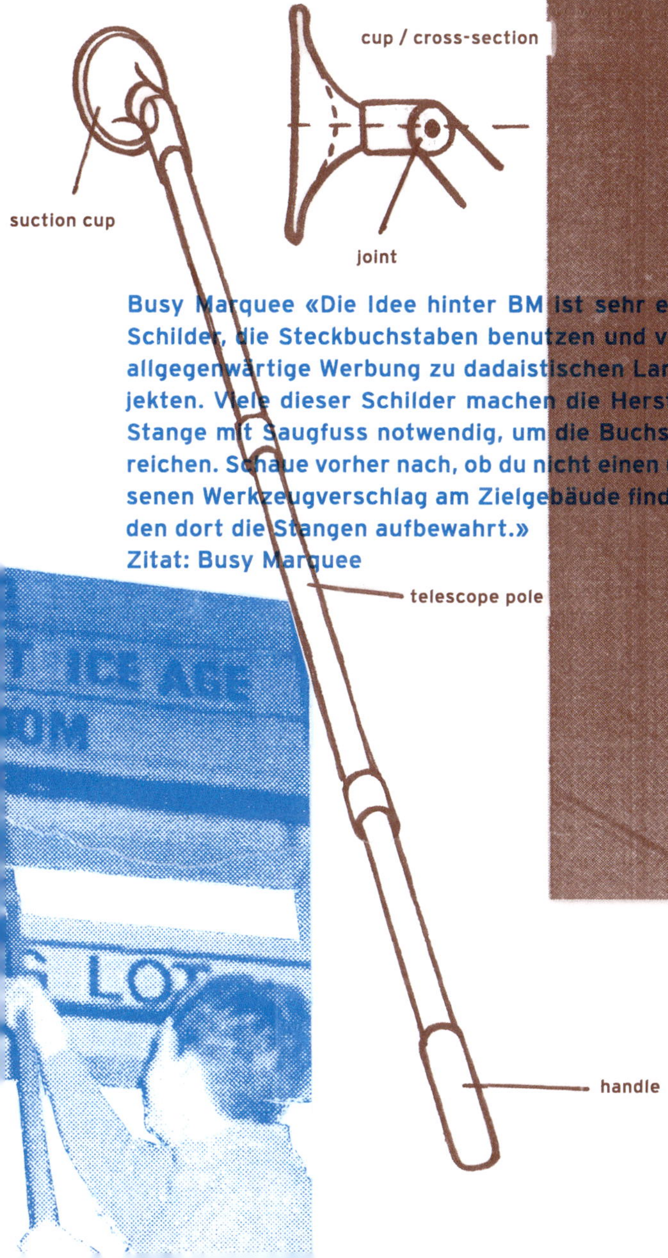

Busy Marquee «Die Idee hinter BM ist sehr einfach: finde Schilder, die Steckbuchstaben benutzen und verändere die allgegenwärtige Werbung zu dadaistischen Landschaftsobjekten. Viele dieser Schilder machen die Herstellung einer Stange mit Saugfuss notwendig, um die Buchstaben zu erreichen. Schaue vorher nach, ob du nicht einen unverschlossenen Werkzeugverschlag am Zielgebäude findest; oft werden dort die Stangen aufbewahrt.»
Zitat: Busy Marquee

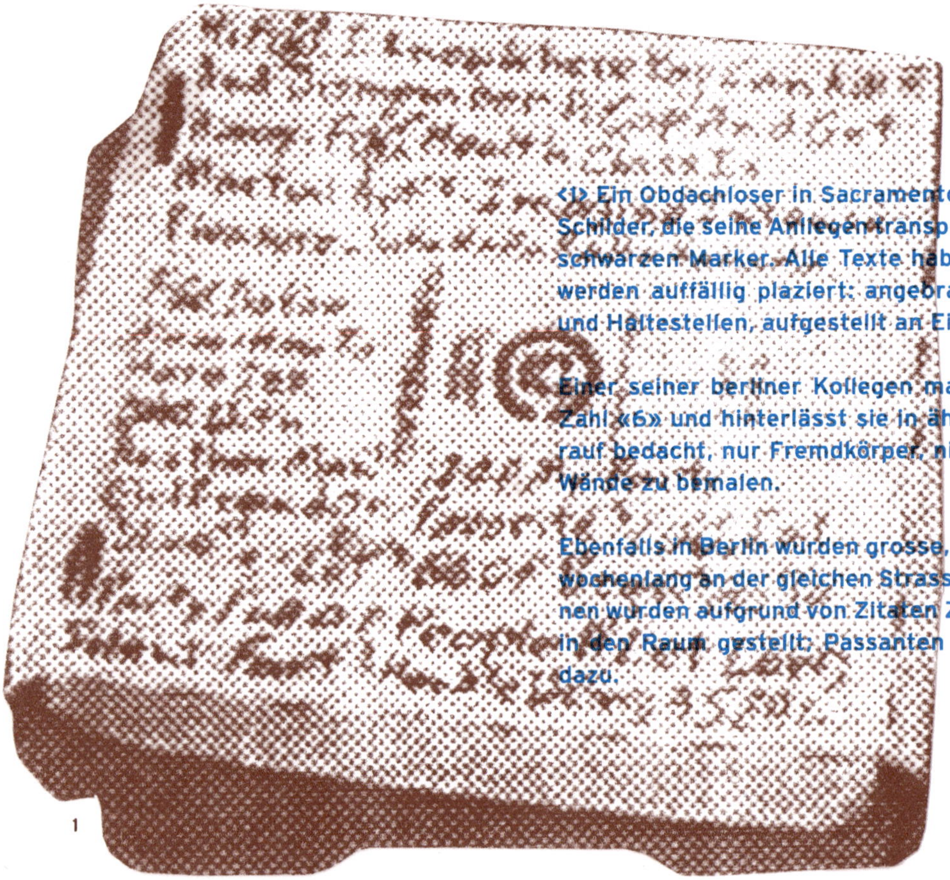

1

<1> Ein Obdachloser in Sacramento (USA) hinterlässt kleine Schilder, die seine Anliegen transportieren. Er benutzt einen schwarzen Marker. Alle Texte haben politische Inhalte und werden auffällig plaziert: angebracht auf Bäume, Pfosten und Haltestellen, aufgestellt an Eingängen und so weiter.

Einer seiner berliner Kollegen malt seit vielen Jahren die Zahl «6» und hinterlässt sie in ähnlicher Weise: immer darauf bedacht, nur Fremdkörper, nie direkt die Strasse oder Wände zu bemalen.

Ebenfalls in Berlin wurden grosse, handgeschriebene Tafeln wochenlang an der gleichen Strassenecke abgestellt. Auf ihnen wurden aufgrund von Zitaten Zweifel am «Terrorkampf» in den Raum gestellt; Passanten schrieben die Antworten dazu.

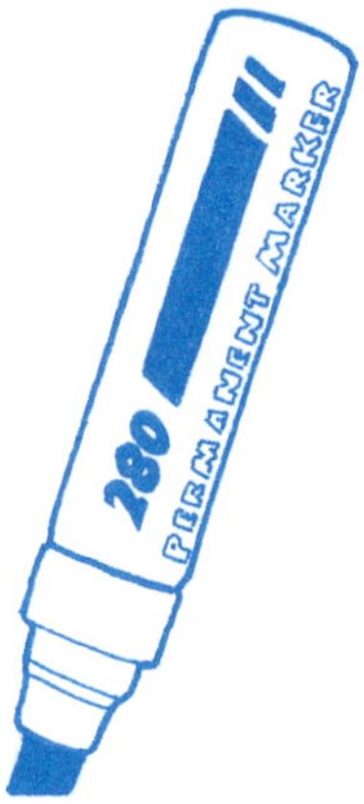

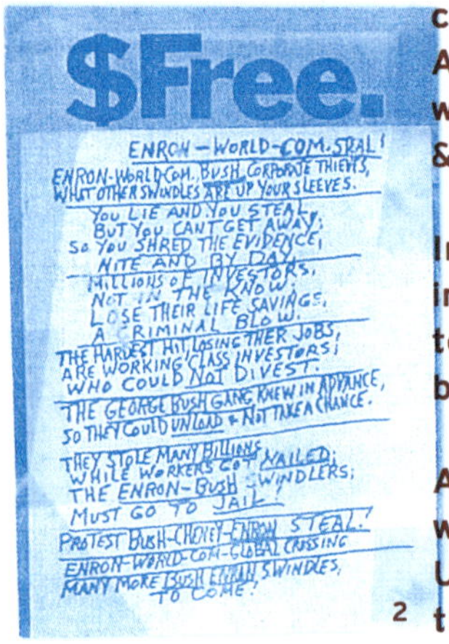

2

<1> A homeless man leaves little signs that address his concerns in Sacramento (USA). He uses a black marker.
All signs have political content and are being left behind in a way that makes them stand out: attached to trees, bus stops & posts, propped up against doorways, etc.

In a similar way, a colleague of his in Berlin keeps on painting the number «6» on surfaces, painstakingly careful never to touch the walls or streets directly, just the objects left by others.

Also in Berlin: for weeks on end, big hand-written placards were left always on the same street corner.
Using quotations, they addressed problems connected to the «War on Terror». Passersby added their comments.

1 in: cockeyed.com, Sacramento (USA) / 2 NYC (USA)

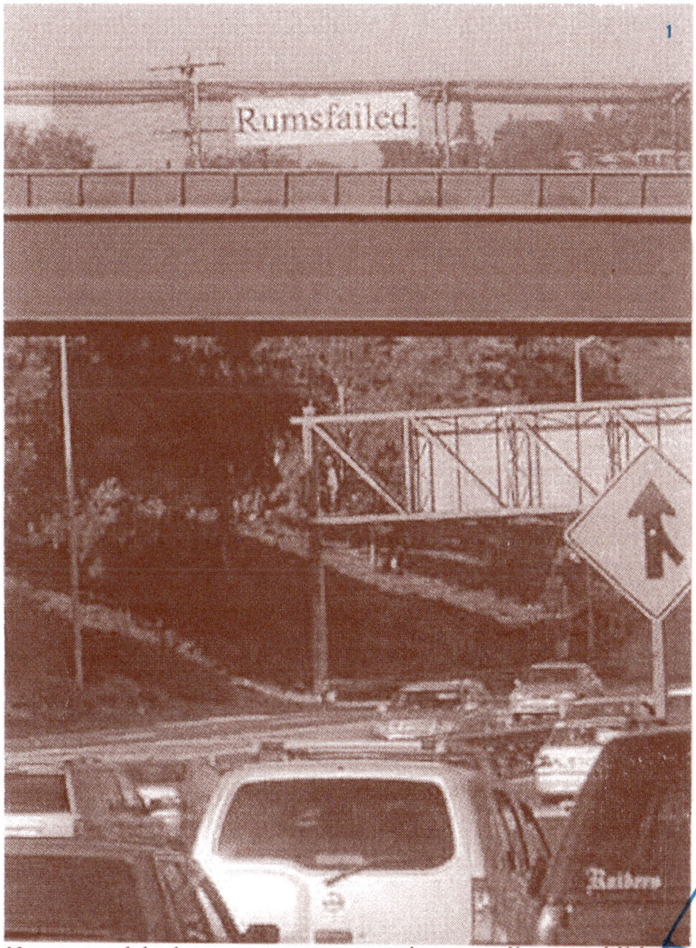

If you want to leave a message grab a pencil; as a child you started to draw and write on the pavement using chalk or brick.

Wer eine Botschaft für andere hinterlassen will greift zum Stift; bereits Kinder beginnen mit Kreide oder einem Stück Ziegel auf die Strasse zu zeichnen und zu schreiben.

Large signs can be made by hand-tracing a text that's projected on a surface with a slide projector or episcope, or by enlarging and tiling with a photocopier. For a detailed description see «Billboard Liberation Front» (pages 43-48).

Grosse Schilder können durch Projektion und Nachzeichnung eines Textes mithilfe eines Diaprojektors oder Episkops hergestellt werden, oder durch Vergrösserung mit einem Fotokopierer. Für eine detaillierte Beschreibung siehe «Billboard Liberation Front» (Seiten 43-48).

2

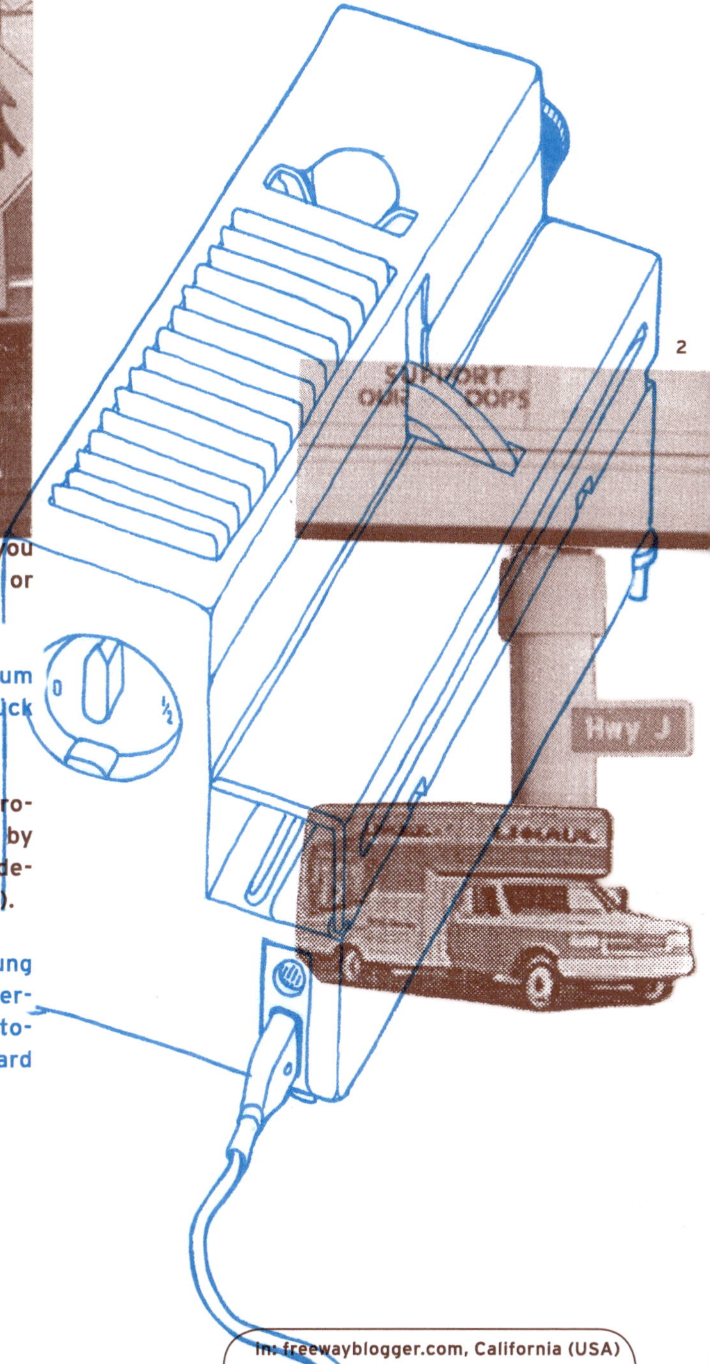

 TWCDC: Stock exchange, May Day 2000 Project

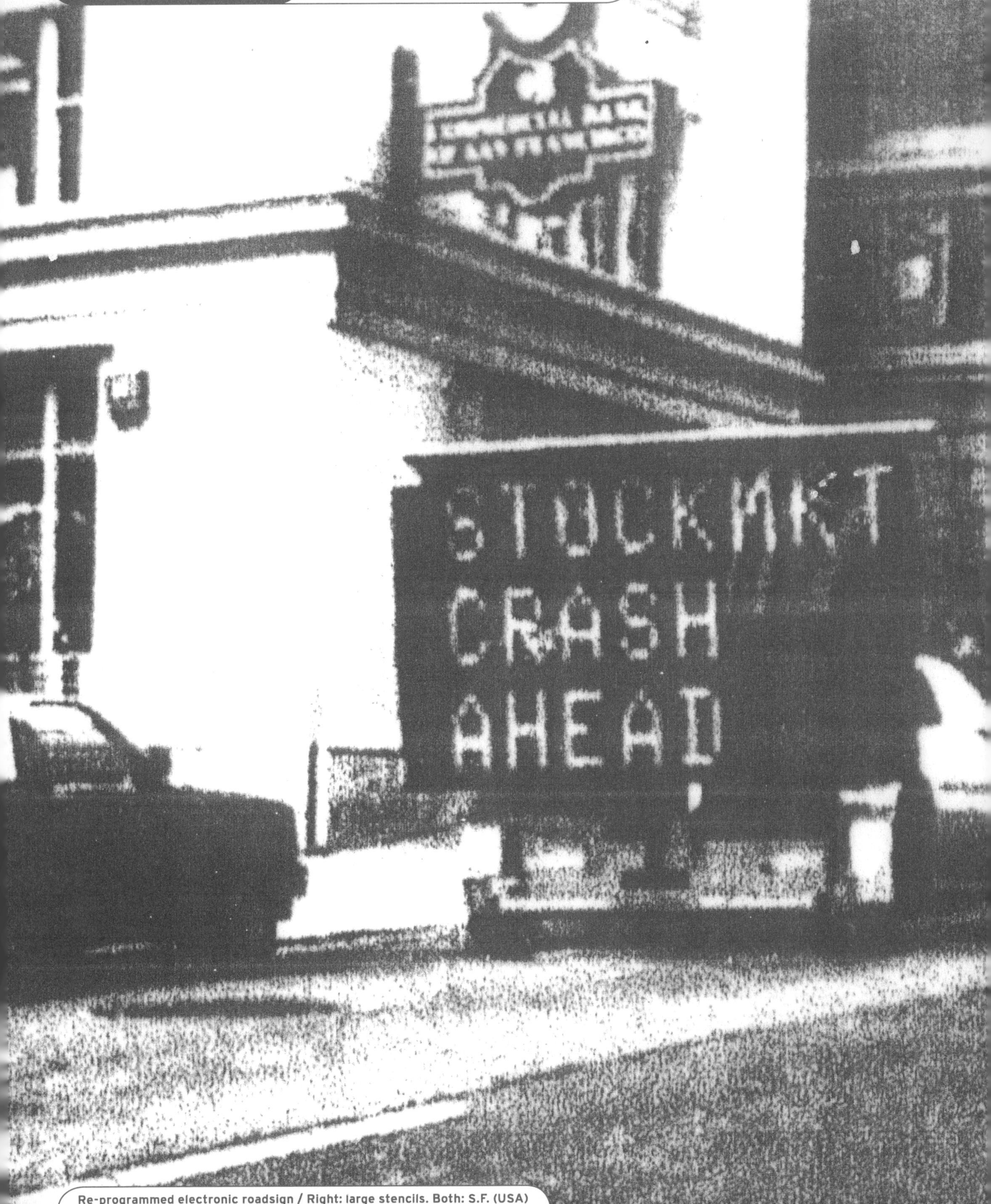

Re-programmed electronic roadsign / Right: large stencils. Both: S.F. (USA)

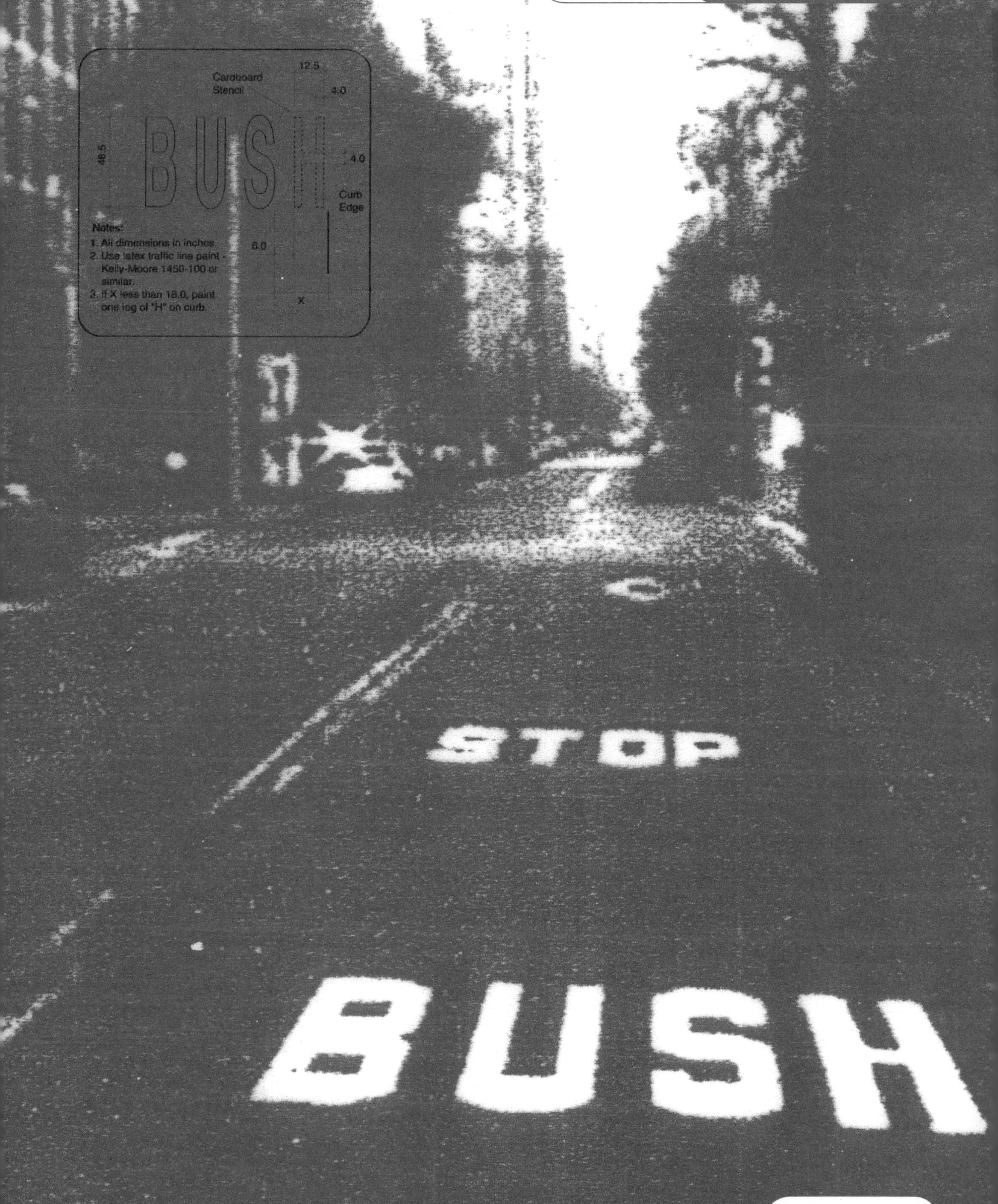

twcdc.com, S.F. (USA)

Cutting

Got a knife in your pocket? Then you could become part of the tradition of the «Affichistes» and «Décollagistes» (Rotella, Hains, Dufrene and others), who introduced to the art world around the end of the 1950s the cutting-up and partial removing of advertisement posters.

The removed espresso-girl is the only cut-and-run work by Zevs, who usually attacks models' images with paint dots and lines. You can cut out whole bodies, parts or just the eyes (and stick them back twisted round), as you wish. The large tarpaulins have the advantage of being fixed on scaffoldings that can be used as comfortable working platforms, without any danger of being spotted from street level.

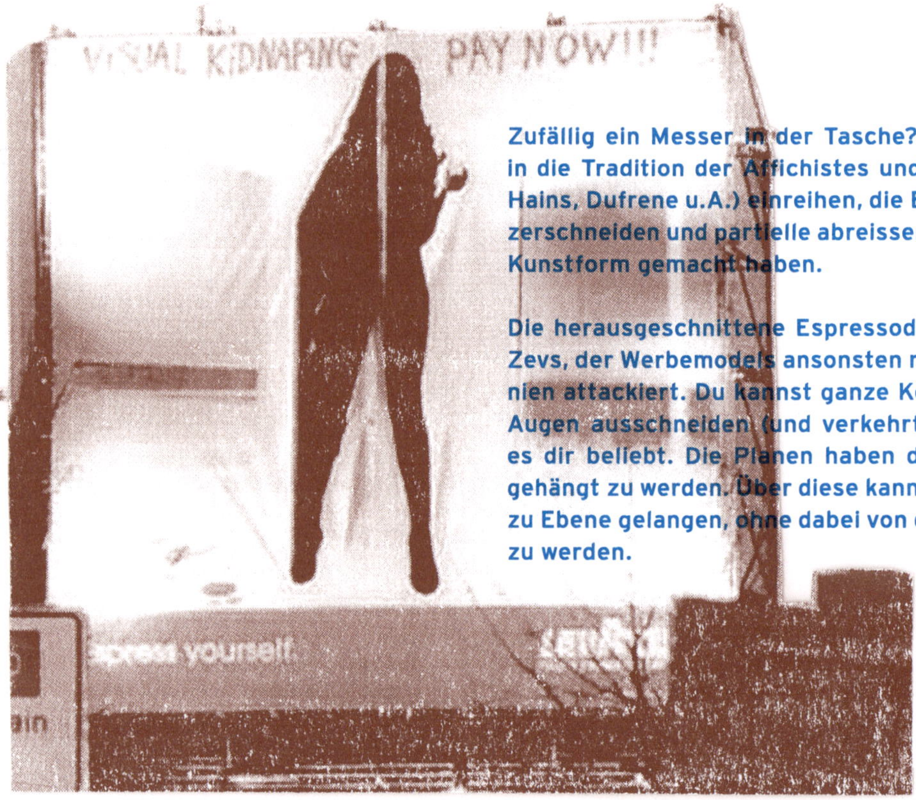

Zufällig ein Messer in der Tasche? Dann könntest du dich in die Tradition der Affichistes und Décollagistes (Rotella, Hains, Dufrene u.A.) einreihen, die Ende der 50er Jahre das zerschneiden und partielle abreissen von Werbeplakaten zur Kunstform gemacht haben.

Die herausgeschnittene Espressodame ist eine Arbeit von Zevs, der Werbemodels ansonsten mit Farbpunkten oder Linien attackiert. Du kannst ganze Körper, Teile oder nur die Augen ausschneiden (und verkehrt wieder einsetzen), wie es dir beliebt. Die Planen haben den Vorteil, auf Gerüste gehängt zu werden. Über diese kann man bequem von Ebene zu Ebene gelangen, ohne dabei von der Strasse aus gesehen zu werden.

up

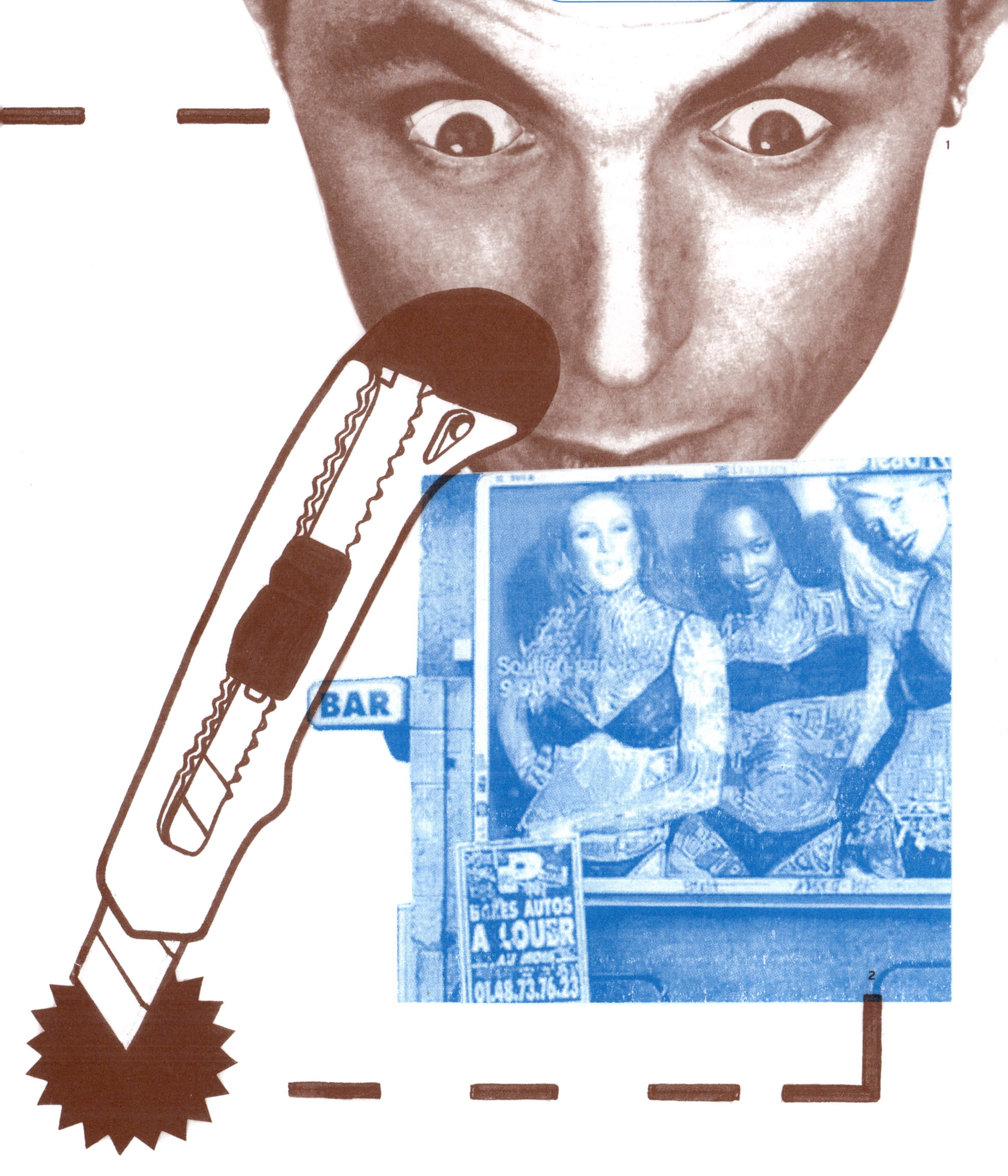

1 Cut and twisted facade ads, Berlin (Germany), int. / 2 Paris (France)

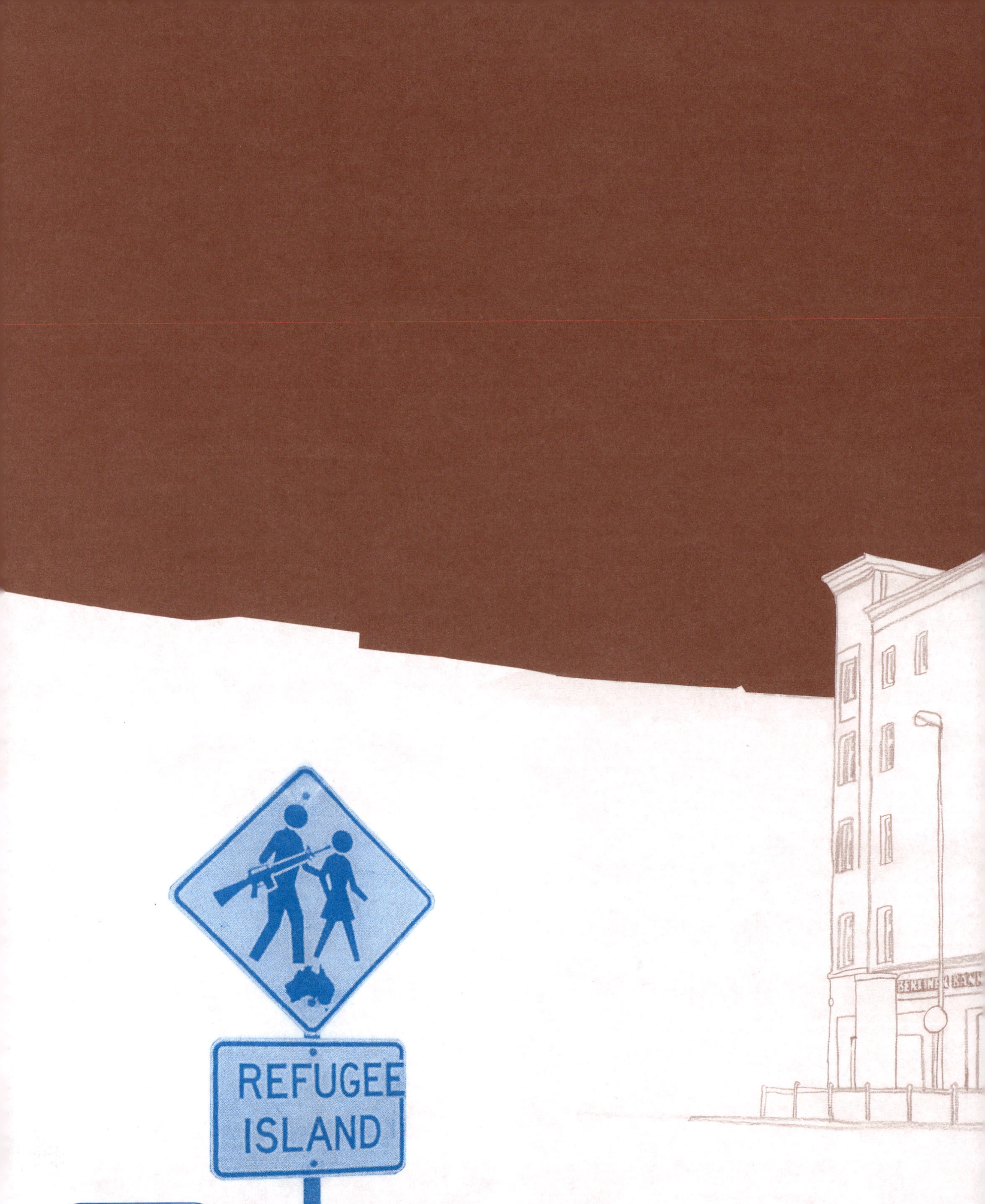

unknown (Australia)

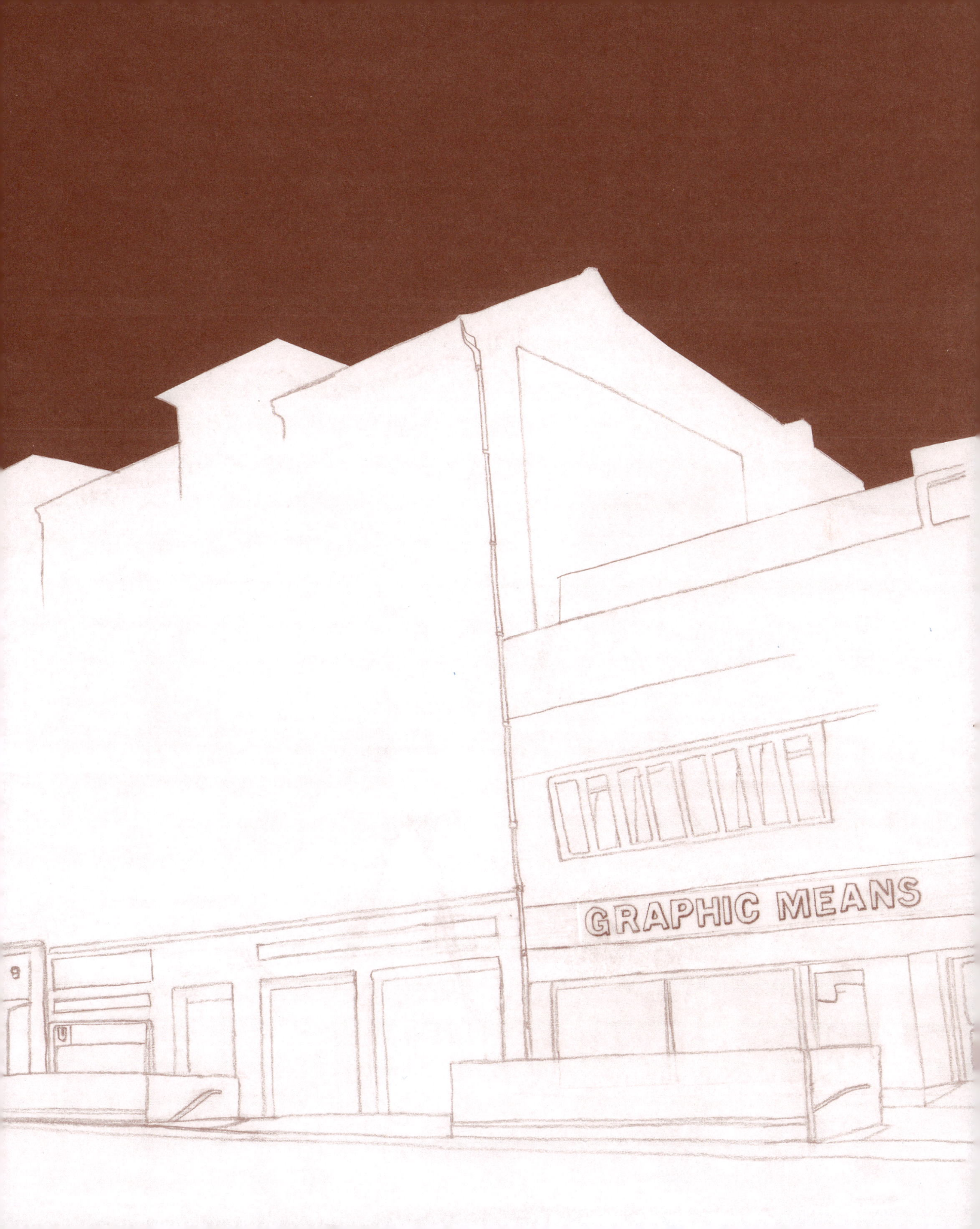
GRAPHIC MEANS

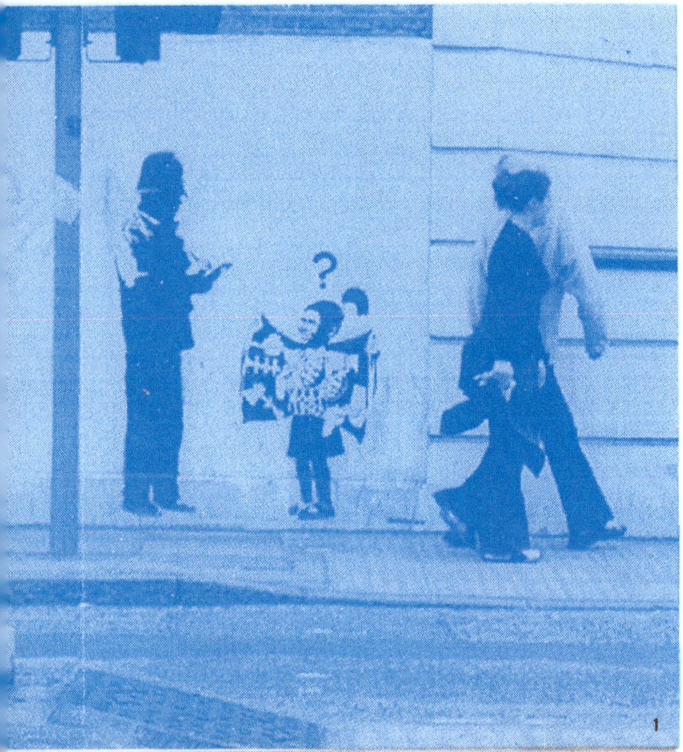
1

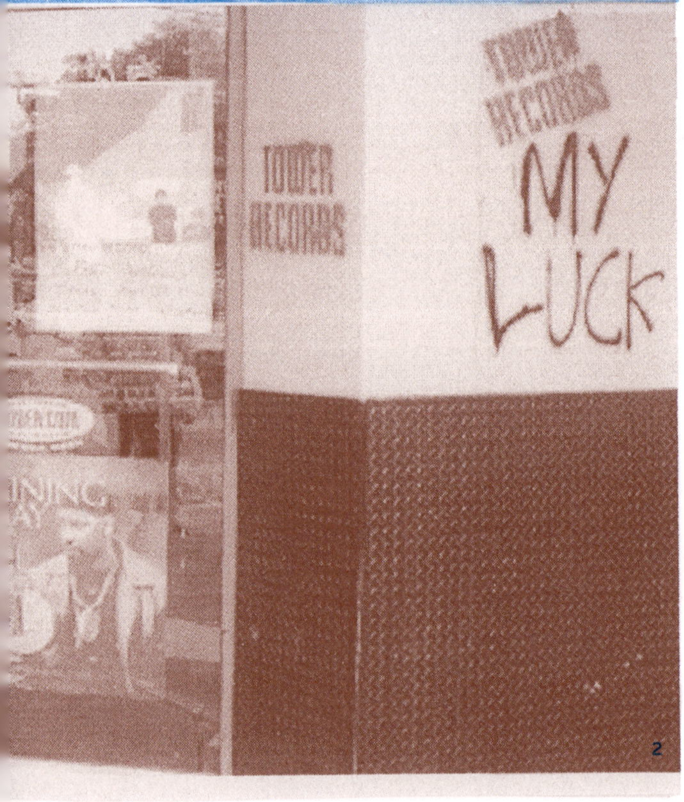

2

Stencils or «pochoirs» are applied with paint or spray paint, a protest technique with a long tradition. Using stiff cardboard and a sharp knife you can cut a form that can be used again and again. Stencils are quick to apply on almost any surface (affix with pieces of Gaffa-tape to avoid spraying your hands).

The protest technique gave birth to an art movement (Paris became its centre in the 80s), and both have complemented each other ever since. There are countless forms of stencils and graffiti, so just a few are shown here. For more go to: > artcrimes.com > stencilrevolution.com or > woostercollective.com

Schablonengraffitis oder 'pochoirs', mit Farbpinsel oder Sprühdose aufgetragen, sind eine Protesttechnik mit langer Tradition. Mit einer Schablone können Bilder oder Texte praktisch endlos wiederholt werden, benötigt werden lediglich Karton und ein scharfes Messer. Sie können schnell und praktisch auf jeder Oberfläche hinterlassen werden (benutze Gaffa-Tape, um dir nicht auf die Hände zu sprühen).

Aus der Protesttechnik ist eine Kunstform hervorgegangen, (Paris in den 80er Jahren war ein Zentrum) welche sich mit dem Protest vermischt und ergänzt. Es gibt endlos viele Arten von 'pochoirs' und Graffiti, hier deshalb nur eine Handvoll. Mehr unter > artcrimes.com > stencilrevolution.com und > woostercollective.com.

<2> The stencils' serial qualities come in handy for the group «Re-Tag» in Austin (USA), who use their own logotype stencils to re-invade the walls of branded stores. According to their philosophy, once a logotype reaches total universal recognition it's time for it to be returned to its sender.

<2> Die seriellen Eigenschaft der Schablonen benutzt die Gruppe «Re-Tag» in Austin (USA) für eine RetourInvasion der Markenlogos. Die globale Verbreitung der Zeichen hätte das Ziel einer totalen Wiedererkennung erreicht, die Logos könnten nun an ihre Ursprünge zurückkehren, so «Re-Tag».

<1,4> If you still need some advice, go to Banksy's homepage (see below).

<1,4> Falls du noch eine Handvoll guter Ratschläge brauchst, lies dir Banksy's Homepage (s. unten) durch.

1 banksy.co.uk, London (UK), in Berlin (Germany) / 2 conglomco.org/retag, Austin (USA)

Worldwide protests were staged in 2003 in an effort to dissuade those national leaders pushing for a renewed war in the Persian Gulf region. Many artists took part in their own way.

<3> Blek's soldier remained for days on end in front of Check Point Charlie in Berlin (Germany).

<5> The collective game «The Art of Urban Warfare» re-enacted fighting in '1st World' cities, with images of toy soldiers competing for urban space:

«THE ART OF URBAN WARFARE IS PLAYED IN THE STREETS OF OUR CITIES + THE ART OF URBAN WARFARE IS MADE VISIBLE BY SPRAYED SILHOUETTE STENCILS ON THE WALLS + THE STENCILS USED IN THE GAME HAVE THE SHAPE OF TOY SOLDIERS IN ACTION + THERE ARE THREE MAJOR TEAMS DISTINCT FROM EACH OTHER BY COLOURS: THE GREEN, THE BROWN AND THE BLUE + THE AIM IS TO OCCUPY THE STREETS WITH THE CHOSEN ARMY COLOUR, MAKING THE GAME VISIBLE TO OTHERS + THERE IS NO LIMIT TO THE NUMBER OF PLAYERS IN THE GAME + EVERY PERSON IS FREE TO JOIN THE GAME AS PARTICIPANT»

2003 wurden weltweite Proteste organisiert in der Hoffnung, kriegswillige Regierungschefs doch noch umstimmen zu können. Viele Künstler nahmen auf ihre Weise teil.

<3> Blek's Soldat blieb tagelang am Checkpoint Charlie in Berlin stehen.

<5> Das kollektive Spiel «The Art of Urban Warfare» brachte den Krieg in die Städte der '1. Welt'. Stellvertretend trugen Bilder von Spielzeugsoldaten den Kampf um den urbanen Raum aus:

«ART OF URBAN WARFARE WIRD IN DEN STRASSEN DER STÄDTE GESPIELT. ART OF URBAN WARFARE WIRD SICHTBAR DURCH GESPRÜHTE SCHABLONEN AN DEN WÄNDEN + DIE SCHABLONEN HABEN DIE FORM VON SPIELZEUGSOLDATEN + ES GIBT DREI TEAMS MIT DEN FARBEN GRÜN, BLAU UND BRAUN + DAS ZIEL DES SPIELS IST ES, DIE STRASSEN MIT DER GEWÄHLTEN ARMEE-FARBE ZU BESETZEN UND SO DAS SPIEL FÜR ANDERE SICHTBAR ZU MACHEN + DIE ANZAHL DER SPIELER IST UNBEGRENZT, JEDER KANN TEILNEHMEN»

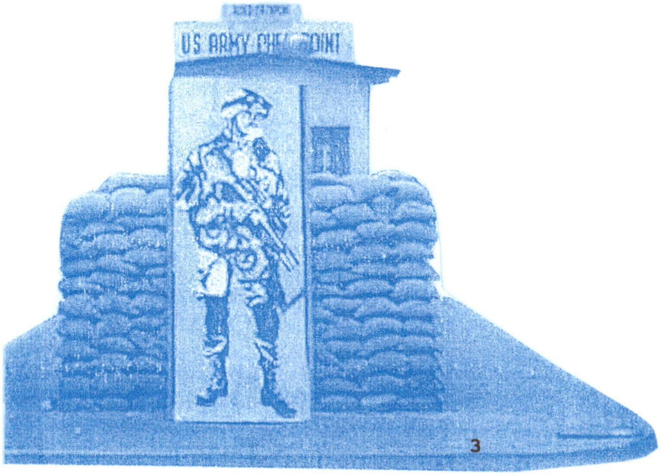

3

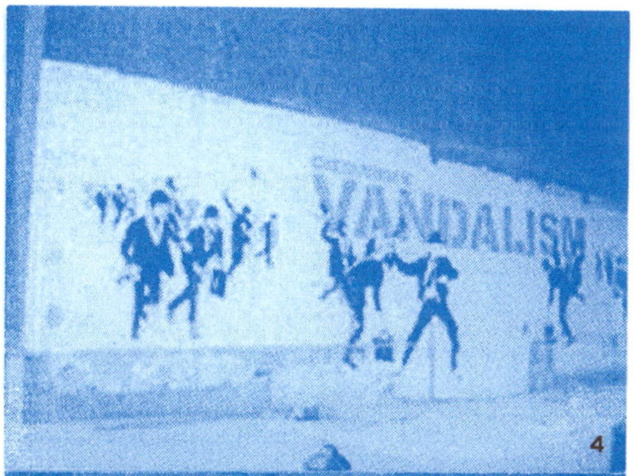

4

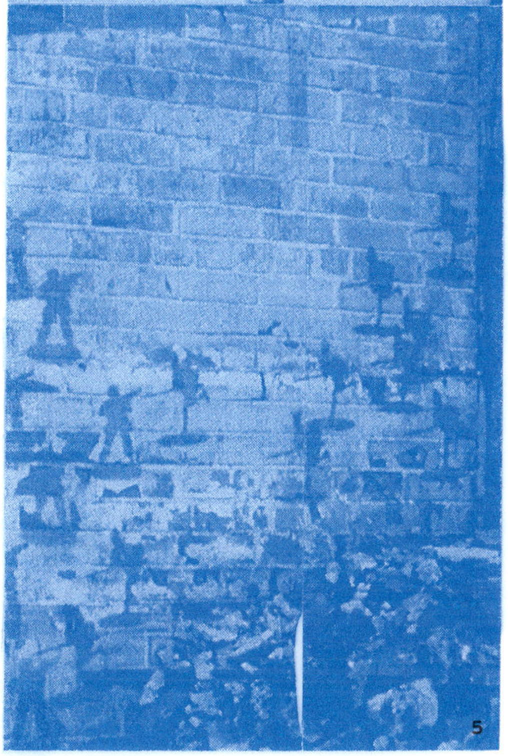

5

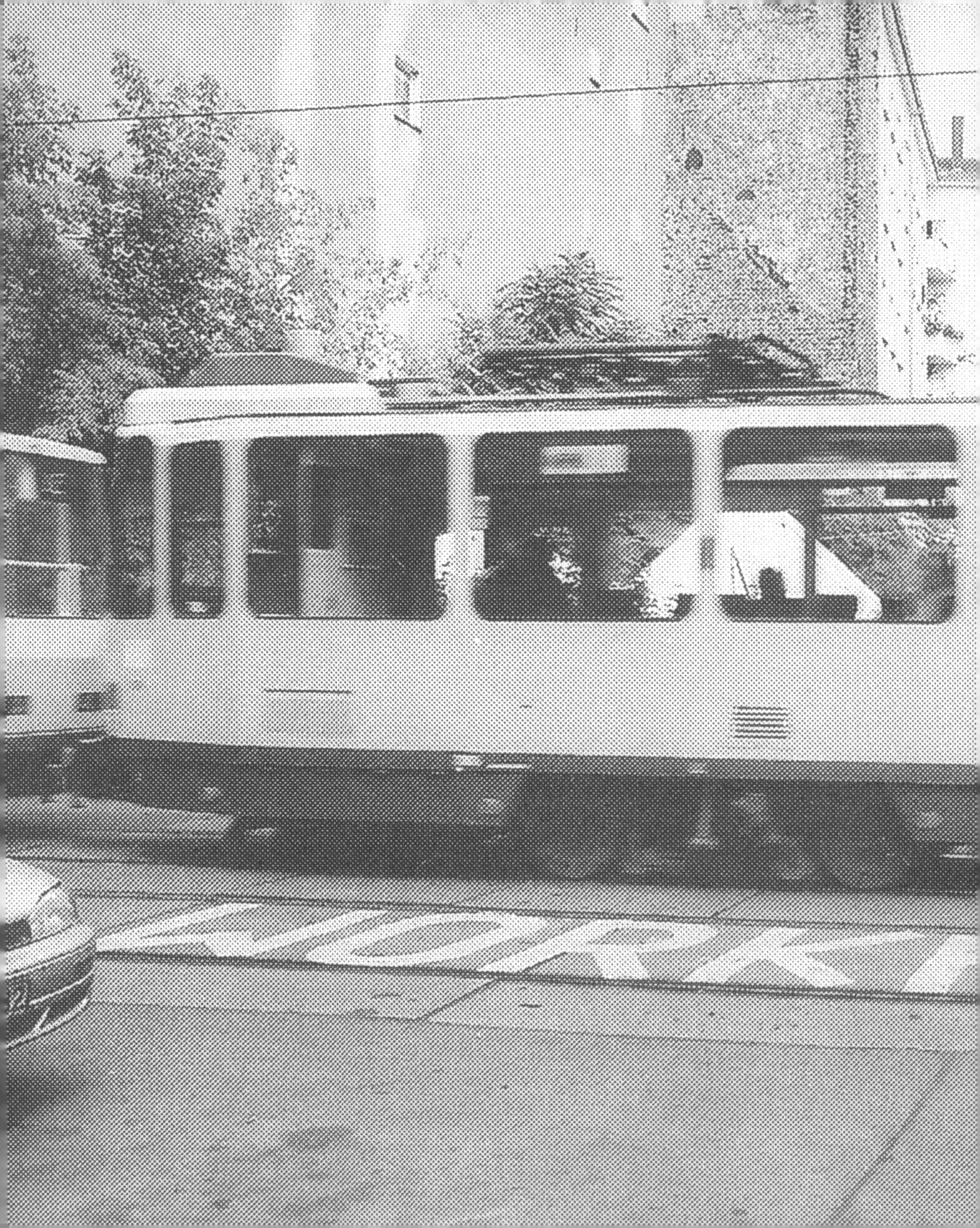

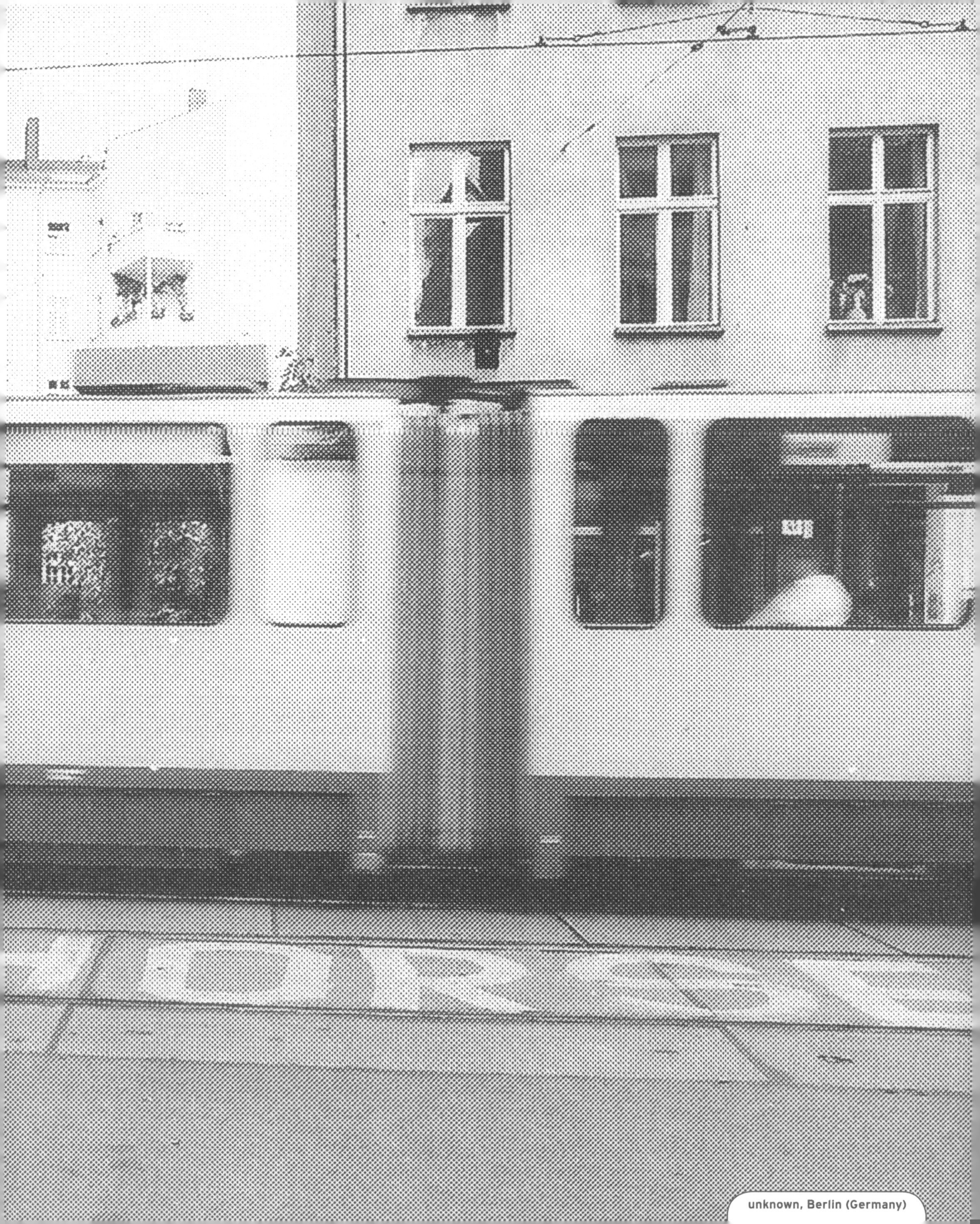

unknown, Berlin (Germany)

GRAFFITI WRITER RESEARCHING PLATFORMS FOR REMOTE TACTICAL CONTENT DEPLOYMENT

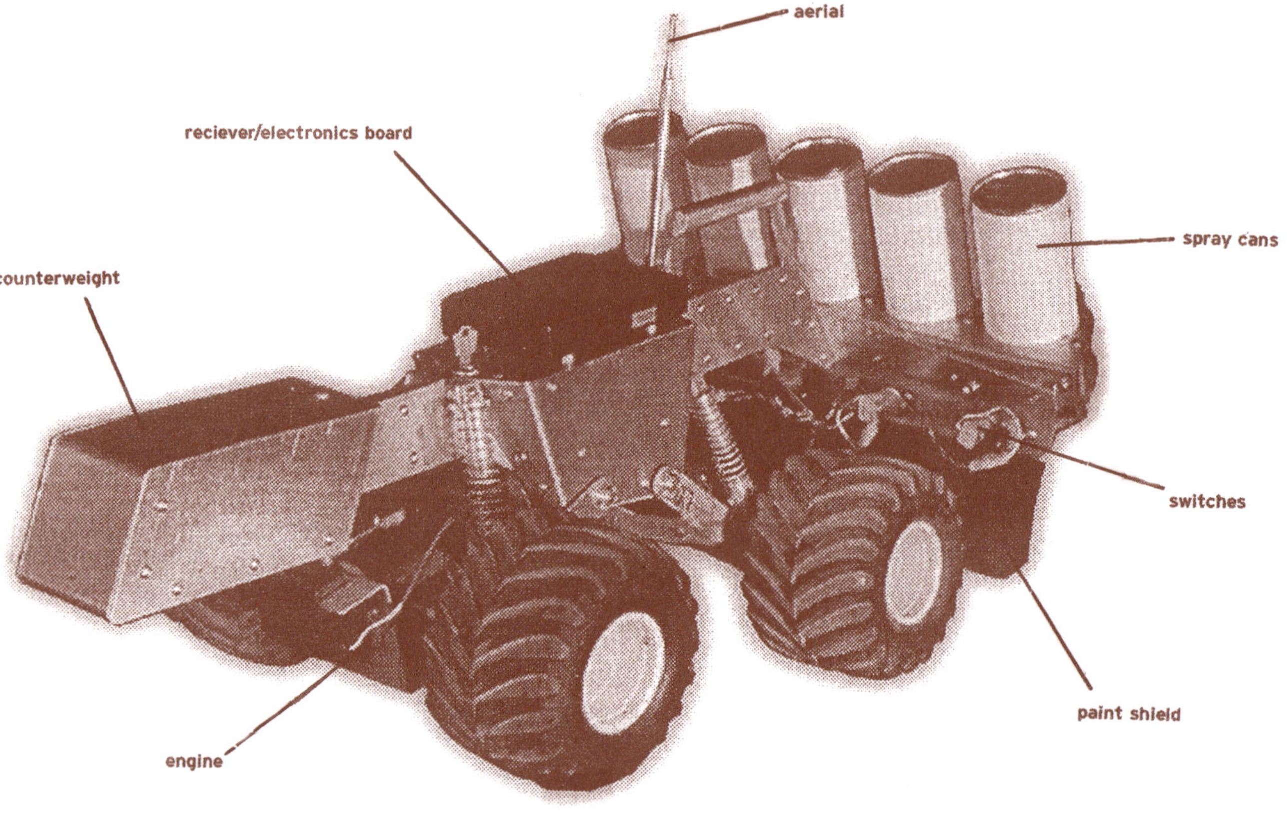

«GraffitiWriter: dank seiner Leichtbauweise und einem leistungsstarken Antrieb gelingt es diesem Textrobot, Botschaften in verbotene Zonen hineinzutragen und zu entkommen, bevor die Autoritäten reagieren können. Der Robot kann über grössere Entfernungen gesteuert werden, der Mann am Kontrollpult bleibt ausser Sichtweite.
Die Robotik ist notwendig, da die neue Generation der urbanen Polizeitechniken die traditionellen Wege des kulturellen Widerstandes erschwert haben. Die Einheit hat ihre Effektivität in wiederholten Versuchen an hochriskanten Zielen unter Beweis gestellt, so im US-Kapitol und in zahlreichen Kommerz- und Verwaltungsgebäuden in- und ausserhalb der USA.

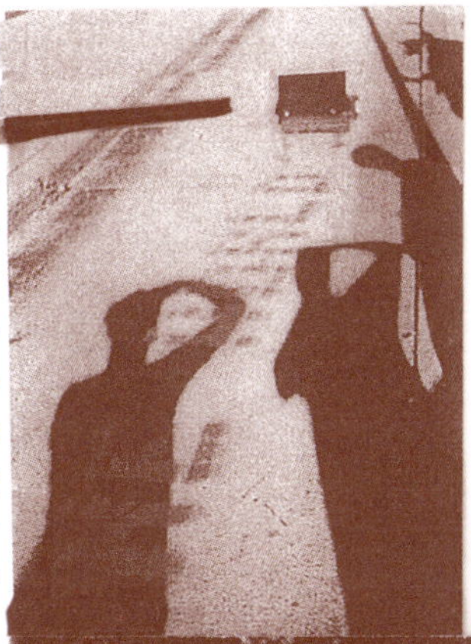

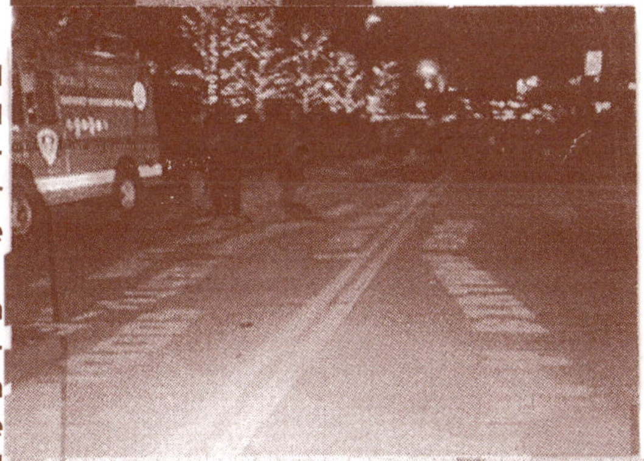

«GraffitiWriter: thanks to its lightweight construction and a powerful engine, this text robot can infiltrate restricted areas, leave messages behind and escape before the authorities have a chance to react. The robot is necessary for the operator to effectively stay behind the line of sight while steering the unit.
The advent of next generation police technologies for urban use has made engaging in active social insurgency an increasingly risky venture. In repeated testing, this system has proven its effectiveness on such high risk targets as the U.S. Capital Building as well as numerous urban commercial and municipal spaces in the U.S. and abroad.

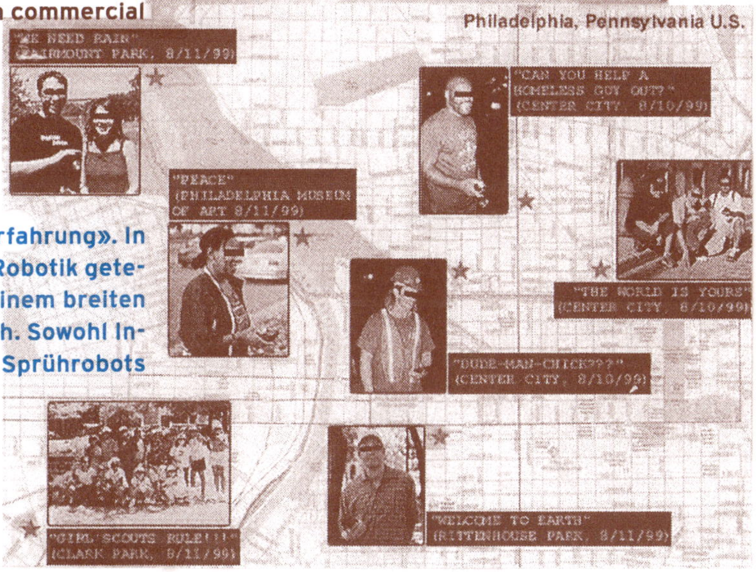

«Schnittstelle einer vermittelten kriminellen Erfahrung». In einem Experiment werden die Fähigkeiten der Robotik getestet. I.A.A.-Tester machen den GraffitiWriter einem breiten Versuchspublikum (Alter 5–74 Jahre) zugänglich. Sowohl Inhalt der Botschaft als auch die Bedienung des Sprührobots werden den Versuchspersonen überlassen.»
Text: IAA

«A public interface to mediated criminal experience». The robotic capacity is tested in an experiment. I.A.A. researchers make the technology available to members of the public (ages 5–74). Both the message content and actual operation of GraffitiWriter is left in the hands of test subjects.»
Text: IAA

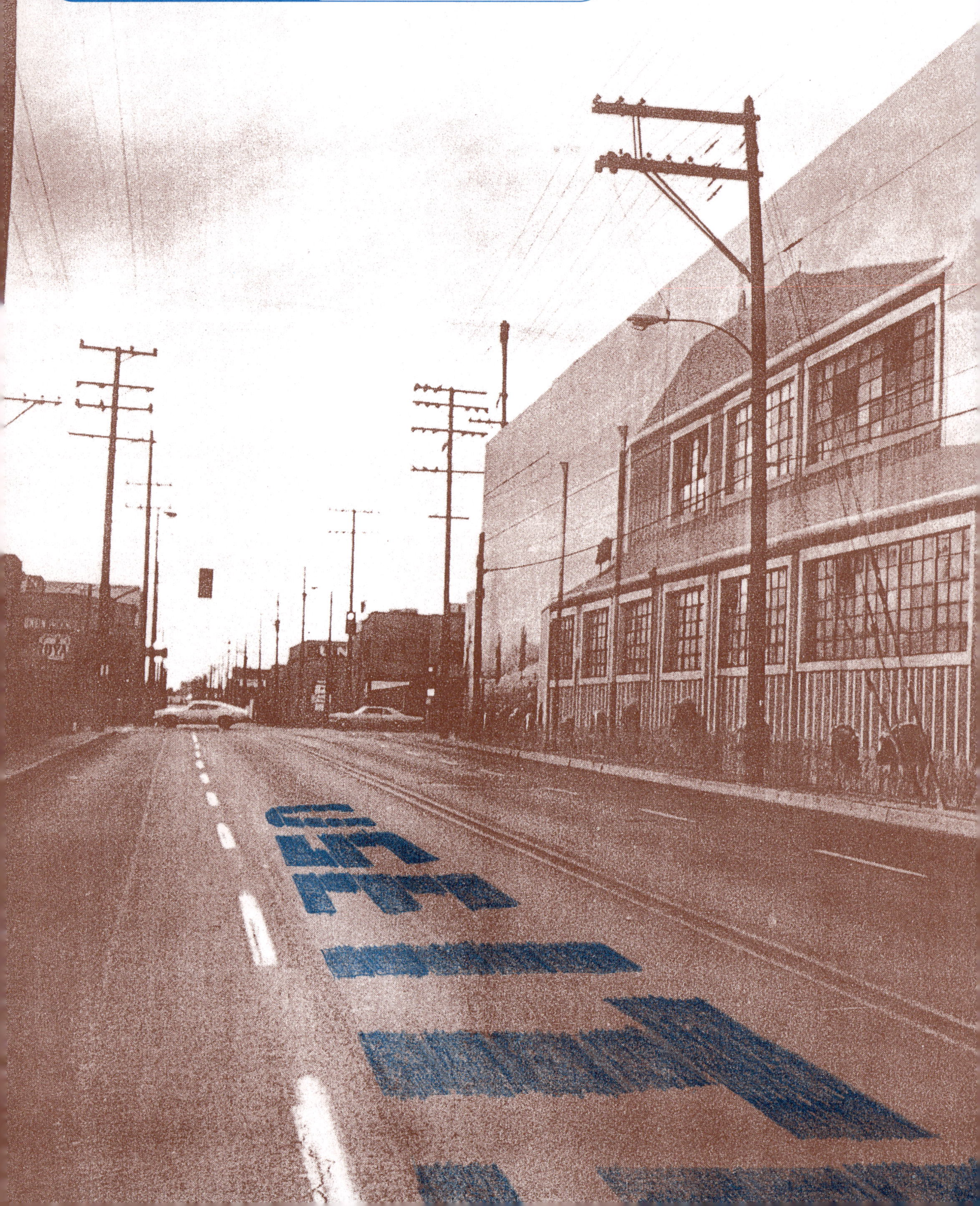

DRIVE-BY MESSAGING THE ULTIMATE TOOL OF EXPRESSION FOR A CAR-CRAZY SOCIETY

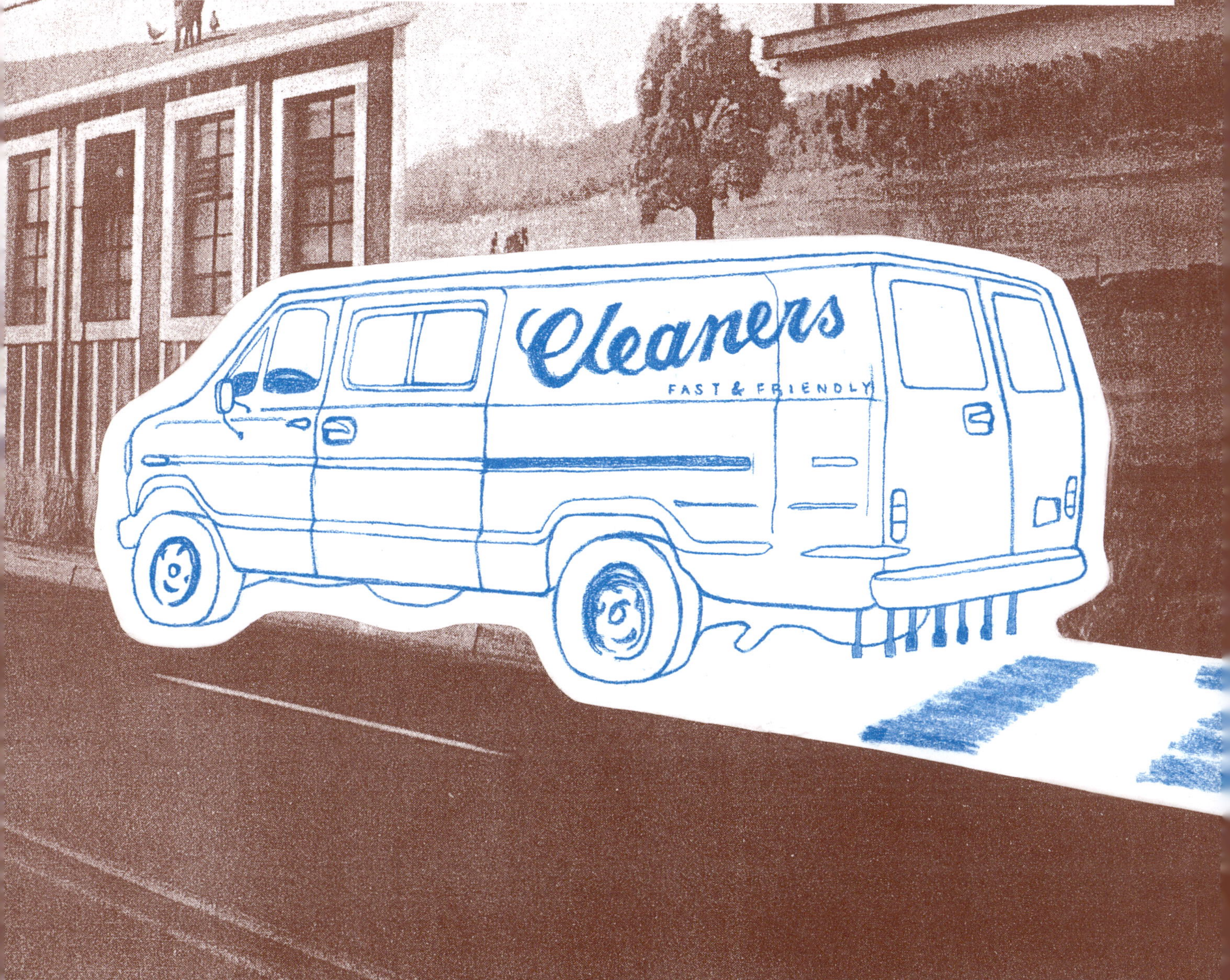

appliedautonomy.com (USA) / backgr.photo: Peter Kenner

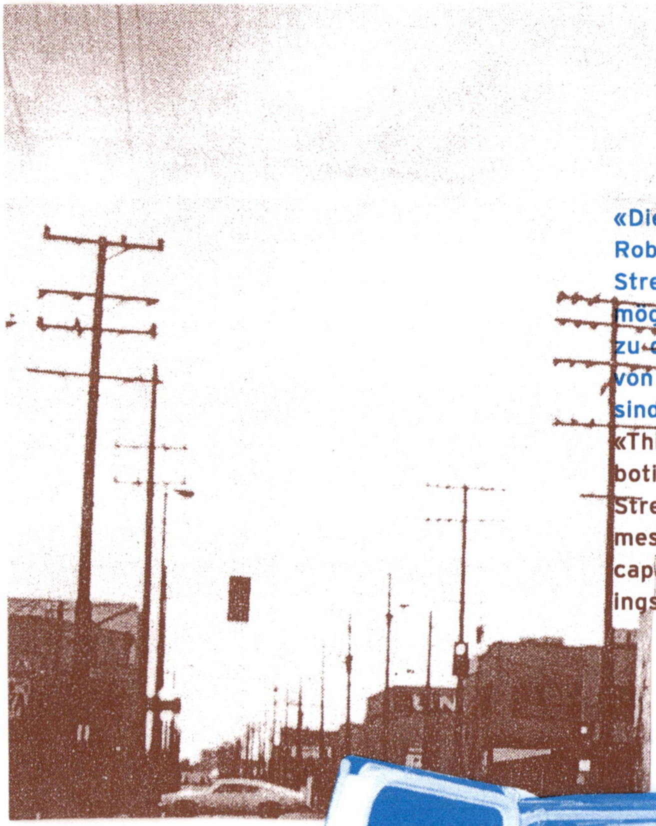

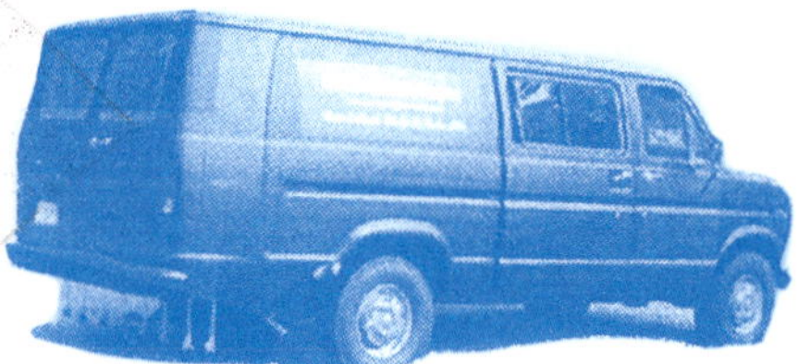

«Dieses Projekt führt die Forschung der anfechtenden Robotik aus dem früheren Projekt GraffitiWriter fort.
StreetWriter ist ein umgebauter Lieferwagen mit dem es möglich ist, während der Fahrt Botschaften auf den Asphalt zu drucken. Das system ist fähig Texte zu generieren, die von hohen Gebäuden und tief fliegenden Flugzeugen lesbar sind.» Text: IAA

«This project continues the research into Contestational Robotics gained from the earlier GraffitiWriter project.
StreetWriter is a modified cargo van, capable of printing messages on to the pavement while driving. The system is capable of rendering texts that are legible from tall buildings and low-flying aircraft.» Text: IAA

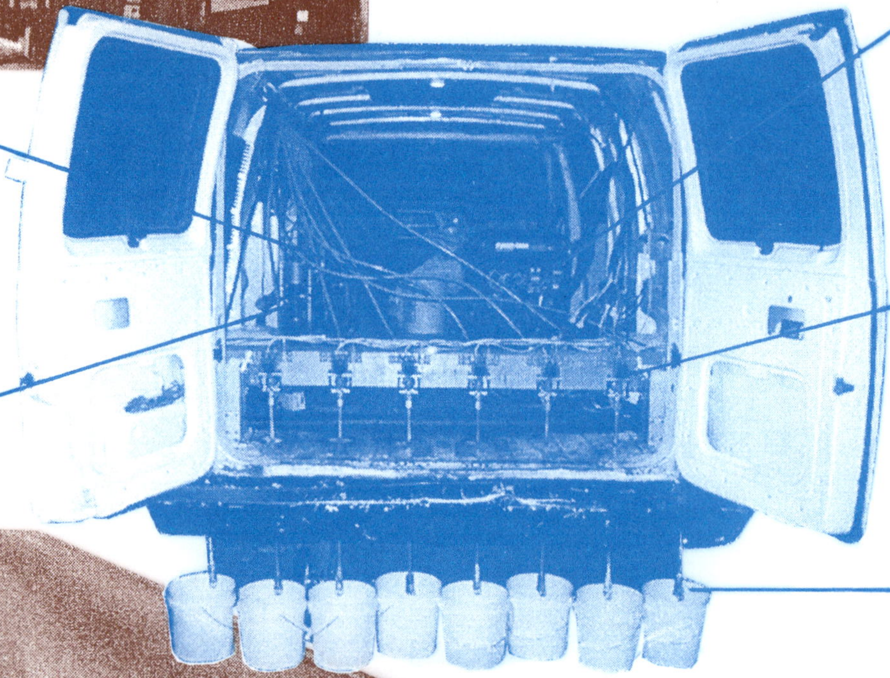

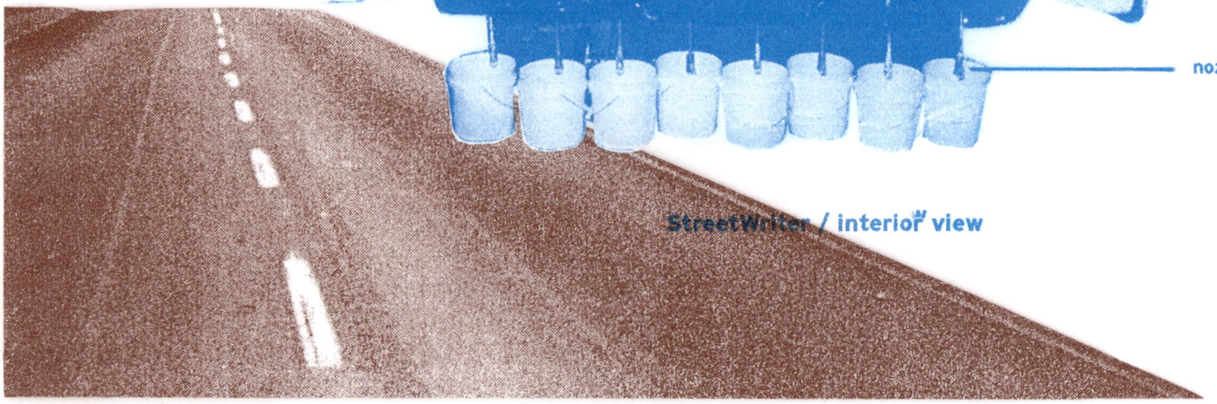

StreetWriter / interior view

Fahrrad-Texter: einfachere Alternative. Schneide den Text aus einem alten (glatten) Schlauch oder Streifen dicken Gummi. Wenn du ein altes Stempelalphabet in die Hände kriegst, kannst du auch das benutzen. Kleb die Buchstaben auf den reifen oder spann sie um die Felge. Farbauftrag: normale Wandrollen.

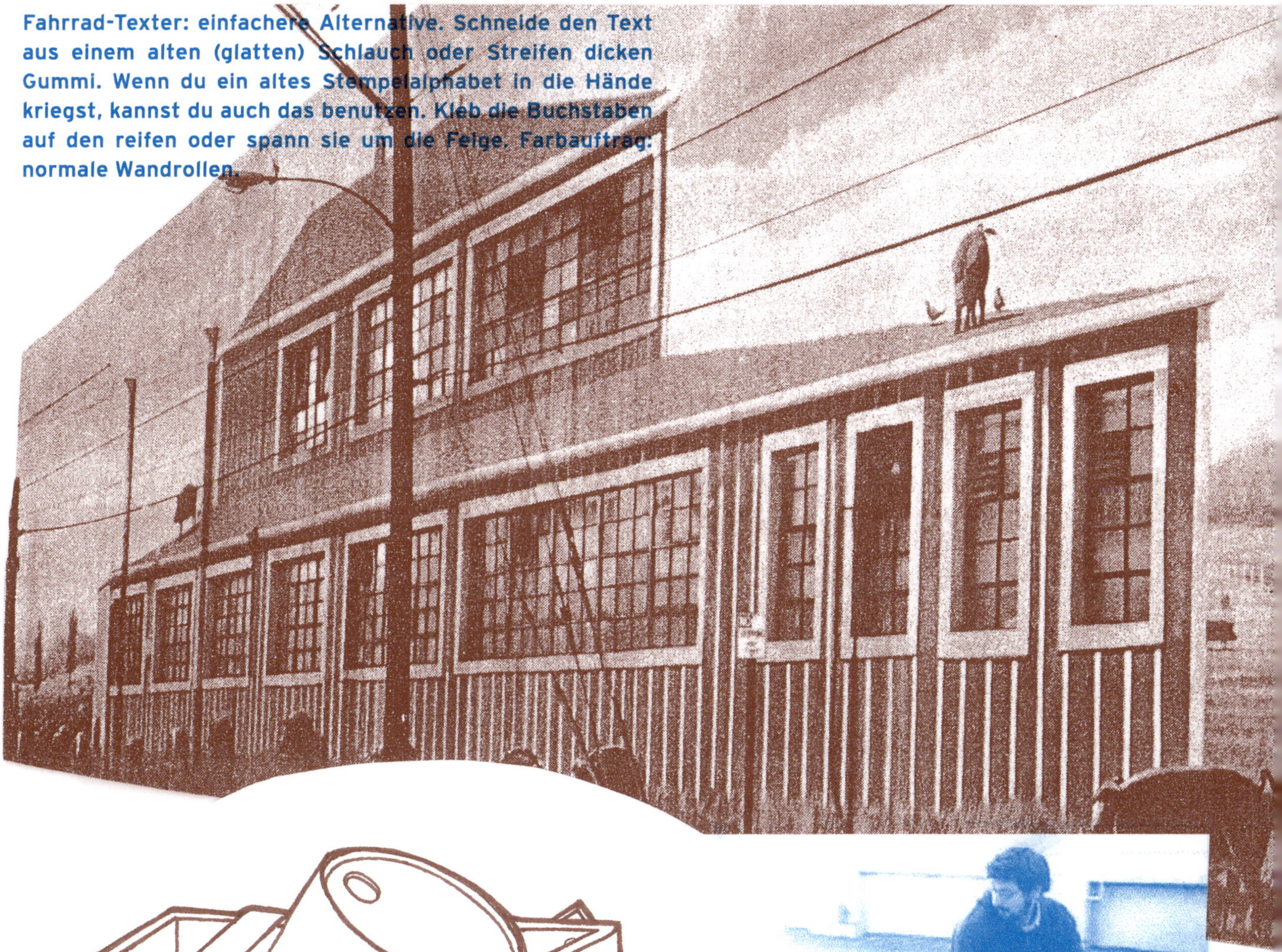

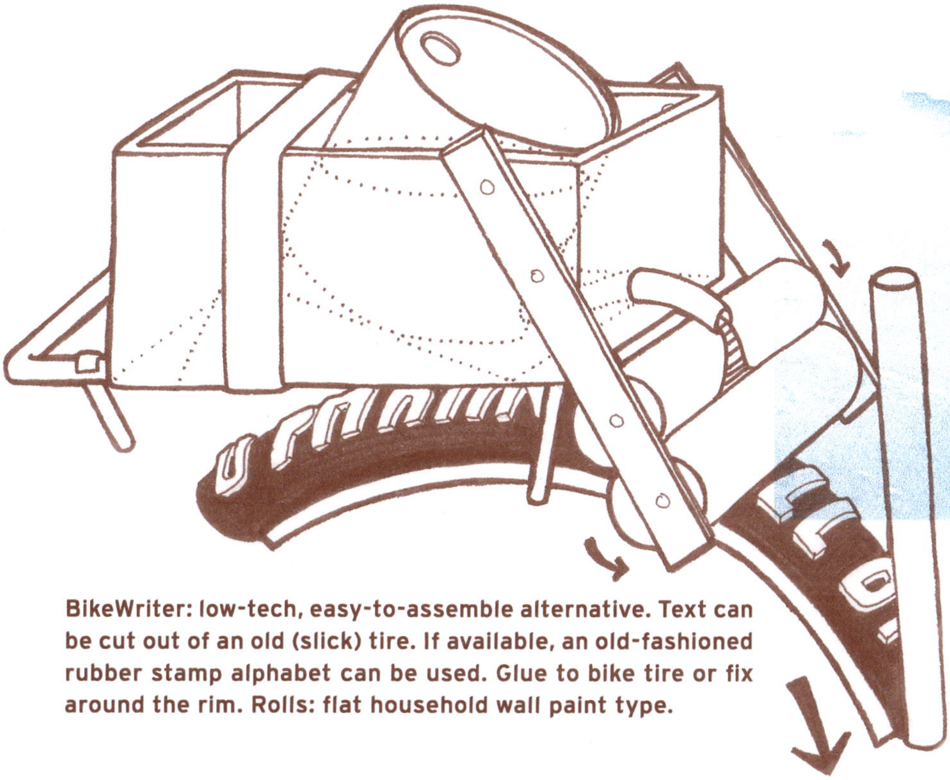

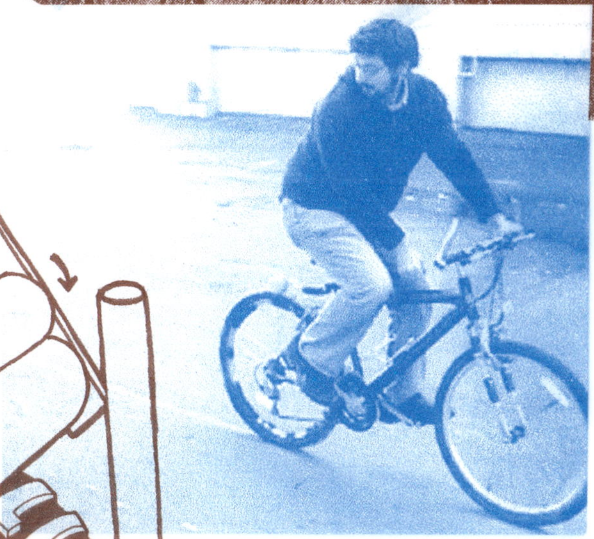

BikeWriter: low-tech, easy-to-assemble alternative. Text can be cut out of an old (slick) tire. If available, an old-fashioned rubber stamp alphabet can be used. Glue to bike tire or fix around the rim. Rolls: flat household wall paint type.

Veränderungen an existierenden Schildern und öffentlichen Einrichtungen zielen auf den Glauben an die offizielle Zeichensprache und versuchen, die routinemässige Akzeptanz der Verhältnisse zu unterbrechen.
Misstrauen zentralisierten Botschaften gegenüber ist der erste Schrift zum anzweifeln des Status Quo, und der Anfang einer intellektuellen Unabhängigkeit.

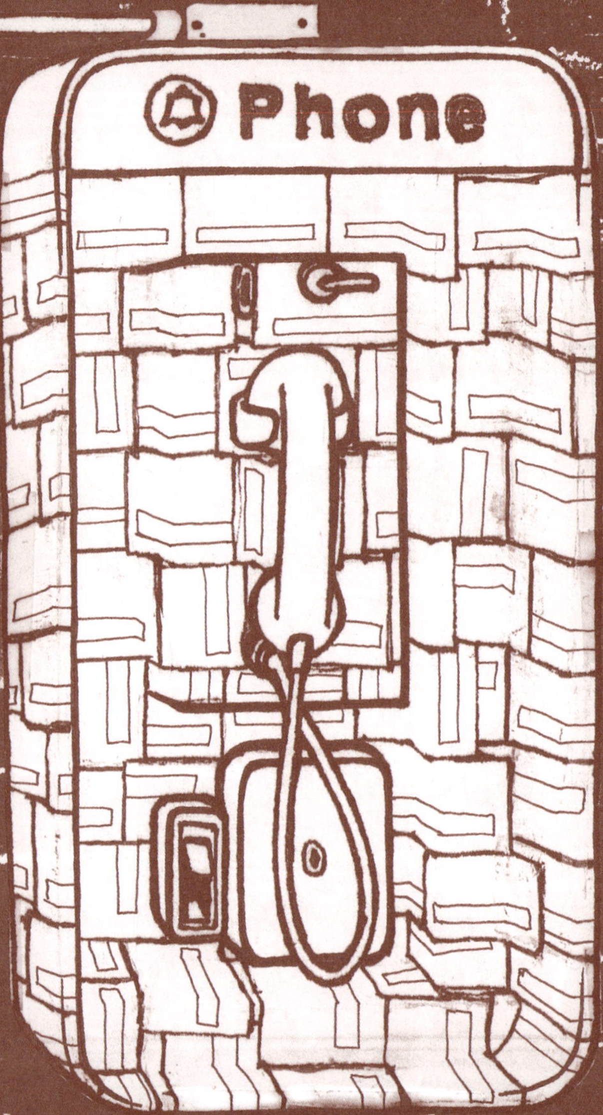

<- Deine Postfiliale stattet dich gerne mit einem Haufen hochklebender Paketaufkleber aus. Sie sind eine ideale Basis zum drucken, schreiben oder zeichnen.

Falls du einen Computer zur Verfügung hast, wirst du mit den simplen Layouts aof der gegenüberliegenden Seite keine Probleme haben. Drucke oder kopiere (wasserfest) auf Selbstklebefolie. Falls du analog arbeitest, kannst du Letraset-Rubbelbuchstaben benutzen und am Kopierer vergrössern.
Falls das Schild erreichbar ist, kannst du es auch mit Transparentpapier direkt vor Ort abpausen. Falls eine Intervention echt aussehen soll, vergewissere dich dass sie genau wie das Original gestaltet ist.

Public phones taped shut with postal stickers. Alias, Berlin (Germany)

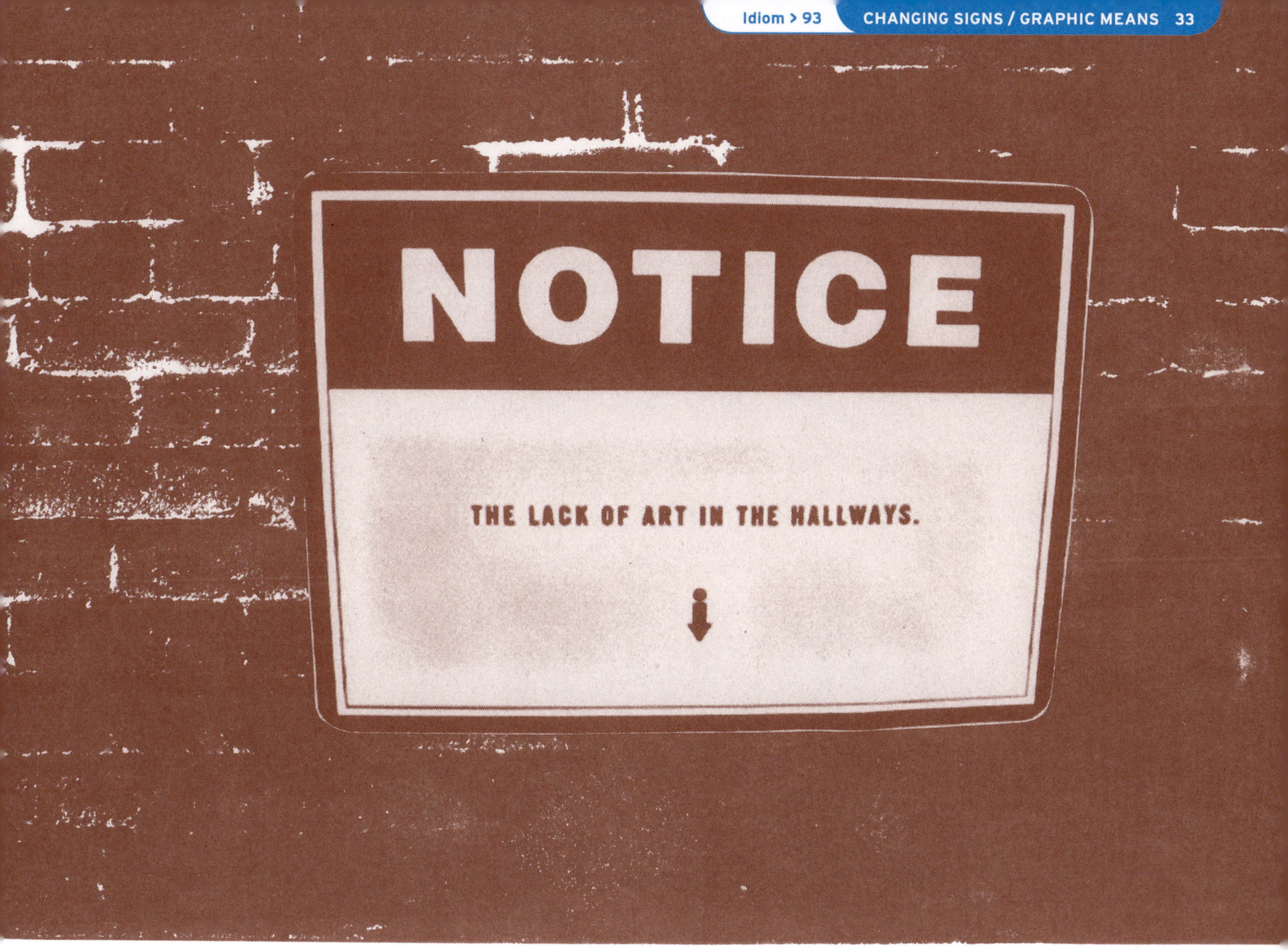

Changes to existing signs and public installations aim at disrupting confidence and consumer routines in relation to advertising signage by creating a fissure in the way things are accepted by routine. Mistrust in centralized messages is the first step on the way to questioning the status quo, and a starting point for intellectual independence.

<Left page> Your local post office will be happy to provide you with a stack of large, permanent-glue parcel stickers for free. They are a perfect base for printed, drawn or written matter.

If you're working with a computer you won't have much trouble forging simple designs such as the ones fetured on this page. Print or copy (waterproof) on sticker foil. Otherwise use Letraset rubbing alphabets and enlarge; if the sign's within reach you might bring some transparent paper and tape and trace the layout on site. If you want an intervention to pass for the real thing make sure that it looks exactly like the original.

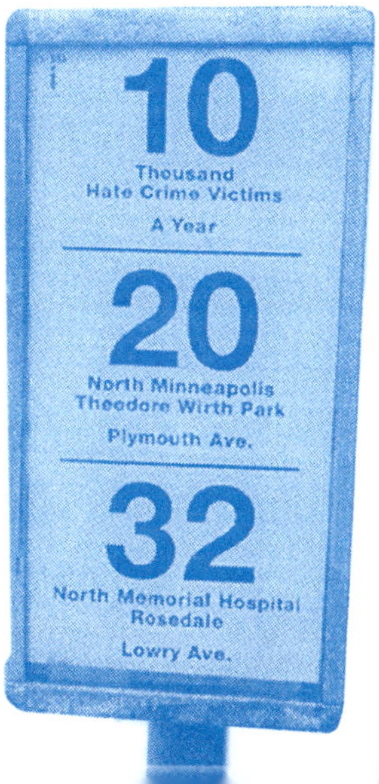

Minneapolis (USA)

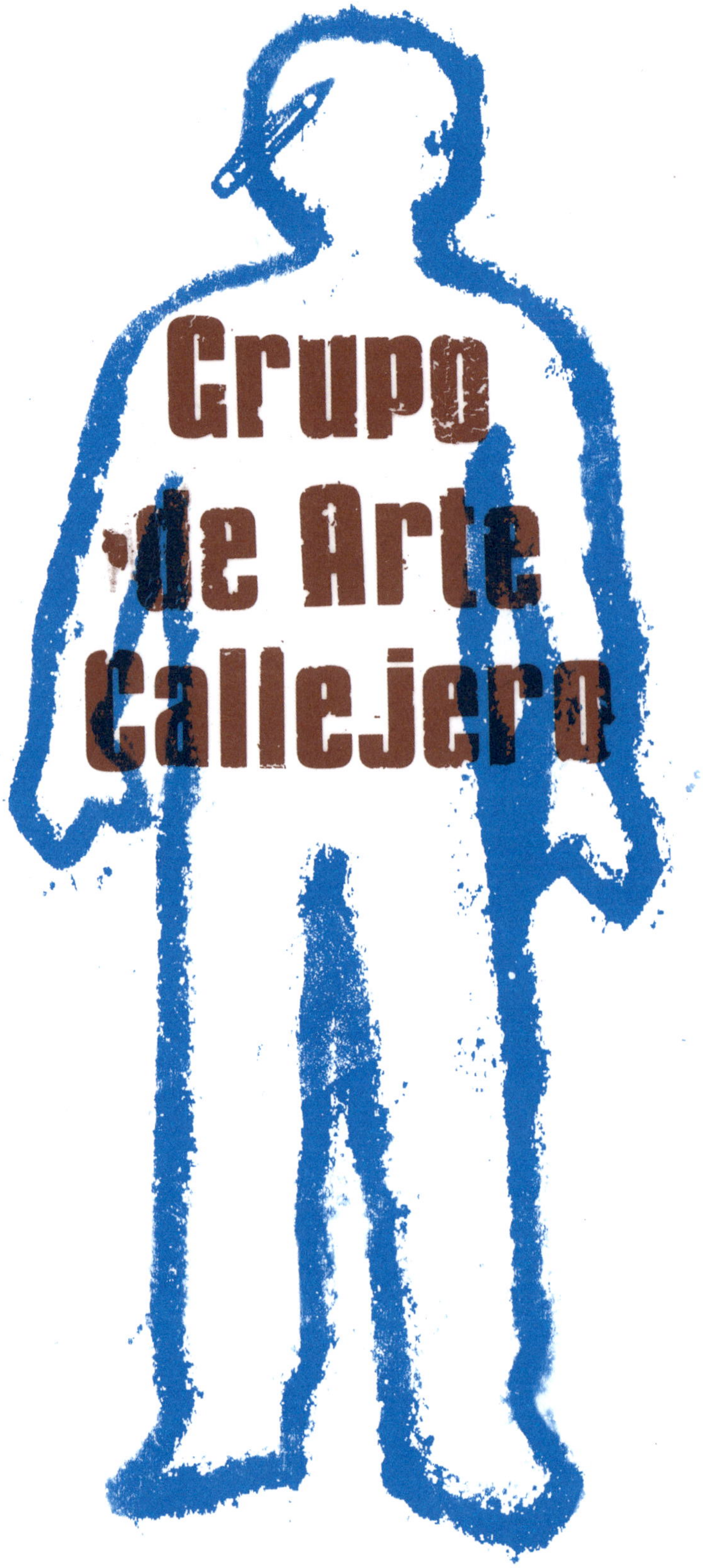
Grupo
de Arte
Callejero

From changing signs to creating new ones, no one has equalled the output of the Argentine 'Grupo de Arte Callejero', who for five years have been bombarding the streets of Buenos Aires with a vast array of different works, ranging from graphic arts to performances and direct actions. They are a loose group of artists from different fields, who work together with members of the public and on occasion with other protest groups, percieving the streets as an open exibition space for visual communication.
They comment on two main problems, the unsolved crimes of Argentina's military dictatorship of the 1970s and the country's recent economic fallout. Their main working method is the subversion of the institutional and popular signs and means, such as traffic signs, ad posters, metro tickets or the aesthetics of TV.

Through these attempts to «infiltrate messages into the system's language» they intend to «provoke fissures that de-mask the workings and structures of power».

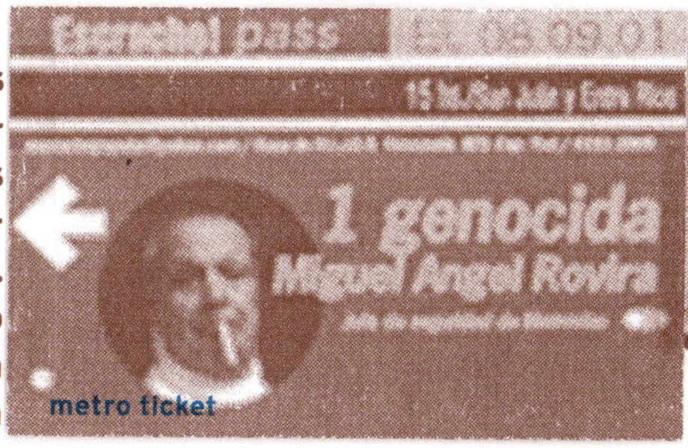

metro ticket

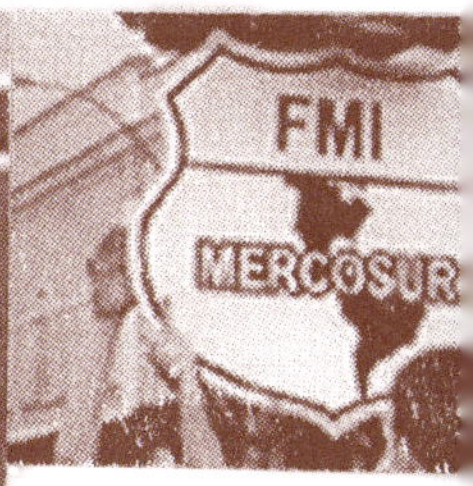

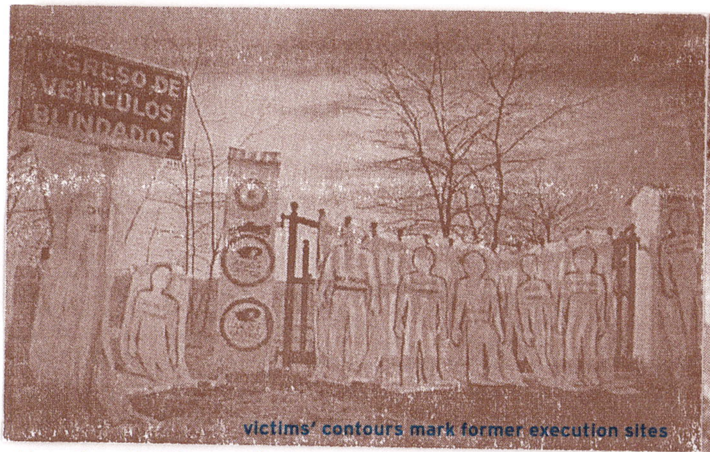

victims' contours mark former execution sites

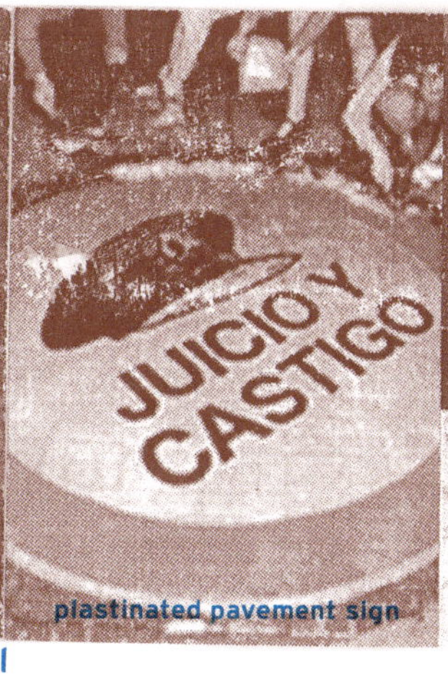

plastinated pavement sign

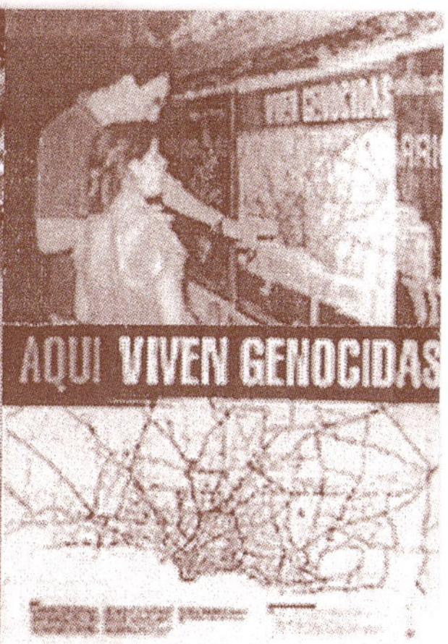

addresses of junta criminals, poster

Von der Zeichenveränderung zur Zeichenschaffung, wohl kaum eine Gruppe hat auf diesem Feld ein solches Output wie die Arentinier 'Grupo de Arte Callejero', die seit fünf Jahren die Strassen von Buenos Aires mit einer Masse verschiedener Arbeiten bombardieren, von Grafiken bis zu Performances und direkten Aktionen. Sie sind eine lose Gruppe mit künstlerischem Hintergrund, die mit dem Publikum und bisweilen mit anderen Gruppierungen zusammenarbeiten; die Strassen sind für sie offene Ausstellungsräume der visuellen Kommunikation.
Sie zielen hauptsächlich auf zwei Probleme, die ungelösten Verbrechen der Militärdiktatur der 70er Jahre und das aktuelle wirtschaftliche Desaster Argentiniens. Ihre Technik ist die Subversion institutioneller und populärer Zeichen und Mittel, wie Verkehrszeichen, Werbung, Fahrkarten und TV-Ästhetik.
Durch diese Versuche der «Infiltration von Botschaften in die Sprache des Systems» wollen sie «Risse provozieren, die die Machtspiele und -strukturen demaskieren».

These very real looking signs have been created using a computer and digital print.

<1> Rome (Italy). Copying the layout of the city's historic sites information system, a number of new panels appeared telling the stories of the unfortunate and forgotten who had lived there. Every story has more than one side, and here different sides are on display.

<2> These posters appeared in June 2004 in the subway system of New York (USA). In a clever twist they combined an image that had become an icon of wrong doing with the aesthetics of the omnipresent iPod adverts, offering «10,000 volts in your pocket – guilty or innocent».

<3> is one of a series of eight billboards that were erected on the west side of Los Angeles (USA). Sporting slick print on a plastic board, they announced in official language the building project of a metro that was to reinforce the city's substandard public transport system. Maybe the disappointed commuters, after they realized that the project's never been on city hall's schedule felt inclined to demand exactly such an undertaking from their city. Then again, maybe not.

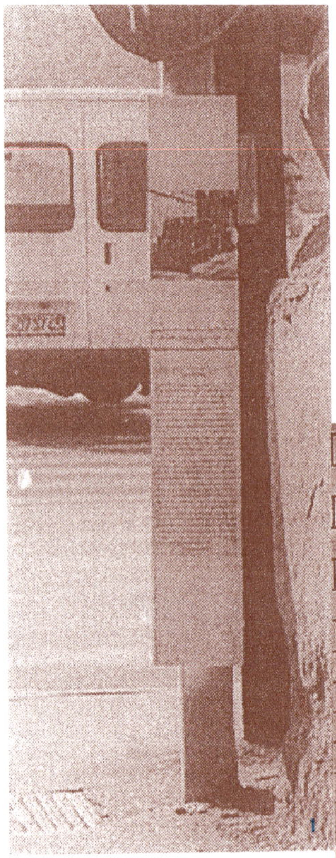
1

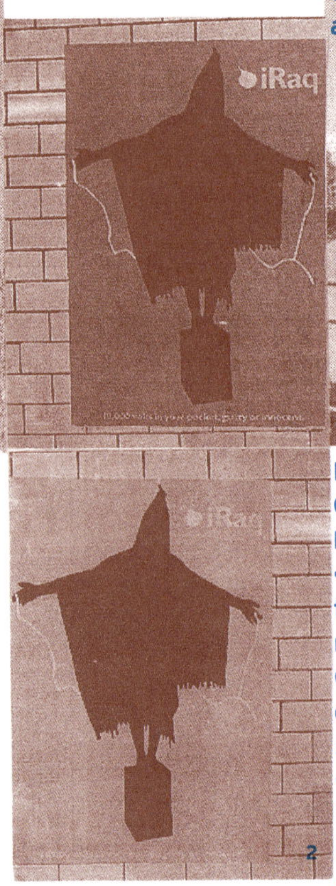

2

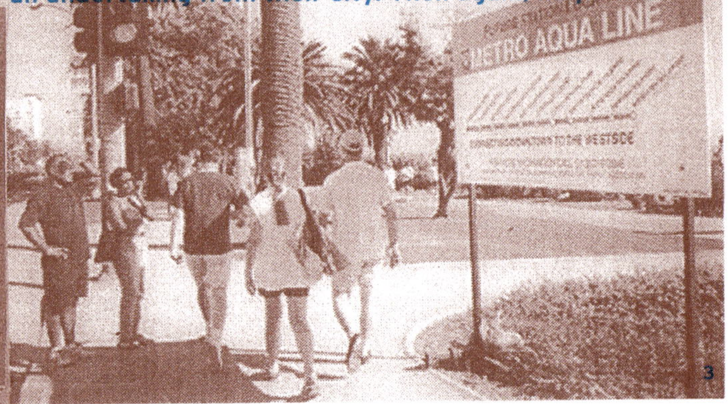

3

Diese täuschend echt aussehenden Zeichen wurden am Computer und unter Verwendung moderner Drucktechniken hergestellt.

<1> Rom (Italien). Das Aussehen des Touristeninformationssystems der Stadt kopierend, erschien eine Anzahl neuer Tafeln welche Anstelle historischer Attraktionen die Geschichten der unglücklichen und vergessenen erzählten, die an diesen Stellen gelebt hatten. Jede Geschichte hat zwei Seiten, hier wurde beiden Raum ge geben.

<2> Diese Plakate erschienen im Juni 2004 Metrosystem von New York (USA). In einem cleveren Dreh kombinierten sie die Bildikone des US-Verbrechens mit der Ästhetik der omnipräsenten iPod-Werbung. Das Poster offerierte «10.000 Volt in der Tasche – schuldig oder unschuldig».

<3> ist eins von acht auf Folien gedruckter Baustellenschilder, die in offizieller Sprachweise den Bau einer Metro für das armselige städtische Transportsystem von L.A., USA ankündigen. Vielleicht hat die Enttäuschung den Pendlern aufgezeigt, was ihnen eigentlich seitens ihrer Stadt fehlt. Vielleicht auch nicht.

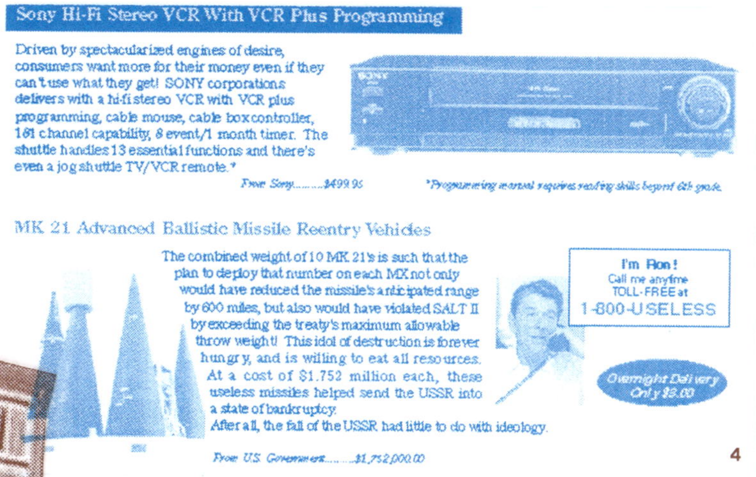

4

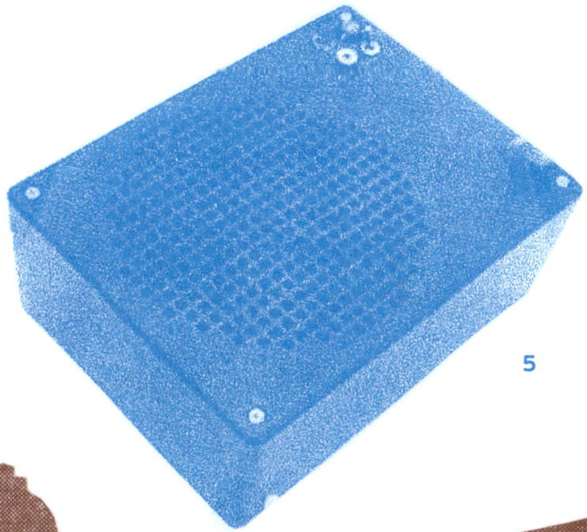

5

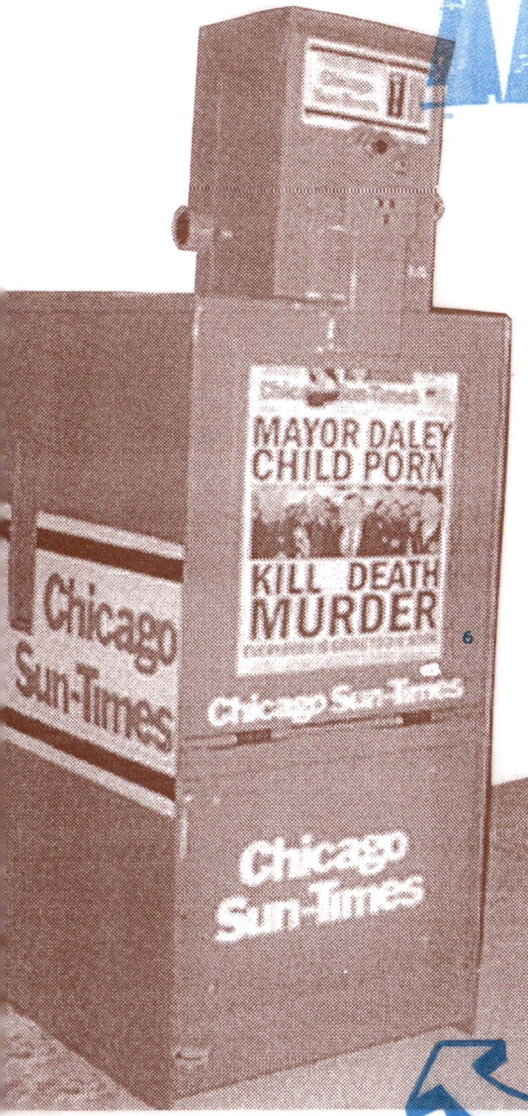

6

4,7 Inserts placed in Sunday newspapers throughout the USA
5 Sound installation, linked to paper dispenser opening

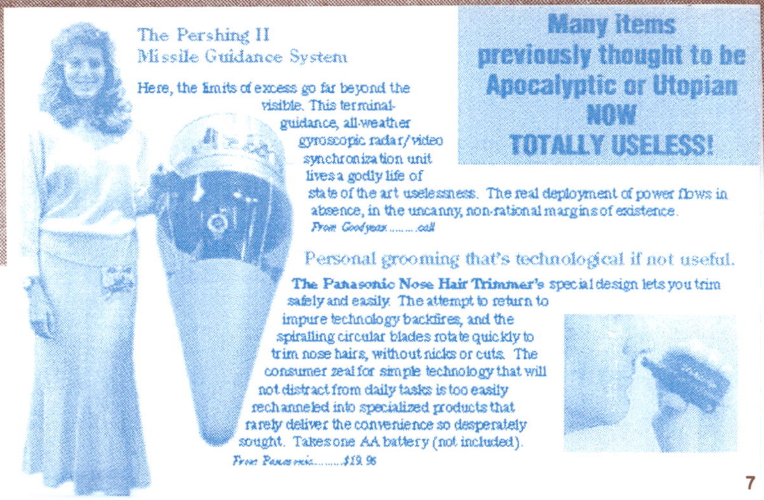

7

«Picture this: a 13-ton hi-tech container right in the middle of Karlsplatz, one of Vienna's historic squares. It's the Nike Infobox: a slick, demountable, walk-in container, two semi-transparent floors, dynamic shapes and a red plastic cover. On the outer windows a curious sign attracts the attention of passersby: 'This square will soon be called Nikeplatz. Come inside to find out more'.

On October 10th 2003, 0100101110101101.ORG claimed publicly to be behind this hyper-real theatrical performance. Their spokeswoman, Eva Mattes, explains: 'For this work we wanted to use the entire city as a stage for a huge urban performance, a sort of theatre show for an unaware audience/cast. We wanted to produce a collective hallucination capable of altering people's perception of the city'.»

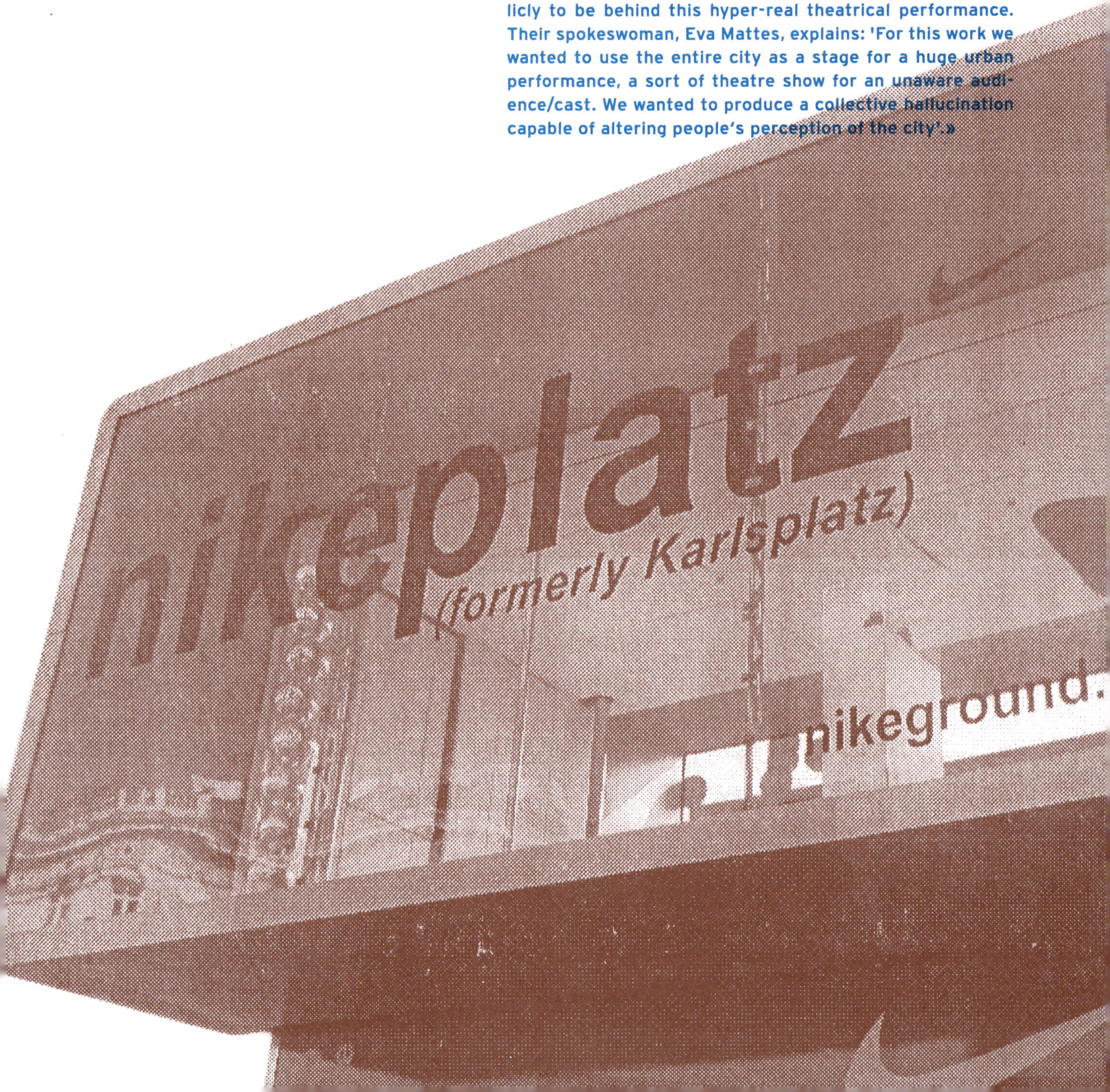

Just four days later, Nike released a 20-page injunction requesting the immediate removal of any reference to copyrighted material, and that any activity related to Nike cease immediately, claiming 78,000 Euro for damages.
While the performance continued until its official takedown on 28 October, Public Netbase's attorney found a formal defect in Nike's complaint. Subsequently, it was rejected by the Commercial Court on formal grounds. After this refusal Nike didn't take further legal action. The match was over: Nike threw in the towel.
This performance was produced by Public Netbase, the Vienna netculture institution.
Text: 0100101110101101.ORG (Eva and Franco Mattes)

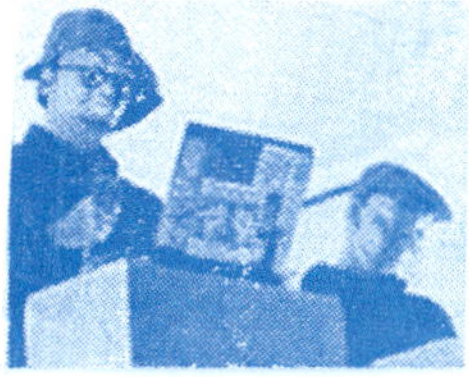

NIKE MONUMENT / PROJECT FOR NIKEPLATZ (FORMERLY KARLSPLATZ) / VIENNA, AUSTRIA 2003

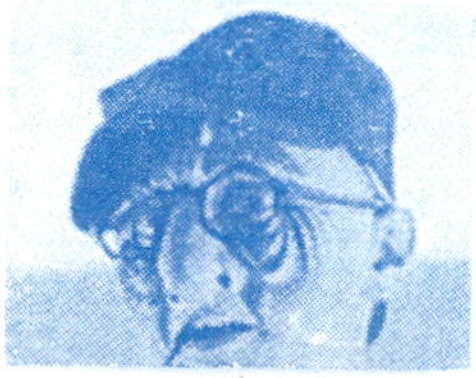

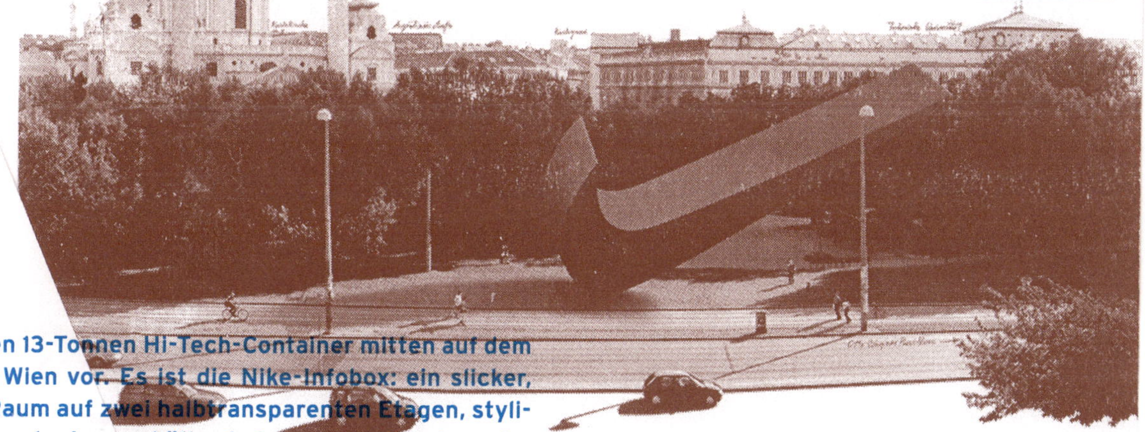

«Stell dir einen 13-Tonnen Hi-Tech-Container mitten auf dem Karlsplatz in Wien vor. Es ist die Nike-Infobox: ein slicker, betretbarer Raum auf zwei halbtransparenten Etagen, stylische Formen, rote Aussenhülle. Auf den Frontfenstern der Text: 'Dieser Platz wird bald in Nikeplatz umbenannt. Mehr Informationen innen'.

Am 10.10.2003 bekennen sich 0100101110101101.ORG, hinter dieser hyperrealen Theaterperformance zu stehen: 'Wir wollten die ganze Stadt als Bühne für diese grossangelegte urbane Performance benutzen,' erklärt Eva Mattes, ihre Sprecherin 'es sollte eine Art Theatervorführung für ein ahnungsloses Publikum sein. Wir wollten einen kollektive Halluzination produzieren, die fähig wäre, die Vorstellung der Leute von ihrer Stadt zu verändern'.»

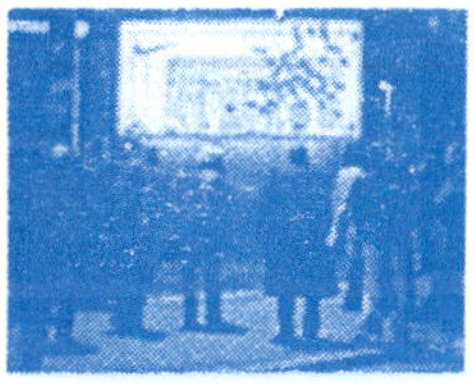

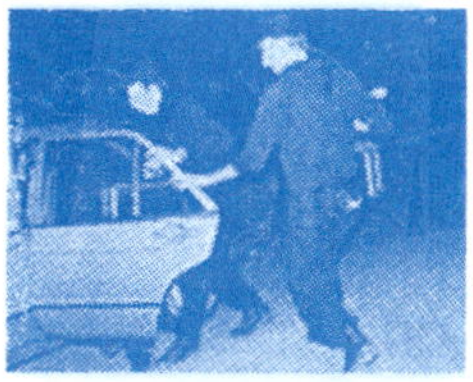

Nike klagte nur vier Tage später auf Abbau des Containers und das Entfernen jeglichen Hinweises auf urheberrechtlich geschützes Material, und machte einen Schaden von 78,000 Euro geltend.
Während die Performance bis zur offiziellen Beendigung am 28.10. weiterging, konnte die Klage aufgrund eines Formfehlers abgewiesen werden. Nach dieser Niederlage unternahm Nike keine weiteren rechtlichen Schritte mehr. Das Match war vorbei: Nike hatte das Handtuch geworfen.
Die Performance wurde von Public Netbase, der Wiener netculture Institution produziert.
Text: 0100101110101101.ORG (Eva and Franco Mattes)

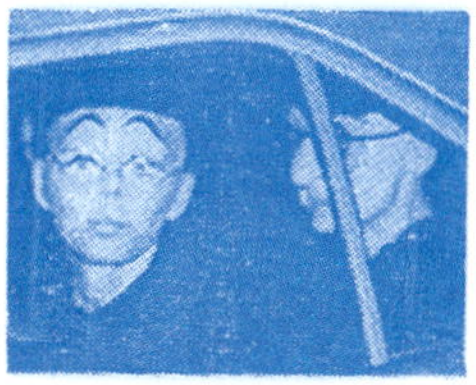

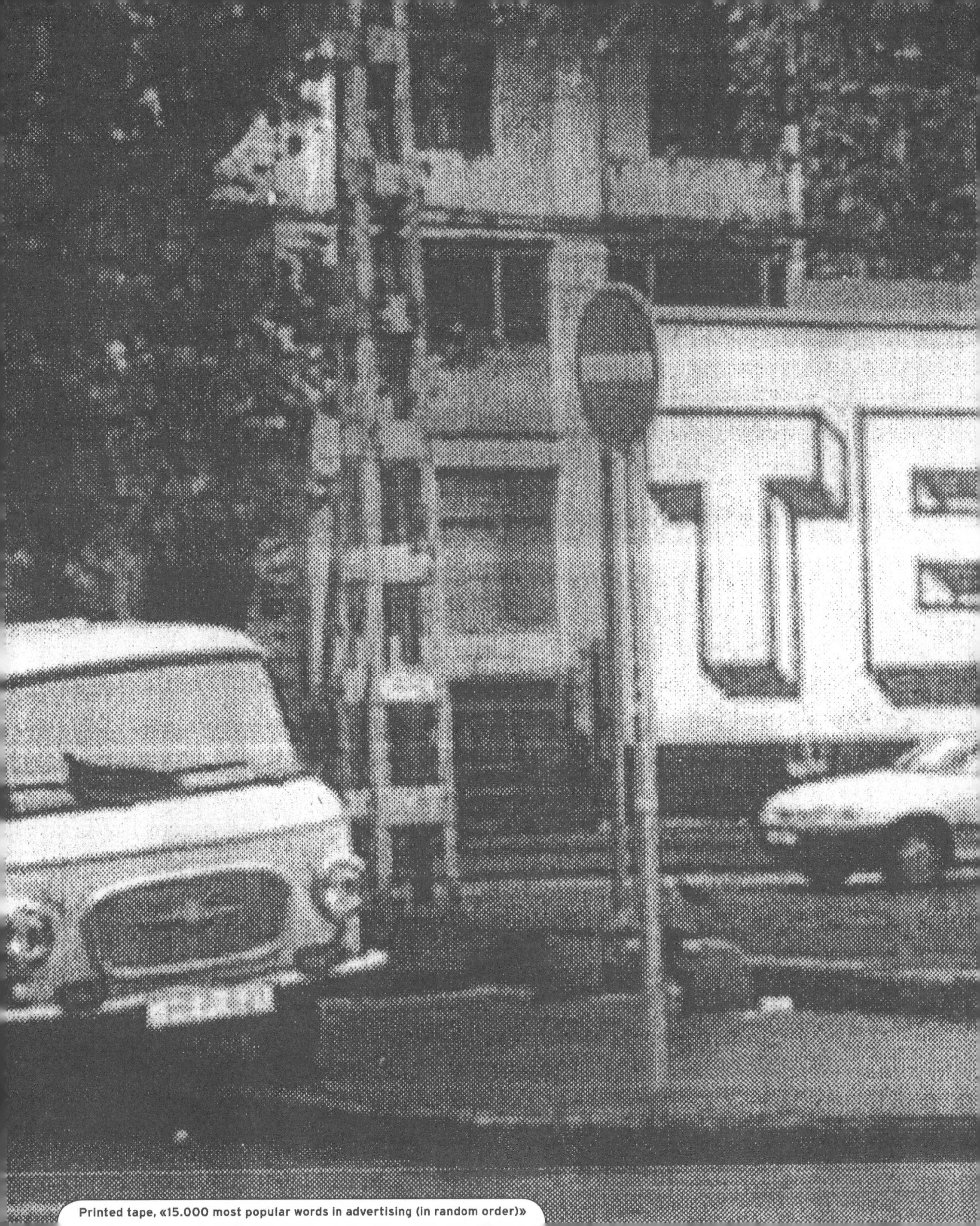

Printed tape, «15.000 most popular words in advertising (in random order)»

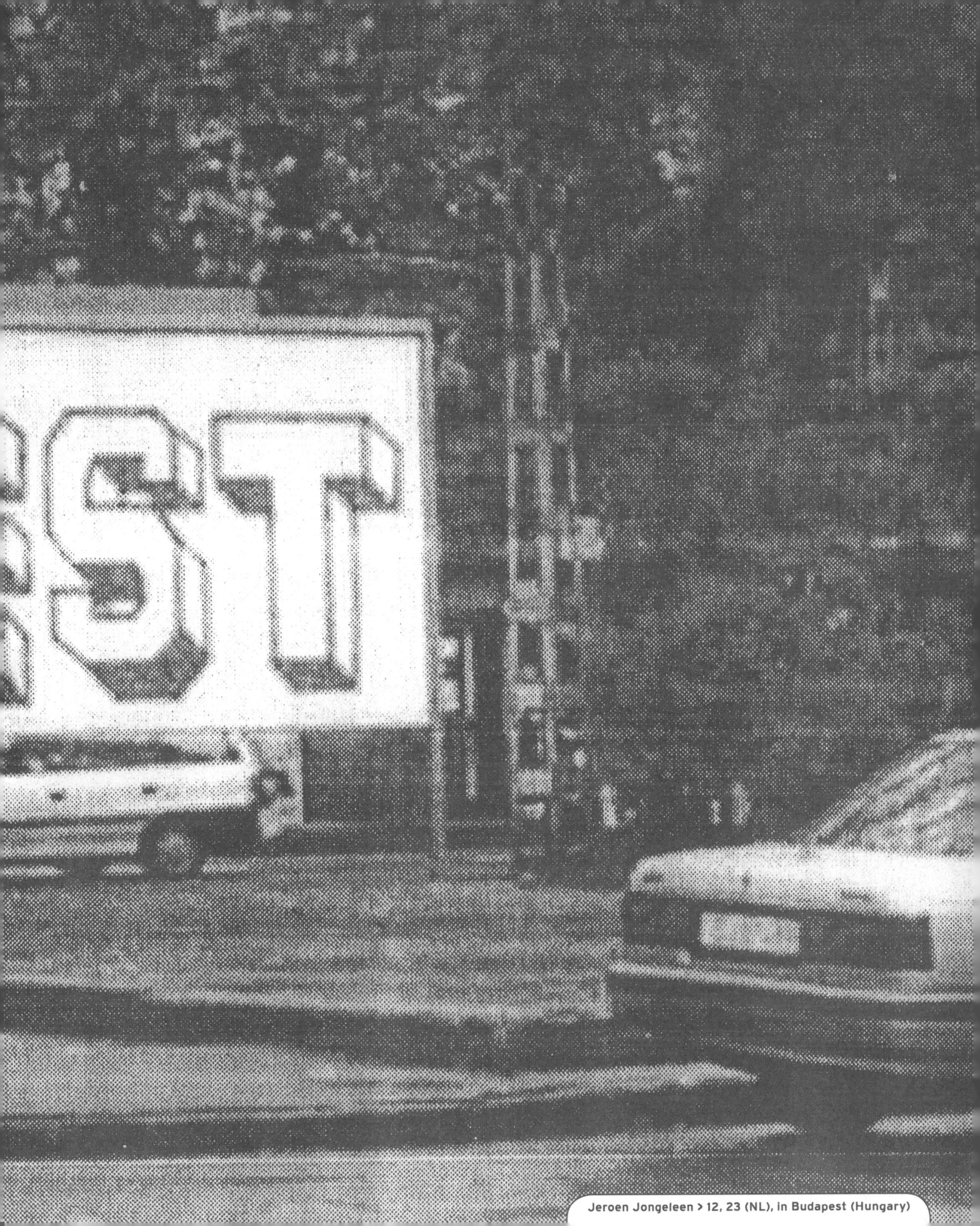

Jeroen Jongeleen > 12, 23 (NL), in Budapest (Hungary)

THE ART AND SCIENCE OF

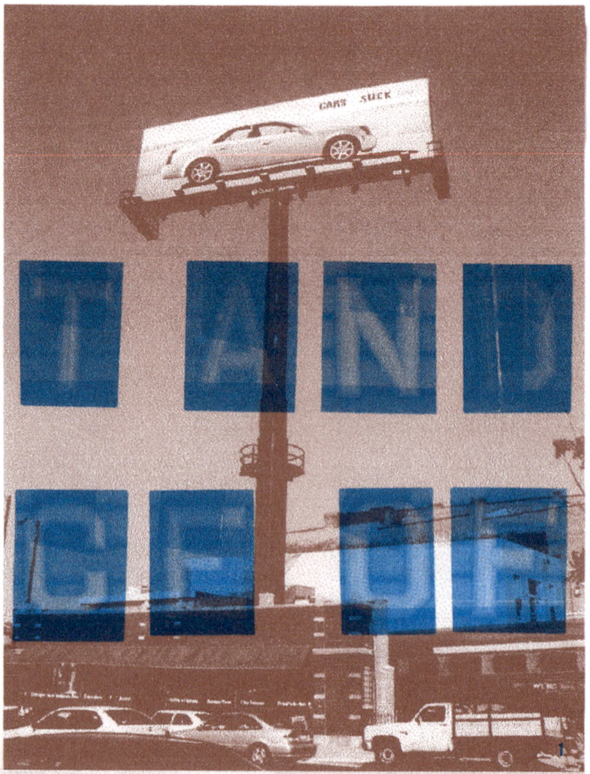

1

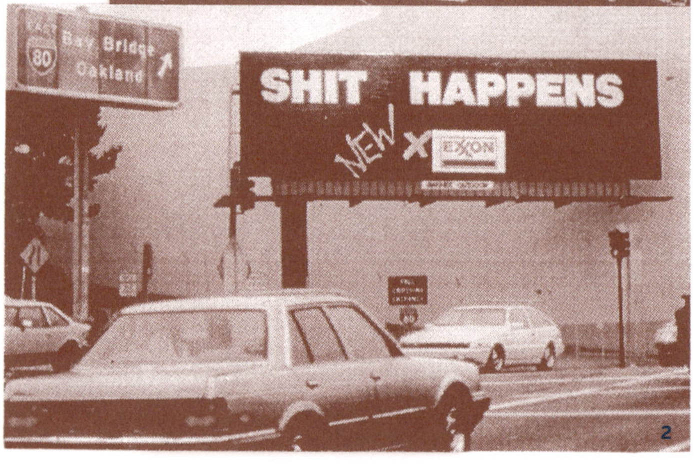

2

A thorough guide for executing billboard alterations can be found on the home page of the «Billboard Liberation Front», an authority in the field. The following text borrows on their field experience.

Eine vollständige Anleitung zur Veränderung von Plakatwänden befindet sich auf der Homepage der «Billboard Liberation Front», einer Autorität auf diesem Feld. Der folgende Text zitiert aus ihrer Expertise.

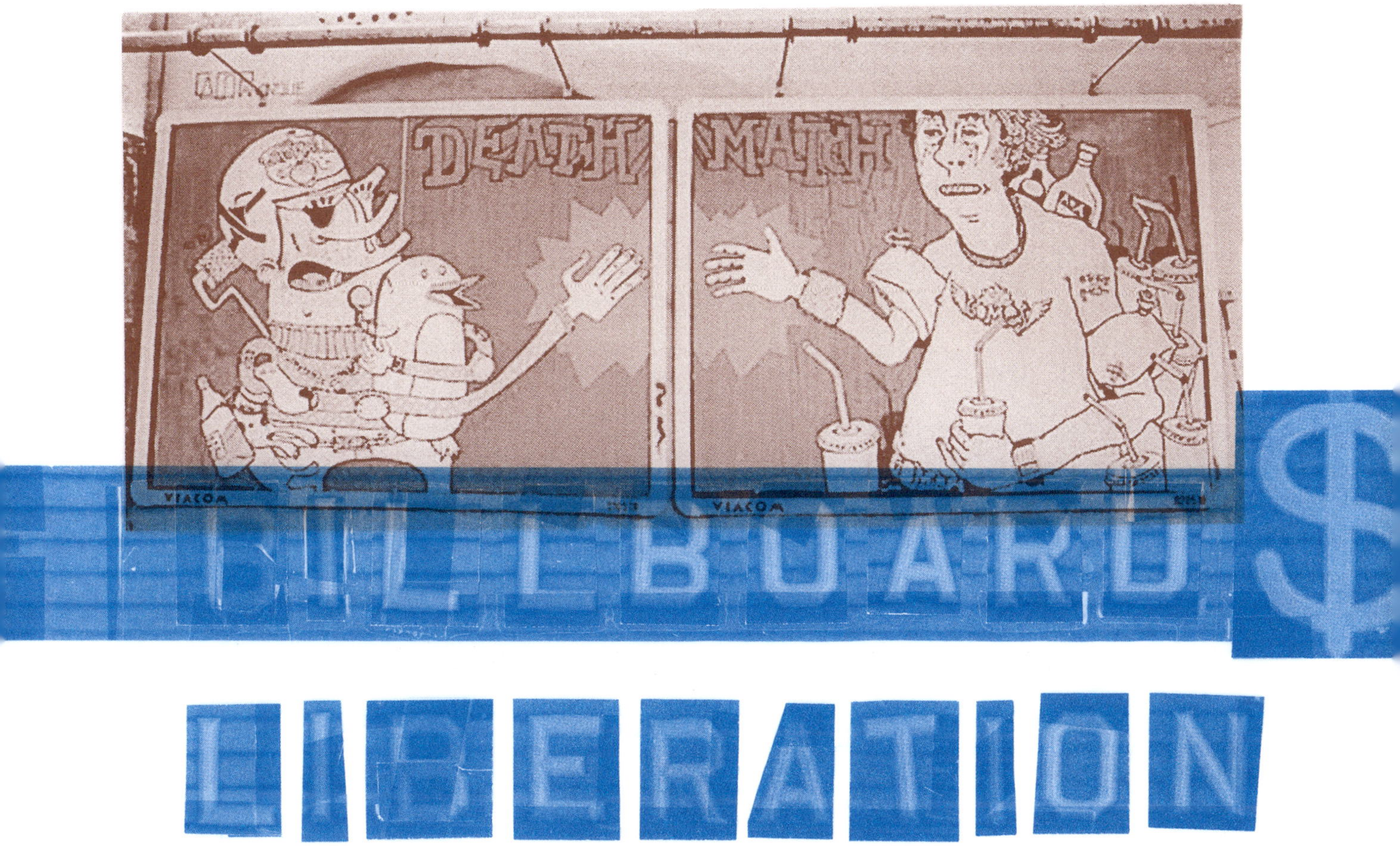

«Plakatflächen sind so allgegenwärtig geworden wie menschliches Leiden, so schwer zu ignorieren wie die ausgestreckte Faust eines Bettlers. Jedes Mal wenn du deine Couch oder Behausung verlässt, für einen Moment die elektronische Nabelschnur unterbrechend, betrittst du den Bereich ihrer Eindrücke. Überlebensgross, subtil wie ein Krieg, greifen sie deine Sinne mit komplexen Codes kommerzieller Anweisungen an. ...

«Billboards have become as ubiquitous as human suffering, as difficult to ignore as a beggar's outstreched fist. Every time you leave your couch or cubicle, momentarily severing the electronic umbilicus, you enter the realm of their impressions. Larger than life, subtle as war, they assault your senses with a complex coda of commercial instructions. ...

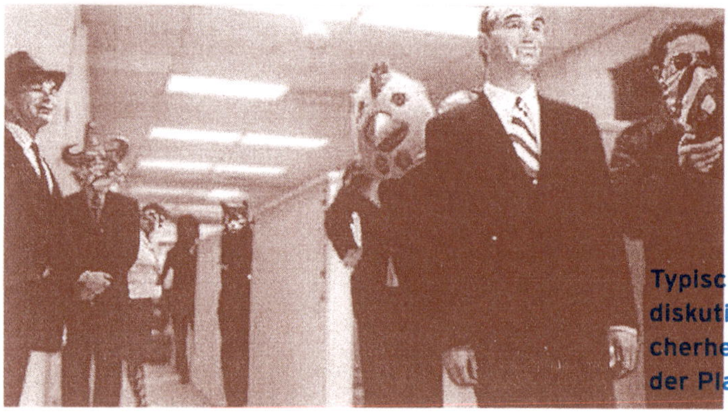

Typischerweise arbeiten 10 – 12 Leute an einem Projekt. Sie diskutieren allgemeine Ideen über Ort und Inhalt und Sicherheitsfragen. Der erste Schritt ist das auskundschaften der Plakatwände.

TECHNIQUES AND

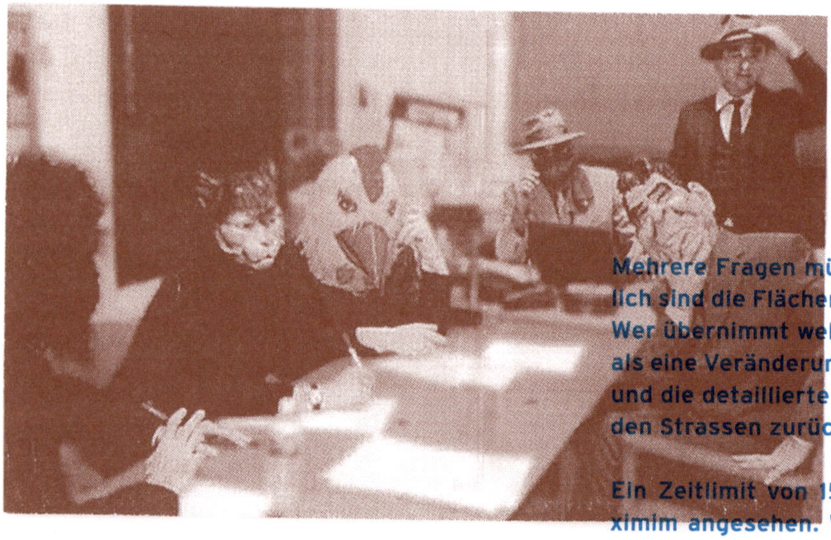

Mehrere Fragen müssen beantwortet werden: wie zugänglich sind die Flächen? Wie hoch? Was soll verändert werden? Wer übernimmt welche Aufgaben? Reicht die Zeit für mehr als eine Veränderung in einer Nacht? Der kollektive Prozess und die detaillierte Planung beginnen, wenn die Scouts von den Strassen zurückkehren.

Ein Zeitlimit von 15 Minuten für jede Aktion wird als Maximim angesehen. Während 4-5 Leute direkt an der Wand arbeiten, fungiert eine ähnliche Anzahl als Posten, Obdachlose, Geschäftsleute oder Betrunkene spielend, können mit Taschenlampen oder Funkgeräten warnen.

Die effektivsten Veränderungen sind oft die einfachsten. Umso besser, wenn mehrere Plakate einer Kampagne verbessert werden können.

...

Typically, 10 to 12 people are involved in any particular effort. They discuss general ideas about locale, content and security. Specific plans follow quickly. The initial step is to scout the billboards in a target area.

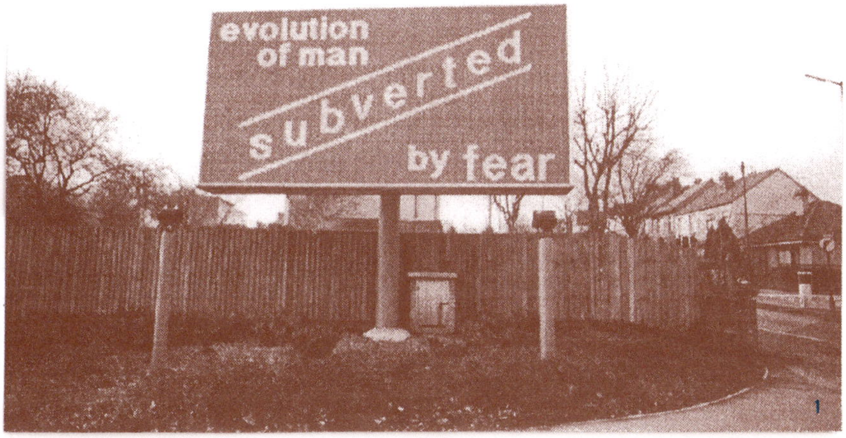

1

APPLICATIONS

Several questions must be raised and answered: How accessible are they? How high? How much physical alteration is necessary? Which members should perform which tasks? Is there time for several alterations during the outing? The collective process continues when scouts return from the streets for more detailed planning.

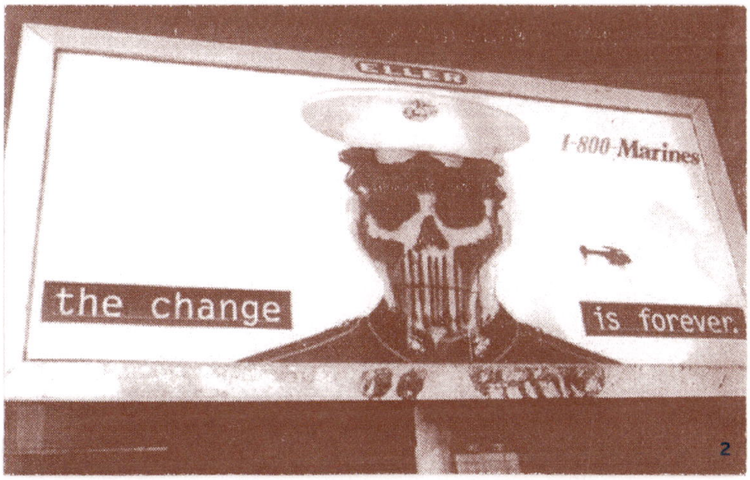

2

A 15-minute time limit is considered a maximum for a single action. While 4 to 5 people are on the actual structure, a similar number, dressed as beggars, business people or drunks, watch for police or others who might interfere. Armed with flashlights or CB radios they warn their cohorts about potential trouble.

Keep in mind that the most effective alterations are often the simplest. Of course, if you can improve more than one board in the same campaign, so much the better. ...

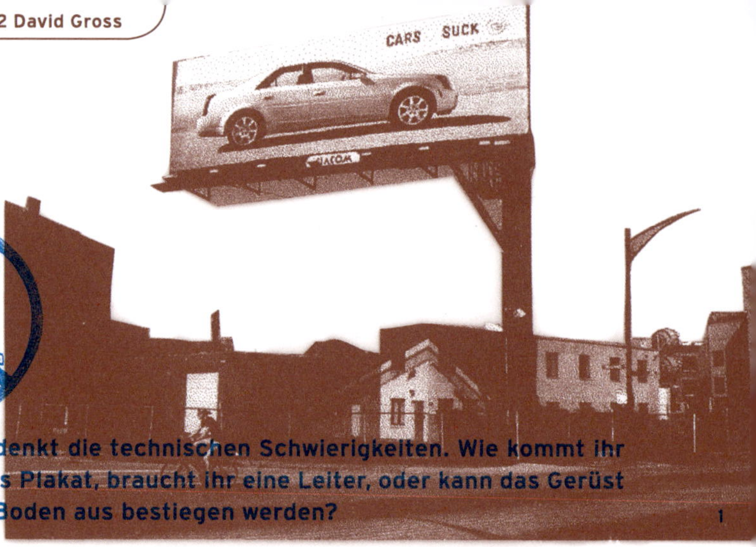

Überdenkt die technischen Schwierigkeiten. Wie kommt ihr an das Plakat, braucht ihr eine Leiter, oder kann das Gerüst vom Boden aus bestiegen werden?

1

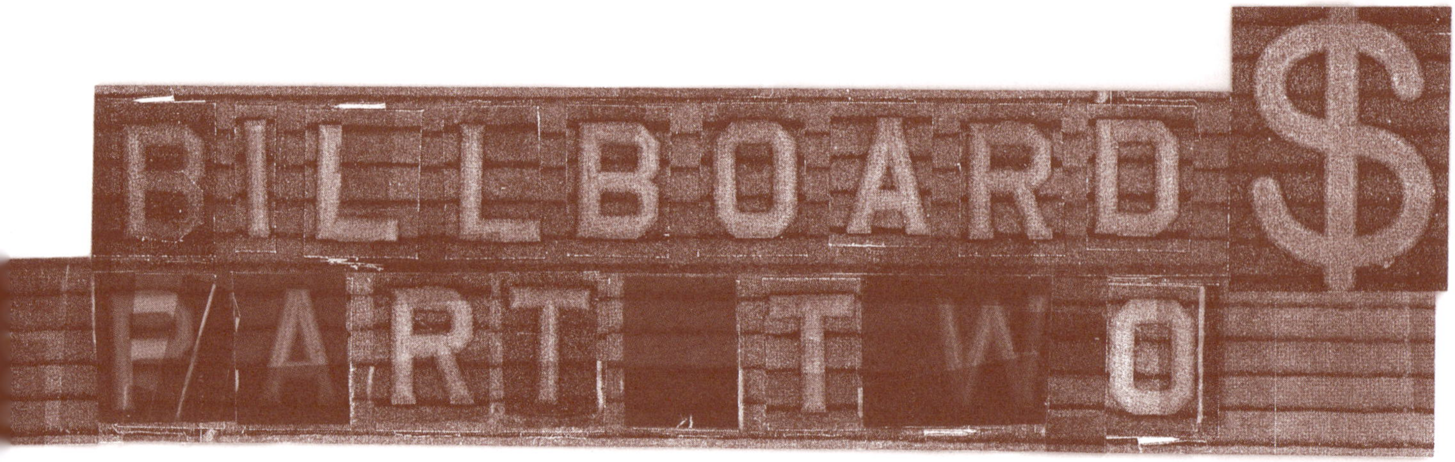

Kleinere Plakate, die nah am Boden hängen und so die Bearbeitung erleichtern, können während des Tages in Angriff genommen werden. Tragt Overalls (mit aufgedruckten Firmennamen?) und Malermützen. Arbeitet schnell.

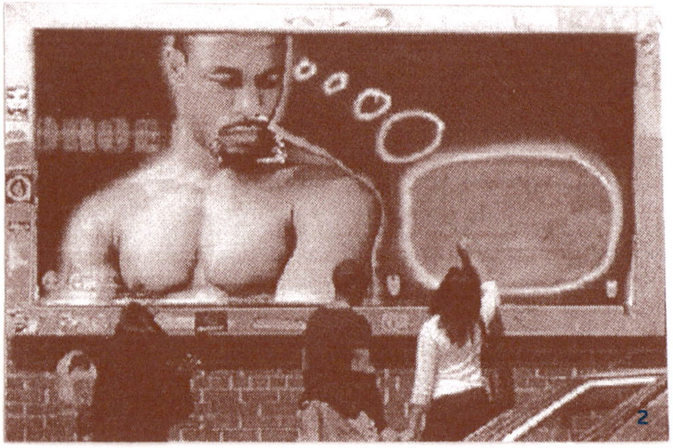

2

Consider the technical difficulties. How do you get up to the billboard? Will you need your own ladder to reach the bottom of the billboard's ladder or can you just climb the structure?

Daytime hits work well for doing smaller billboards lower to the ground where the alteration is relatively quick and simple. If you do choose to work in the light, wear coveralls (company name on the back?) and painters' hats. Work quickly.

Large boards: the finished layout's scale can be planned with photographs of the target. Colour-match by cutting a sample from the board or use a colour sample book. Letter styles can be found in font books.

2 sniggle.net/chalkboard (USA, int.)

Enlarge your improved layout through tiling. This can be done automatically using popular computer programs like QuarkXpress and PageMaker, or with a good copier. Draw a grid that's equivalent to the copier's largest paper size on the scaled drawing or printout, then cut along the grid and enlarge each panel for as many times as necessary. Then cut-and-glue to heavy pattern paper.
Be sure to photograph and publicize your hit to the local media. The more creative you are when relaying the message, the more attention it'll get.»

Quotes from:
BLF, «The Art & Science of Billboard Improvement»

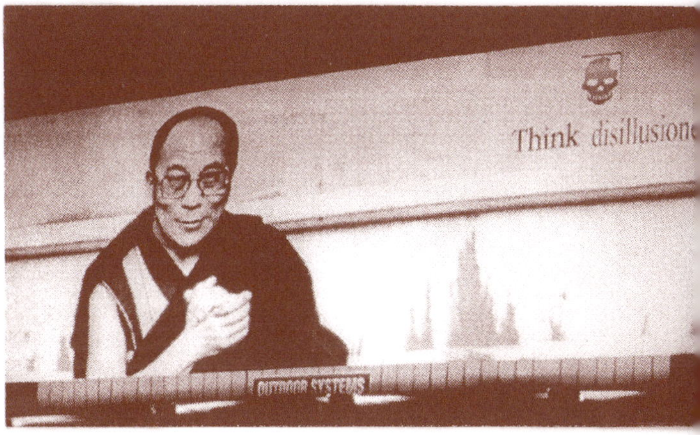

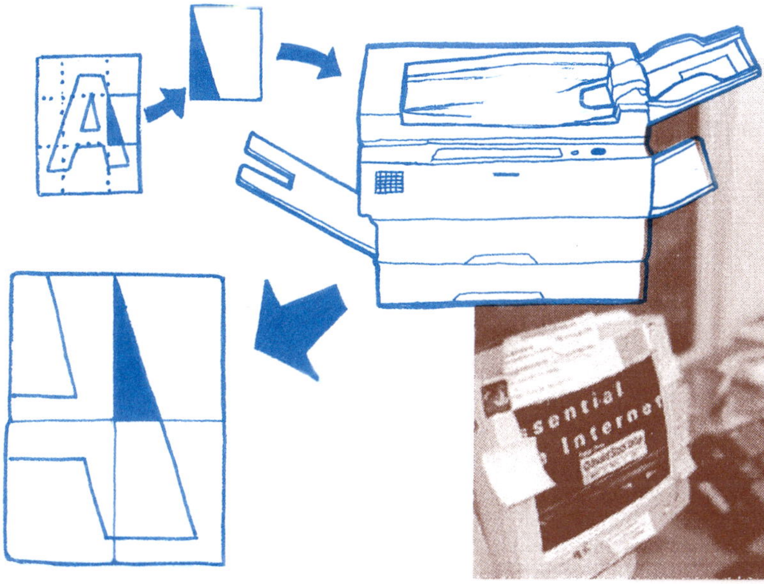

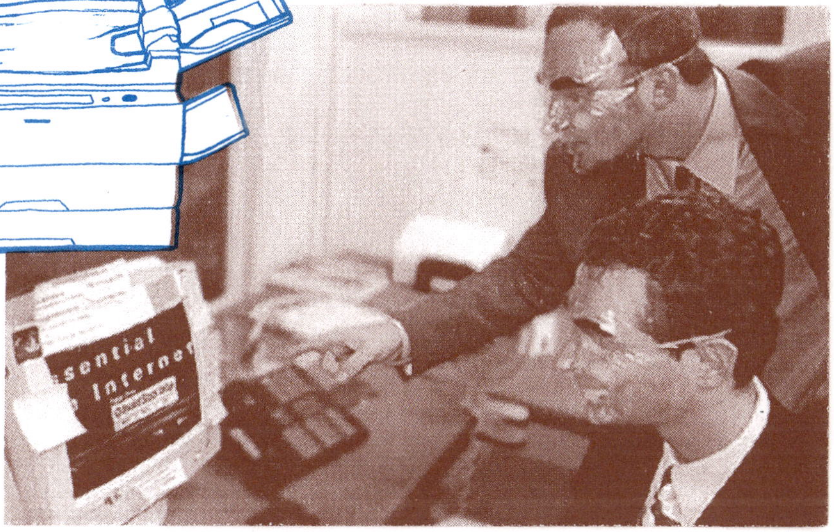

Auf Grossflächen: die Masse des fertigen Layouts können anhand eines Frontalfotos bestimmt oder direkt abgemessen werden. Farben können über Plakatproben oder Farbfächer bestimmt werden, Schriften anhand von Schriftbüchern.
Vergrössert das überarbeitete Layout durch die Druckoption «Montagefläche» der Computer-Printprogramme oder benutzt eienen Kopierer mit Vergrösserungsfunktion: über Entwurf oder Ausdruck wird ein Raster gezeichnet, dessen Felder den Seitenverhältnissen des verfügbaren Papierformats entsprechen. Ausgeschnitten können die Felder nun sooft es nötig ist vergrössert und auf reissfestem Papier zum fertigen Bild zusammengefügt werden.
Fotografiert den Eingriff und benachrichtigt die lokale Presse. Je phantasievoller die Nachricht überbracht wird, desto mehr Aufmerksamkeit wird sie bekommen.»
Zitate aus:
BLF, «The Art & Science of Billboard Improvement»

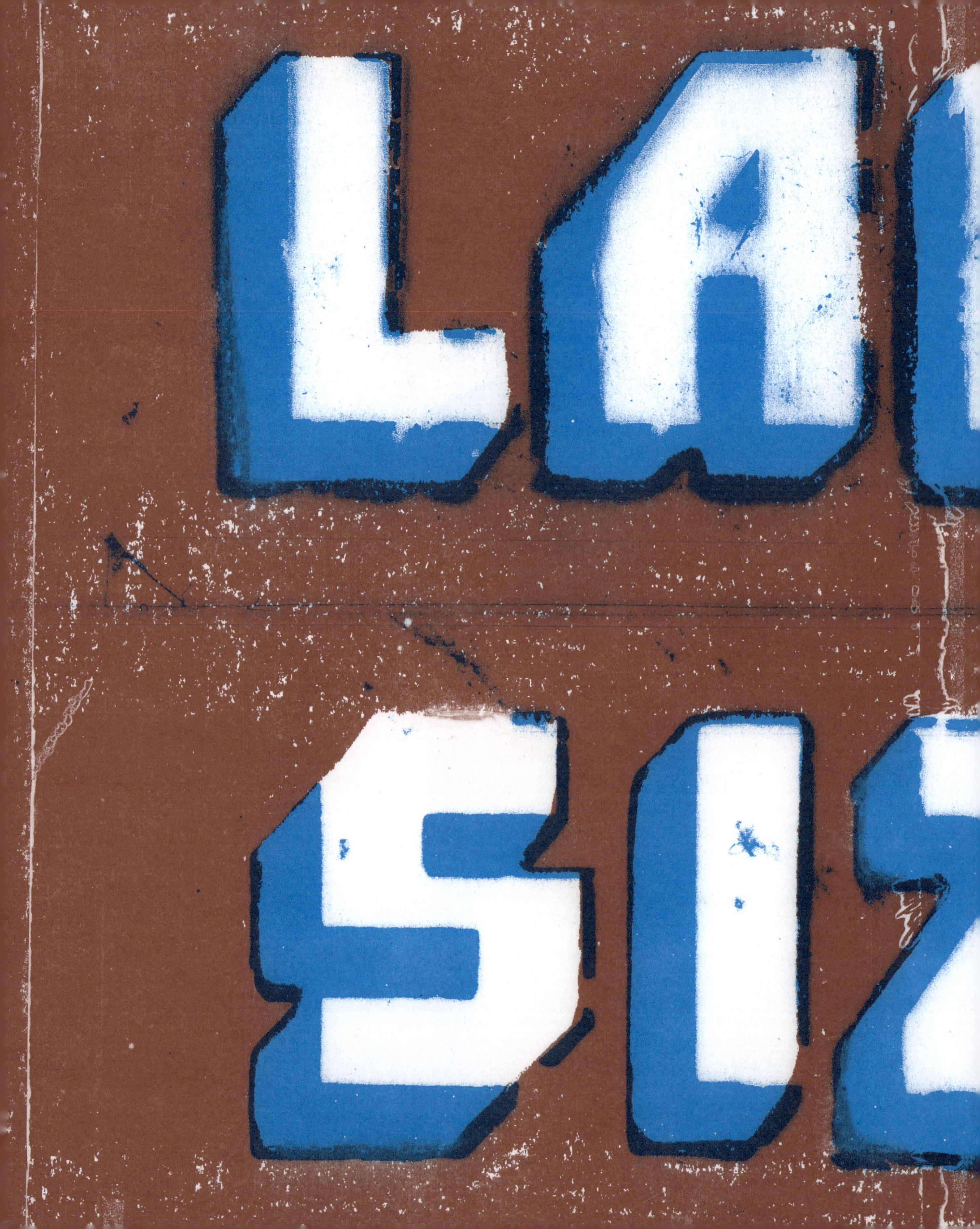
LA
SI

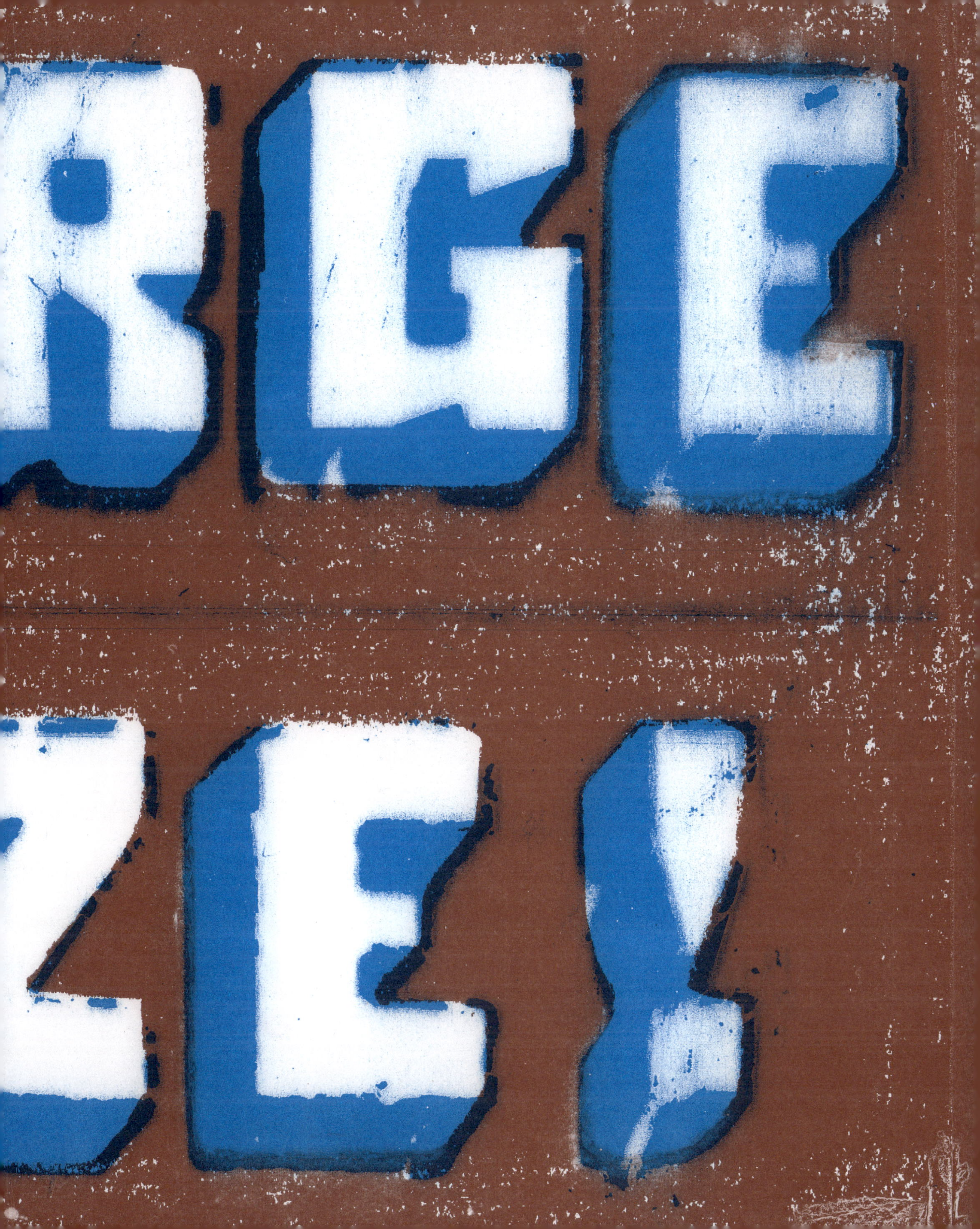
RGE
ZE!

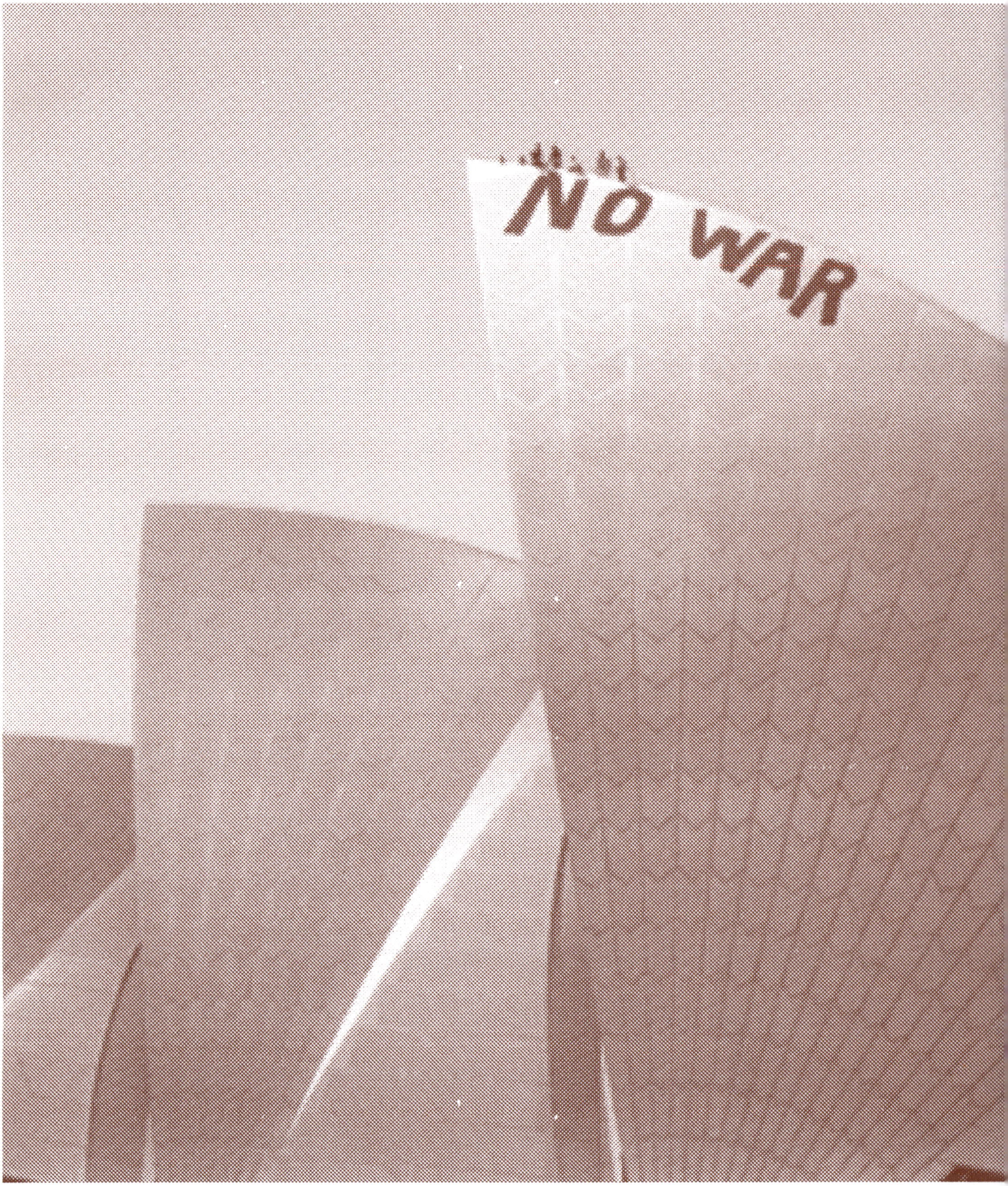

Sydney opera, 2003, Sydney (Australia)

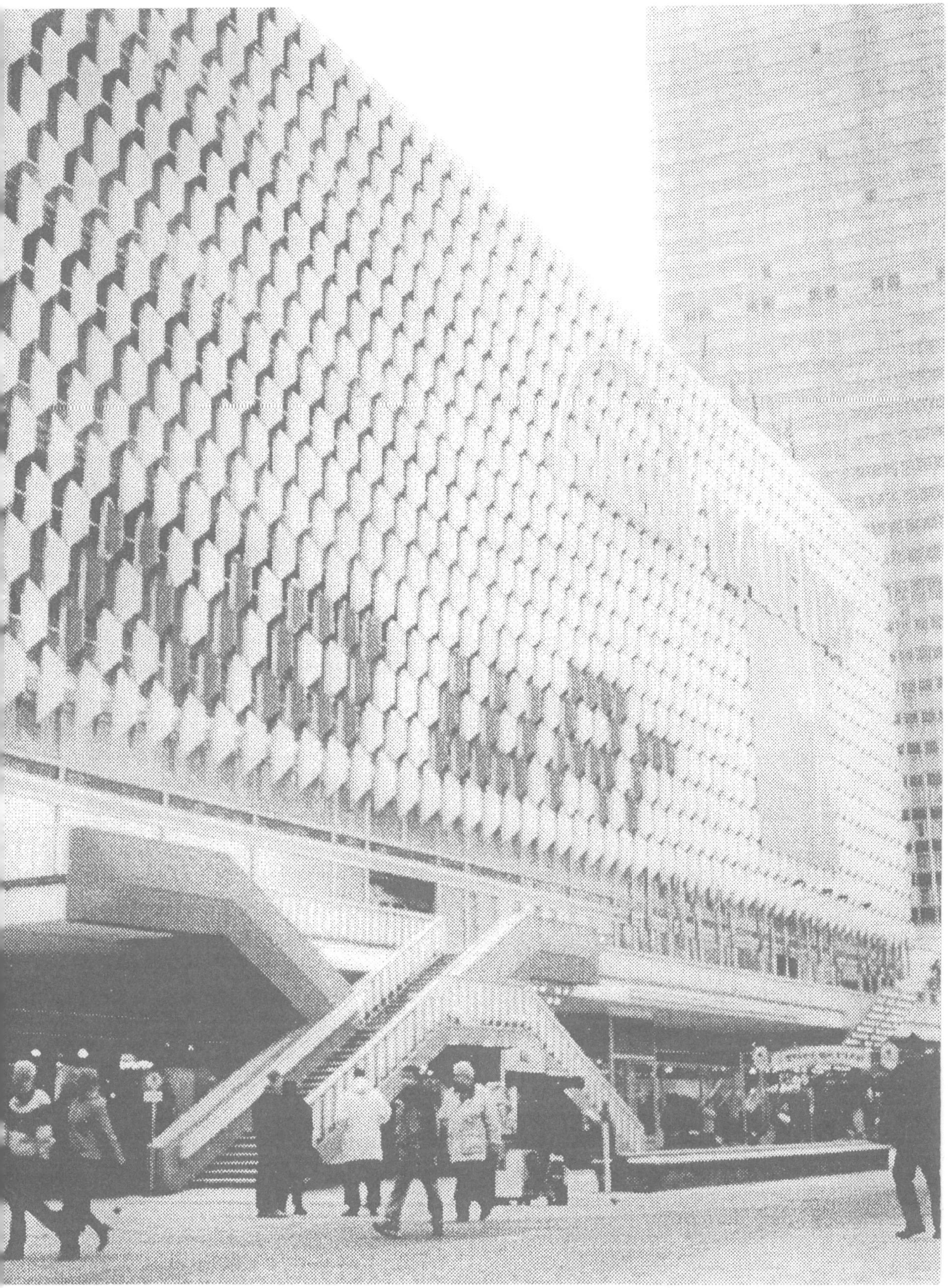

Alexanderplatz, 2003, Berlin (Germany)

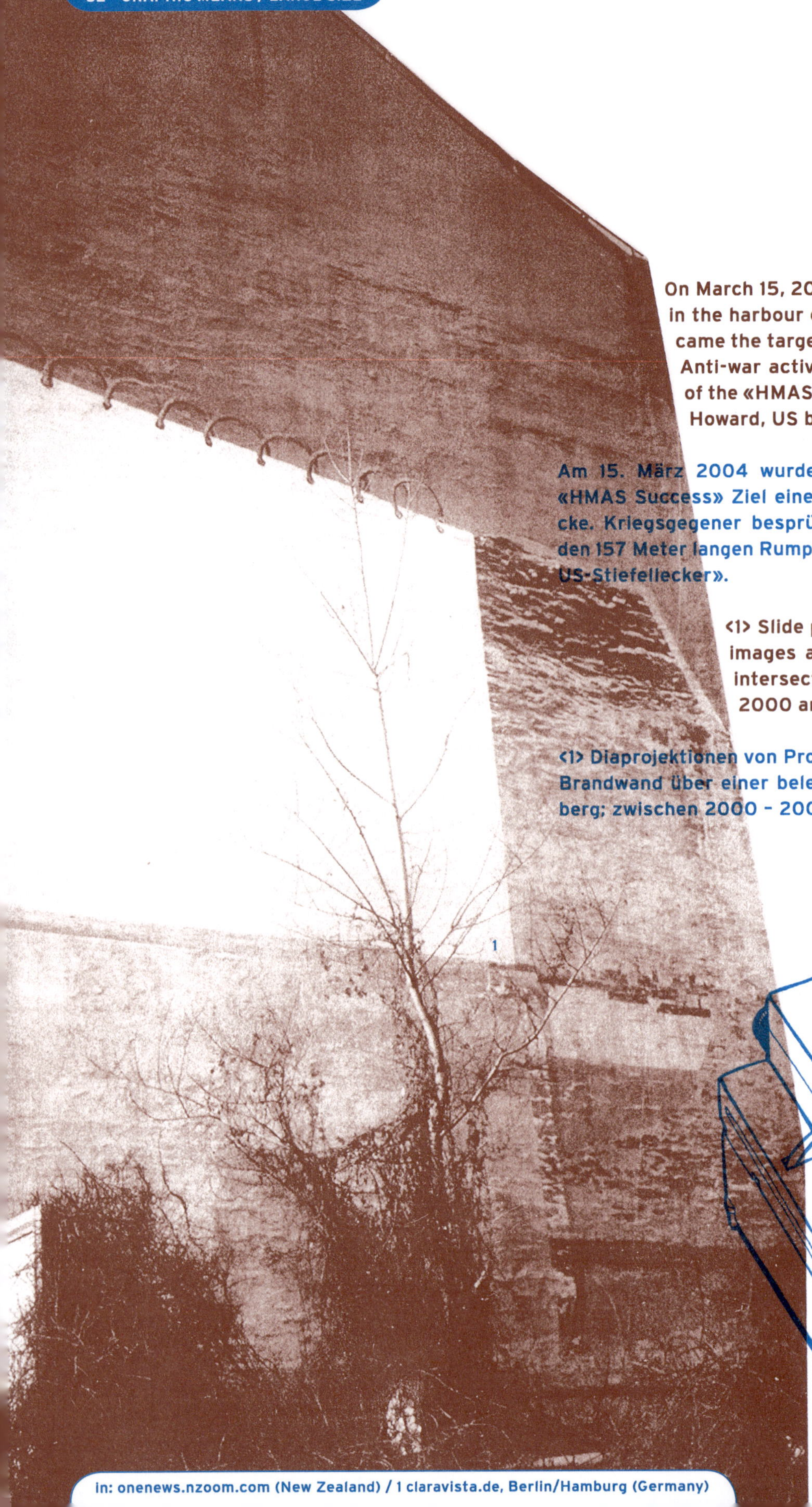

1

On March 15, 2004 an Australian warship laying in the harbour of Wellington (New Zealand) became the target of a large scale graffiti attack. Anti-war activists sprayed the 157-metre hull of the «HMAS Success» with the words: «John Howard, US bootlicker» in fluorescent green.

Am 15. März 2004 wurde das australische Kriegsschiff «HMAS Success» Ziel einer gross angelegten Graffitiattacke. Kriegsgegener besprühten in leuchtendgrüner Farbe den 157 Meter langen Rumpf mit den Worten: «John Howard, US-Stiefellecker».

<1> Slide projections of self-made protest images and texts on a wall over a busy intersection in Berlin (Germany) between 2000 and 2002.

<1> Diaprojektionen von Protestbildern und -texten an einer Brandwand über einer belebten Kreuzung in Berlin Kreuzberg; zwischen 2000 – 2002.

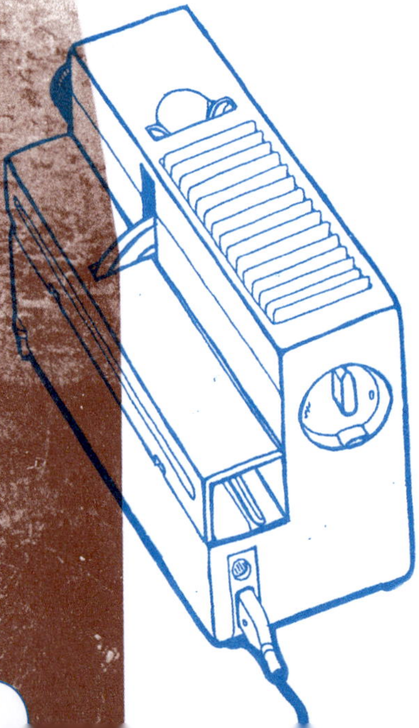

in: onenews.nzoom.com (New Zealand) / 1 claravista.de, Berlin/Hamburg (Germany)

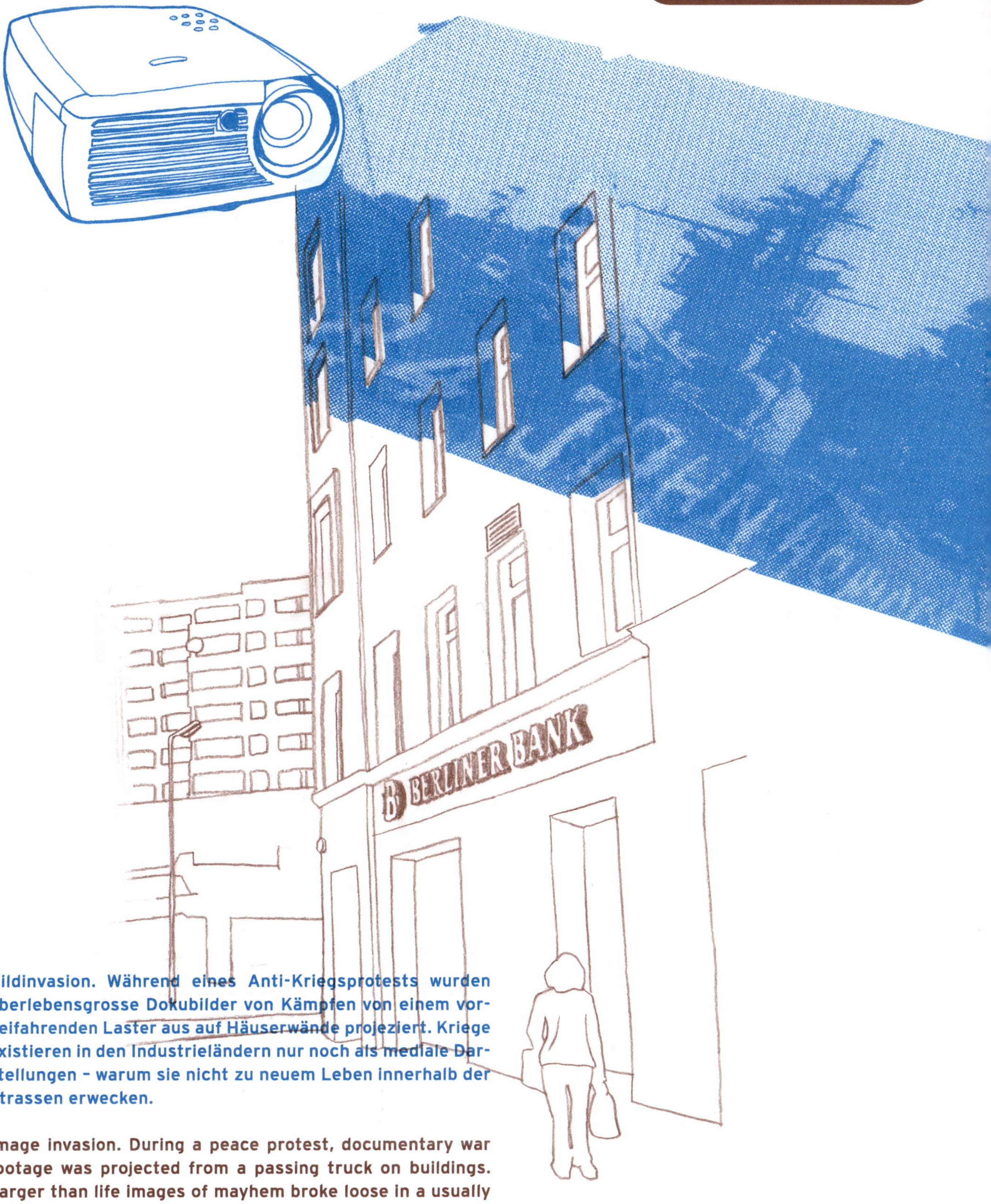

Bildinvasion. Während eines Anti-Kriegsprotests wurden überlebensgrosse Dokubilder von Kämpfen von einem vorbeifahrenden Laster aus auf Häuserwände projeziert. Kriege existieren in den Industrieländern nur noch als mediale Darstellungen – warum sie nicht zu neuem Leben innerhalb der Strassen erwecken.

Image invasion. During a peace protest, documentary war footage was projected from a passing truck on buildings. Larger than life images of mayhem broke loose in a usually quiet city. Wars are known to those living in the industrialized nations merely as media images. So why not bring them back to life in the streets again?

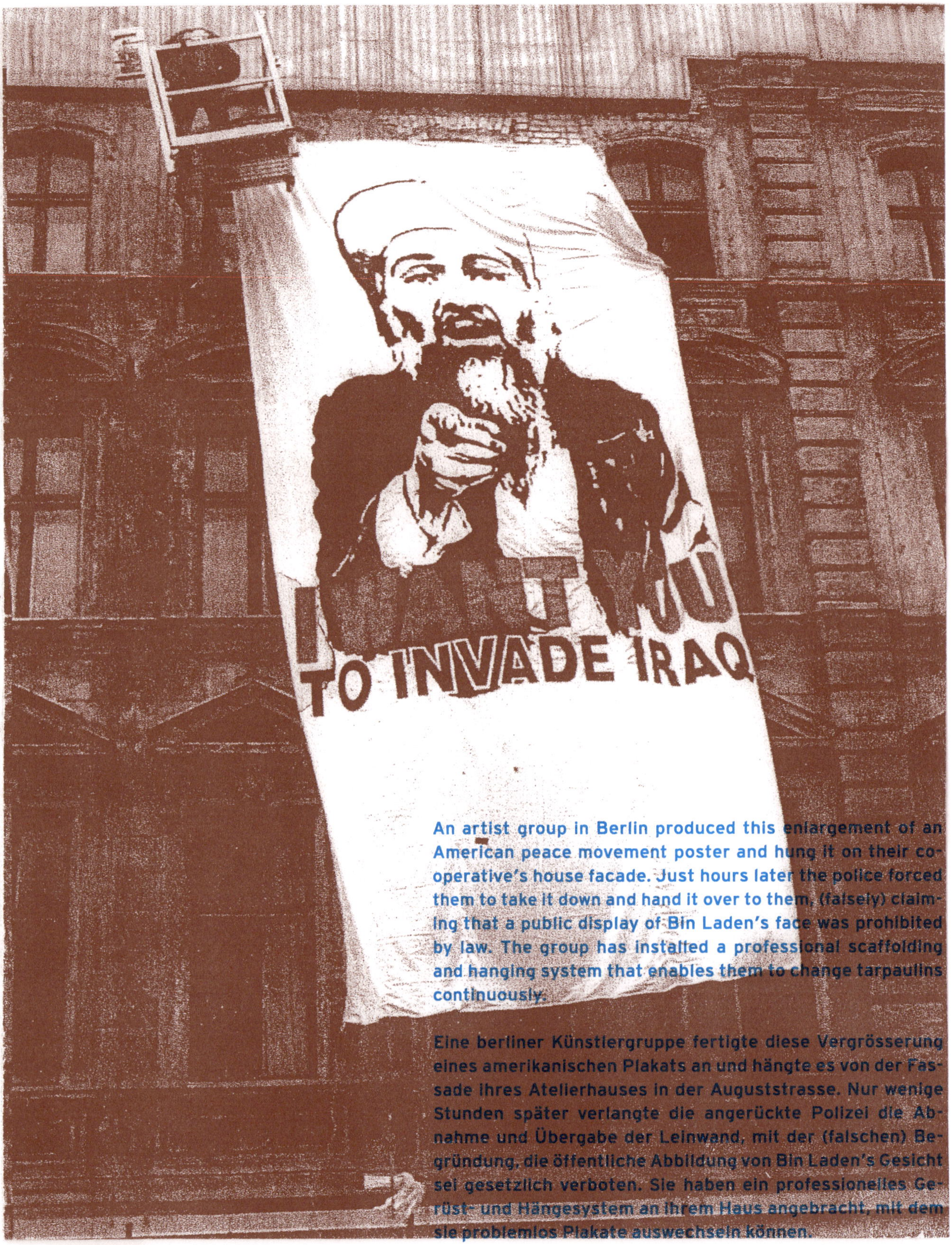

An artist group in Berlin produced this enlargement of an American peace movement poster and hung it on their co-operative's house facade. Just hours later the police forced them to take it down and hand it over to them, (falsely) claiming that a public display of Bin Laden's face was prohibited by law. The group has installed a professional scaffolding and hanging system that enables them to change tarpaulins continuously.

Eine berliner Künstlergruppe fertigte diese Vergrösserung eines amerikanischen Plakats an und hängte es von der Fassade ihres Atelierhauses in der Auguststrasse. Nur wenige Stunden später verlangte die angerückte Polizei die Abnahme und Übergabe der Leinwand, mit der (falschen) Begründung, die öffentliche Abbildung von Bin Laden's Gesicht sei gesetzlich verboten. Sie haben ein professionelles Gerüst- und Hängesystem an ihrem Haus angebracht, mit dem sie problemlos Plakate auswechseln können.

This image became an icon of the evolving «No Global» movement. The action took place during the G8 protests in Seattle in 1999, and had been executed by the «Ruckus Society», a training group that promotes and teaches the implementation of strategic nonviolent direct action, organized strategic development and planning, effective media work and IT activism.

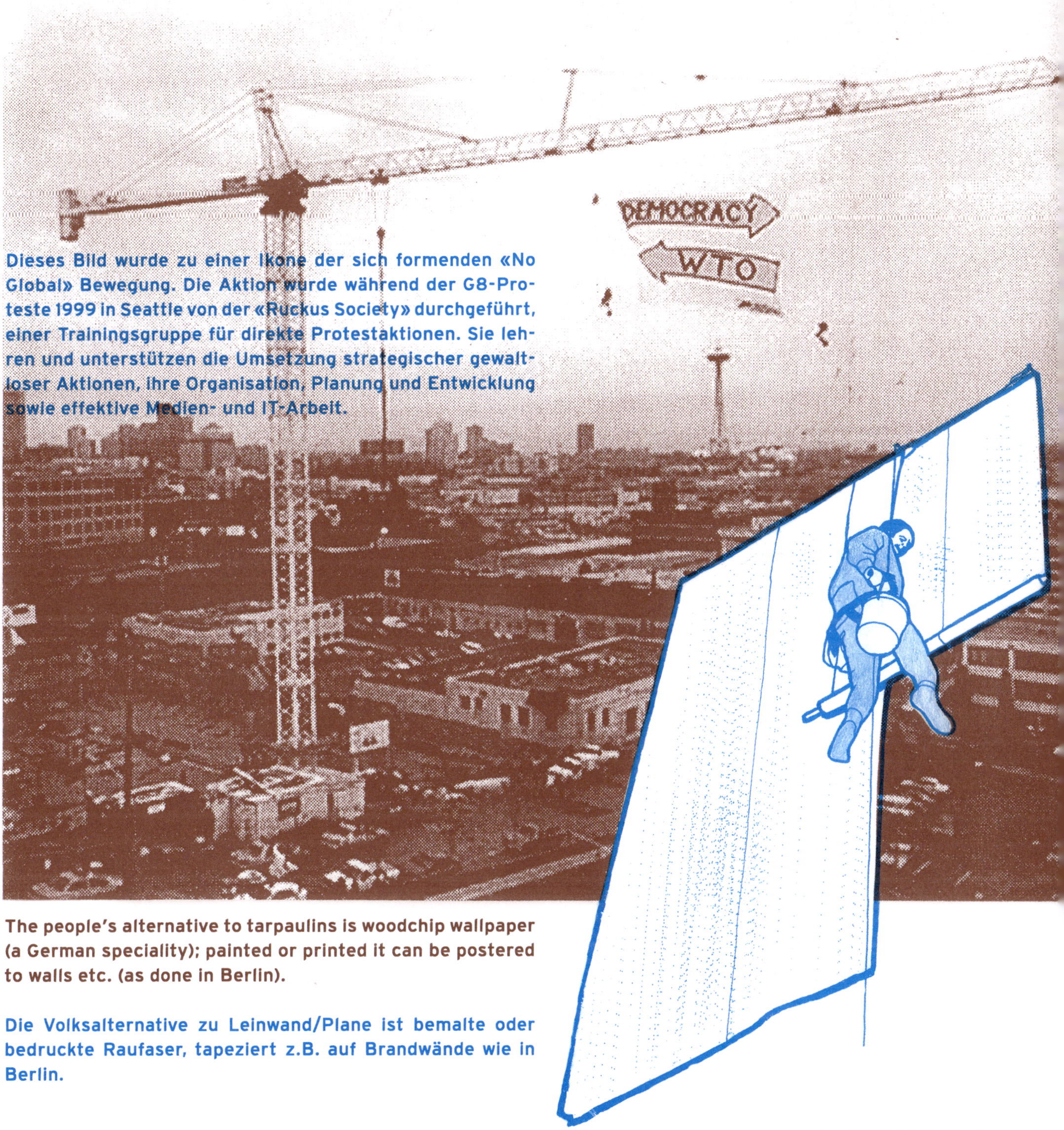

Dieses Bild wurde zu einer Ikone der sich formenden «No Global» Bewegung. Die Aktion wurde während der G8-Proteste 1999 in Seattle von der «Ruckus Society» durchgeführt, einer Trainingsgruppe für direkte Protestaktionen. Sie lehren und unterstützen die Umsetzung strategischer gewaltloser Aktionen, ihre Organisation, Planung und Entwicklung sowie effektive Medien- und IT-Arbeit.

The people's alternative to tarpaulins is woodchip wallpaper (a German speciality); painted or printed it can be postered to walls etc. (as done in Berlin).

Die Volksalternative zu Leinwand/Plane ist bemalte oder bedruckte Raufaser, tapeziert z.B. auf Brandwände wie in Berlin.

 Critical Art Ensemble > 37, 77, 83, 97, 120

TRANSPORT

«Critical Art Ensemble and Beatriz de Costa / Digital Tags»: During a workshop participants learned how to build autonomous digital screens that displayed a pre-programmed moving text. The finished tags were arranged in different places in New York City (USA).

The workshop explored new ways of making a message visible; an electronic device gets much more attention and respect in the eyes of most people than a painted or sprayed message ever will.

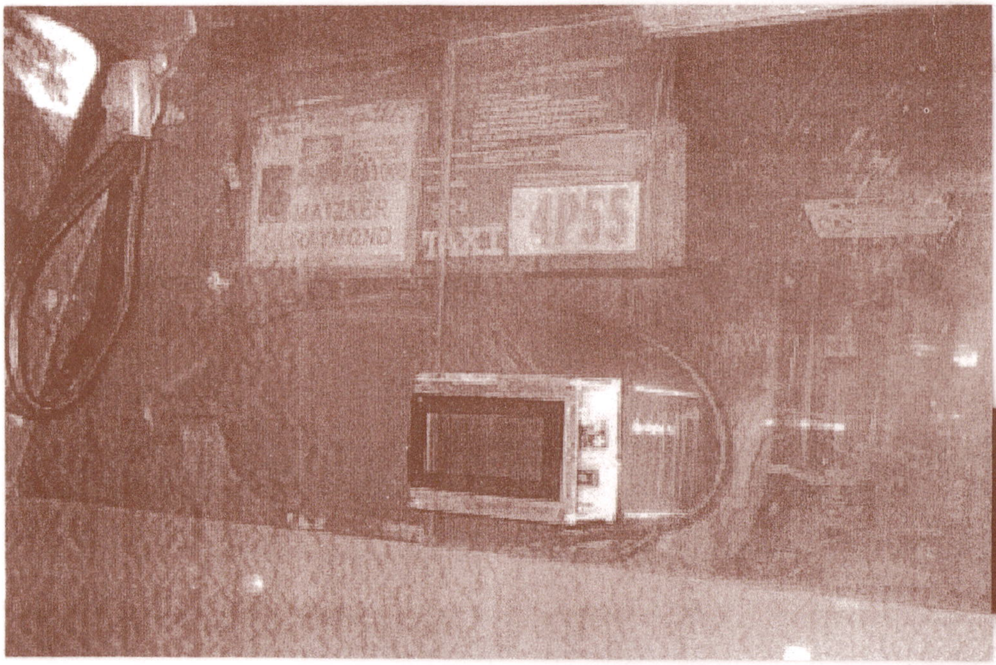

«Critical Art Ensemble and Beatriz de Costa / Digitale Tags»: In einem Workshop lernten die Teilnehmer kleine LCD-Anzeigen zu bauen, die von äusseren Stromquellen unabhängig, einen programmierten Text ablaufen liessen. Die Tags wurden an verschiedenen Orten in New York (USA) angebracht.

Der Workshop untersuchte neue Wege der sichtbarmachung von Botschaften. Einem elektronischen Gerät wird eine ganz andere Bedeutung und Stellenwert beigemessen als etwas geschriebenem oder gesprühtem.

«Bitcab: BIT inserts geospecific data directly into NYC taxi display units, which are used for advertising, financial, sports or weather data. The Bureau has secured access to the signage and will be inserting critical location-based data (such as details of toxic residues) at current GPS positions of the vehicle, and real-time news alerts for street-based actions.

The «BIT Cab Information» overlays advertising, moving through the taxi display with a velocity related to the cab's speed. While this will not obscure the original message, the layering will provide a reason to look. The Bureau explored use of the system for strategic news alerts at the WEF street actions in February 2002. The BIT insertions can be seen as electronic graffiti.» Text: Bureau IT

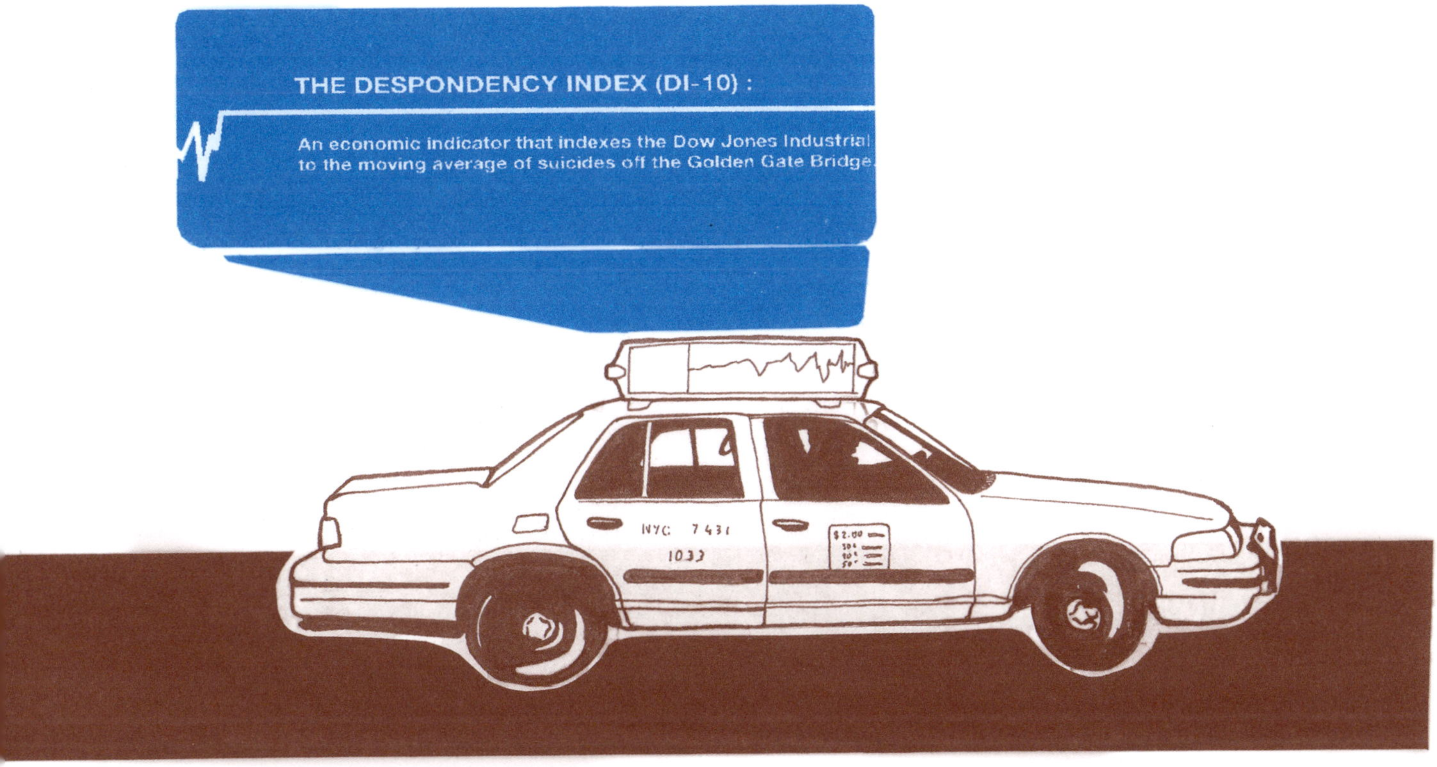

«BITcab: BIT überspielt geospezifische Daten direkt auf die elektonischen Dachdisplays von New Yorker Taxen. Diese werden normalerweise zur Anzeige von Werbung, Finanz-, Sport- und Wetterdaten genutzt. Das Bureau hat den Code der Anzeigen geknackt und wird kritische, ortsrelevante Daten (wie Details über giftige Rückstände, Echtzeit-Bulletins für Strassenaktionen) in die Anzeigen einspeisen, sobald sich Fahrzeuge an betreffenden GPS-Positionen befinden.

Die «BIT Cab Information» überblendet die Werbung und bewegt sich mit einer Geschwindigkeit über das Display, die der Fahrtgeschwindigkeit des Taxis entspricht. Die Originalanzeige wird nicht gelöscht, es ist die Überblendung, die den Blick auf sich zieht. Das Bureau hat die Nutzung des Systems bereits während der WEF-Strassenaktionen im Februar 2002 erforscht.

Die BIT-Infiltration kann als eine Art von elektronischem Graffiti angesehen werden.» Text: Bureau IT

<1> Paint the town... rosé. A number of subway entrances in Boston (USA) have been painted pink by unknown villains. No political motives could be identified – but it added a nice touch to the commuter everyday.

<2> France, 2004/05. In all big French cities, but especially in Paris, every Friday a crew of ad-sick youth has started to descend in large mobs into the tunnels to cover the omnipresent advertisement posters with paint and text. Going into the hundreds, they share one common point of view: I'm fed up with ads!

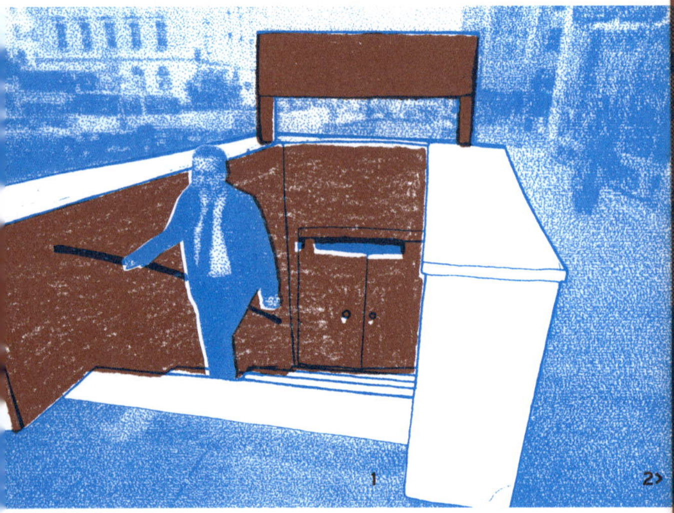

1

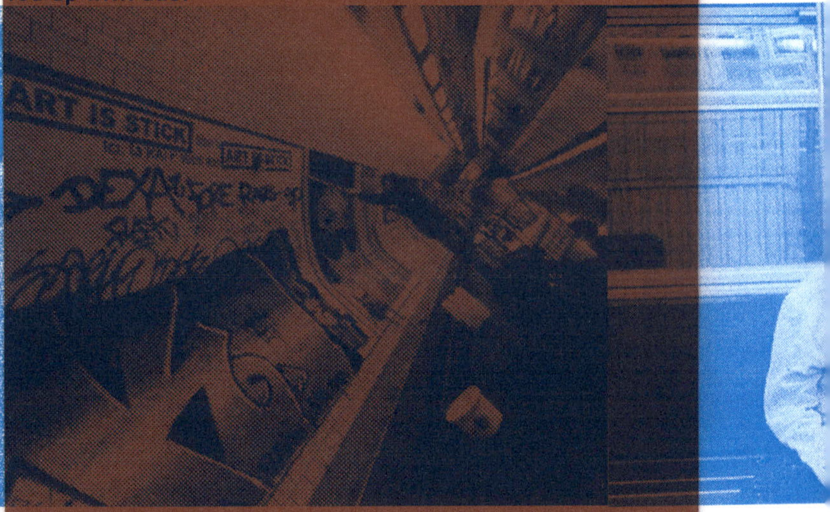

2>

Fed up, too were Akay & the Toyshop Collective. The former covered all of the ads in a Stockholm train with the word «sorry», adding small hanging notes that apologised for everything he had sprayed, painted or changed in his life.
The Collective's approach is rather artistic, turning trains into travelling showrooms <3,4>.

Small sizes can be printed or glued on adhesive film; study the ad frames on the walls: some need to be opened with a simple key, others have an opening on top, stiff material can be slid in.

New York City Transit
Going your way

<1> Mal die Stadt rosa... unbekannte Vandalen haben eine Serie von U-Bahneingängen in Boston (USA) pink bemalt. Politische Motive waren nicht erkennbar – dafür eine surreale Überraschung für das Pendlerleben.

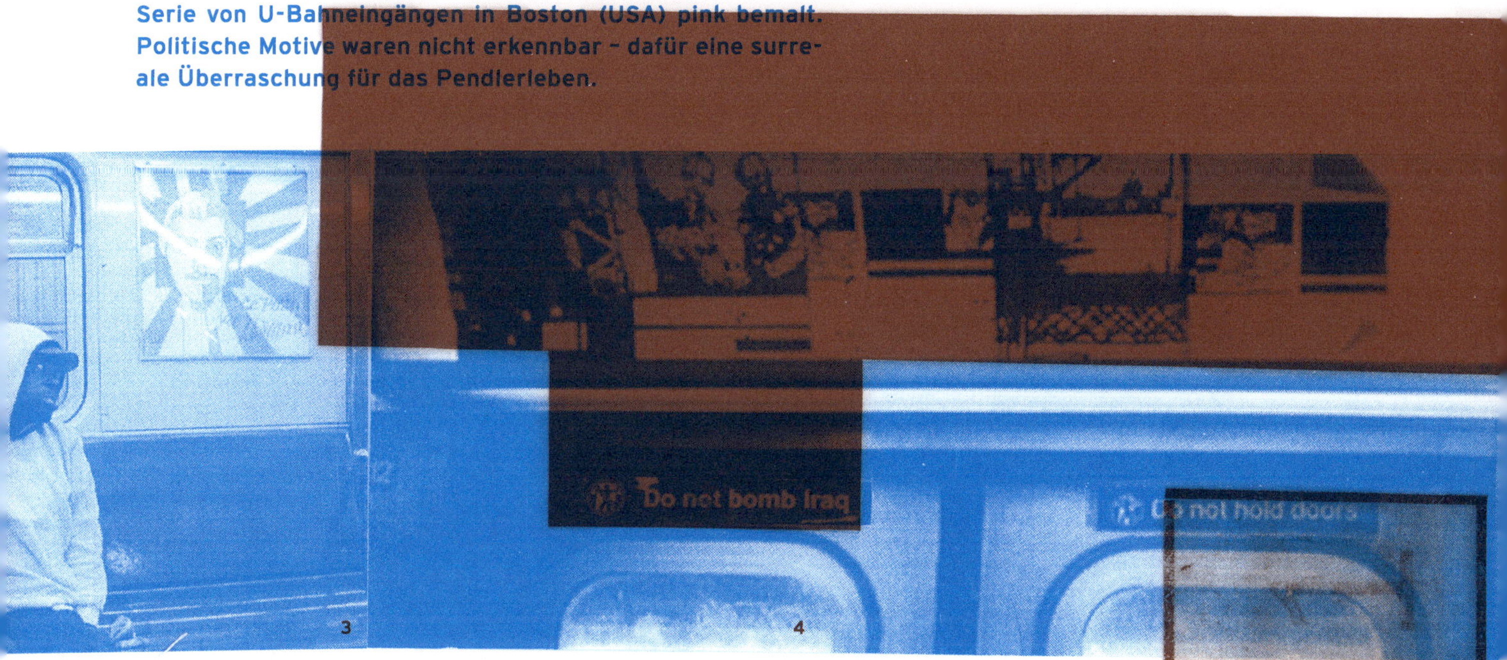

3 4

<2> Frankreich, 2004/05. In den grössten Städten, vor allem jedoch in Paris entsteht eine 'Anti-Werbe-Militia', die freitags in grossen Gruppen die Metrotunnel stürmt und die Werbeplakate bemalt. Sie sind hunderte und haben eines gemeinsam: den Hals voll von Werbung.

Genug hatten auch Akay und die Toyshop Collective. Der erstere deckte alle Werbeflächen in einem stockholmer Zug mit dem Wort «entschuldigung» ab und hängte kleine Zettel mit der Beichte aller seiner Sprüh- und Veränderungsattacken dazu. Die «Collective» ist eher künstlerisch unterwegs und verwandelt U-Bahnwaggons in fahrende Ausstellungen ihrer Zeichnungen <3,4>.

Kleine Formate können auf Klebefolie gedruckt oder kopiert werden. Anzeigenrahmen lassen sich entweder mit einem einfachen Vierkantschlüssel öffnen, oder sie sind oben offen: steife Materialien können eingeschoben werden.

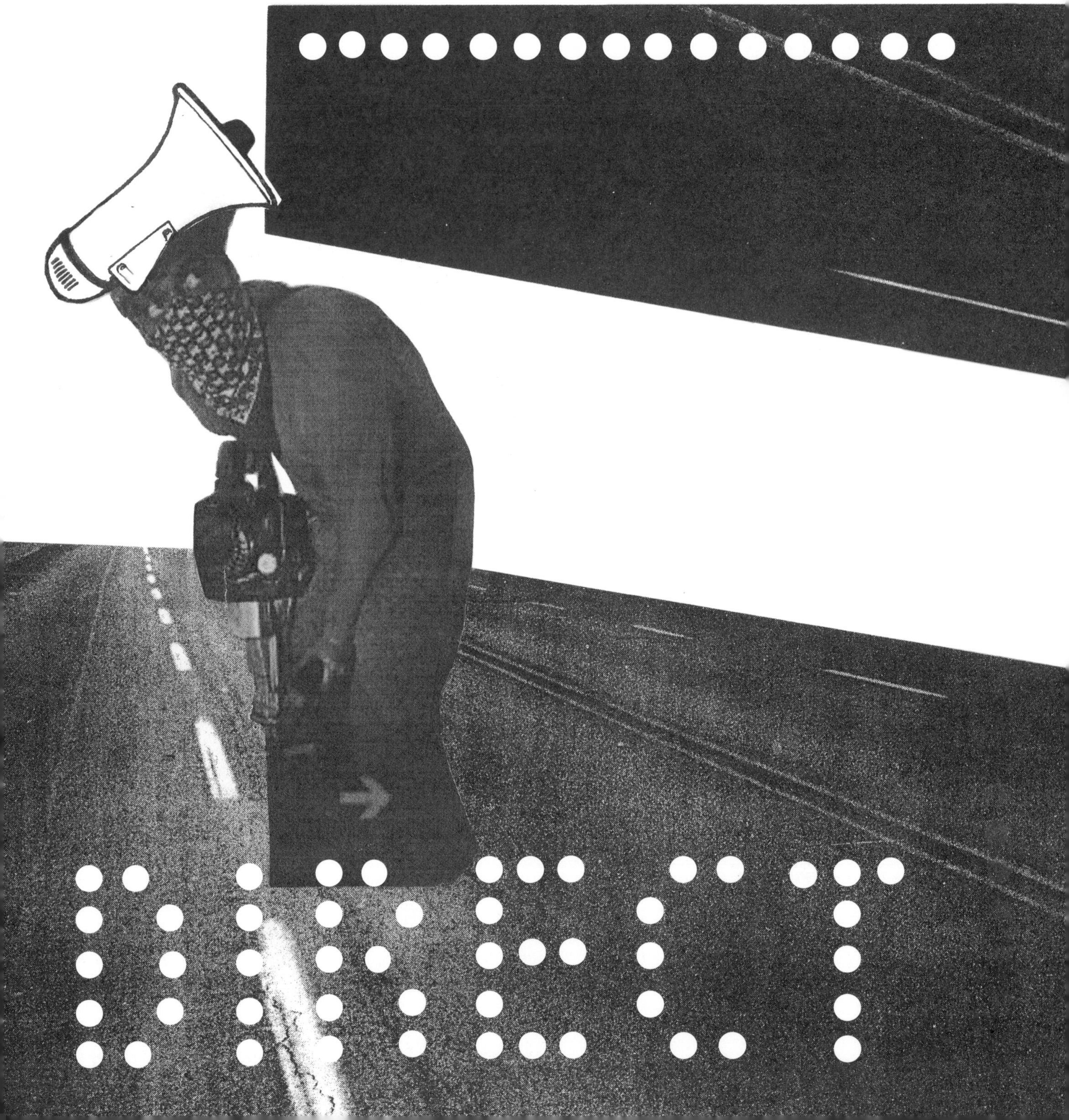
DIRECT

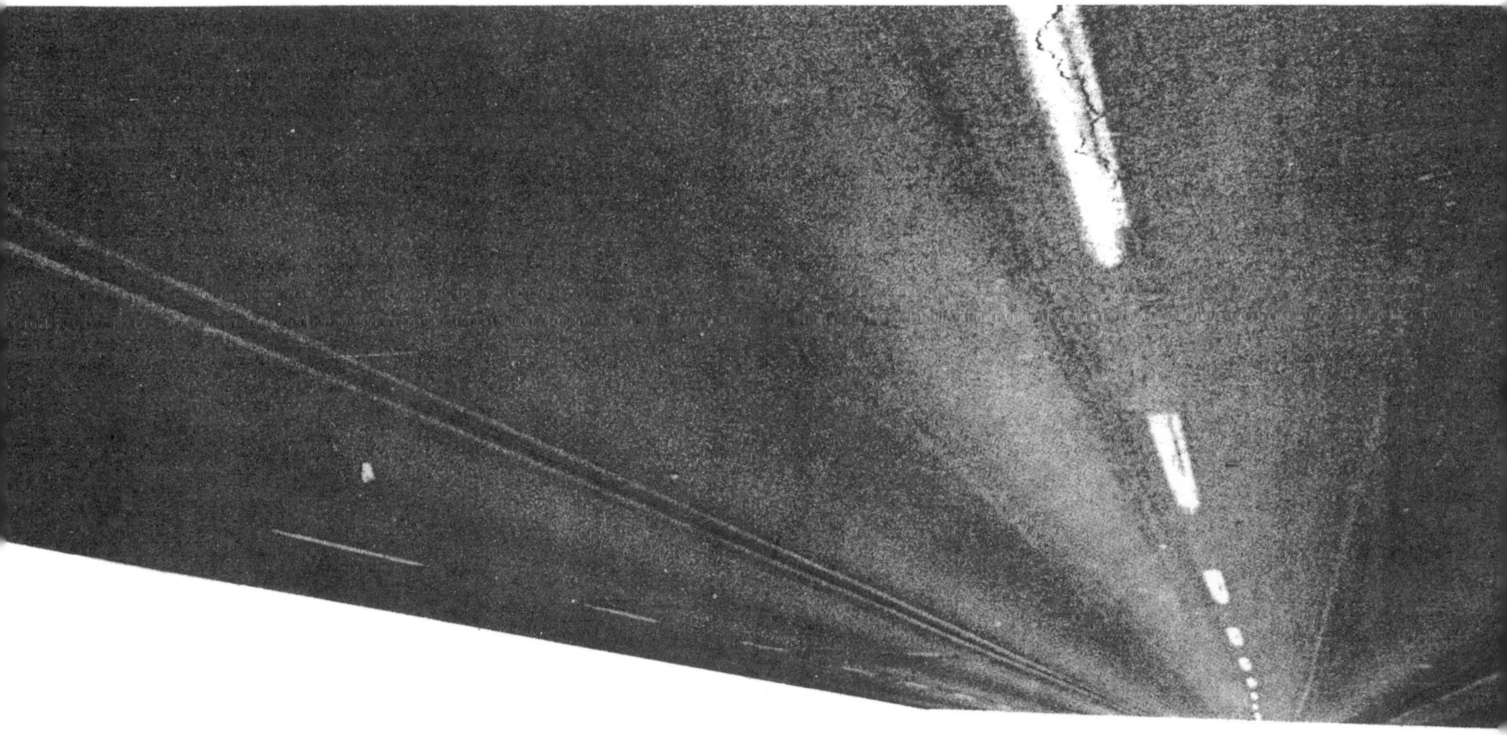

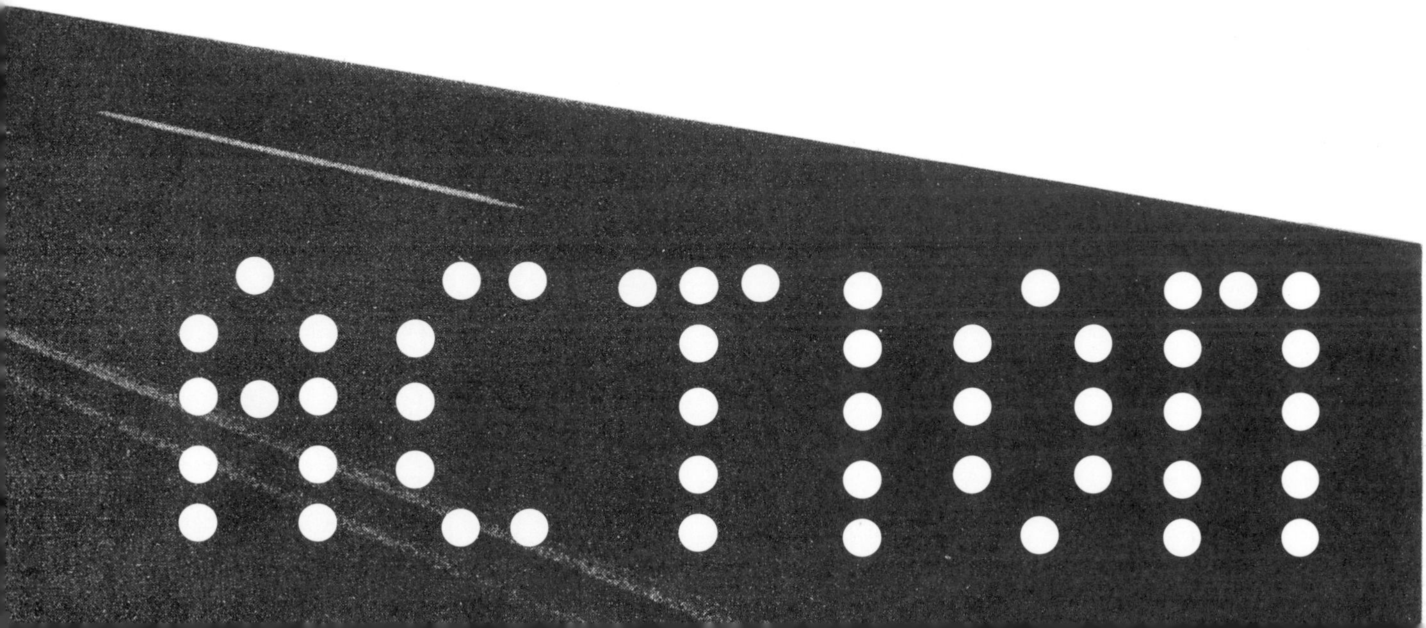
ACTION

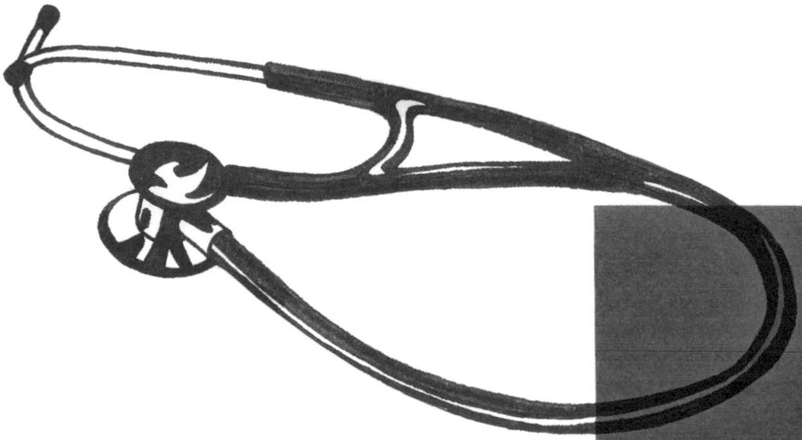

'Escrache' means to make visible, to out. 'Escraches' are an answer to the impunity of junta members from Argentina's military dictatorship of the 1970s. The 'escraches' were used to mark the houses of military criminals, thus exposing their presence in the neighbourhoods. The effect surpassed all expectations: facing their neighbors' loathing, many had to move away.

'Escrache' on Sánchez Ruiz, May 24, 1999: Ruiz was a military medic who, starting in 1976, had been present at tortures, killings and forced births of pregnant prisoners. These newborns have often been offered for adoption to childless military couples; many discovered their real origins as adults only by chance. They founded their own protest group, «H.I.J.O.S.» (children), which organized many of the 'escraches' against military criminals.

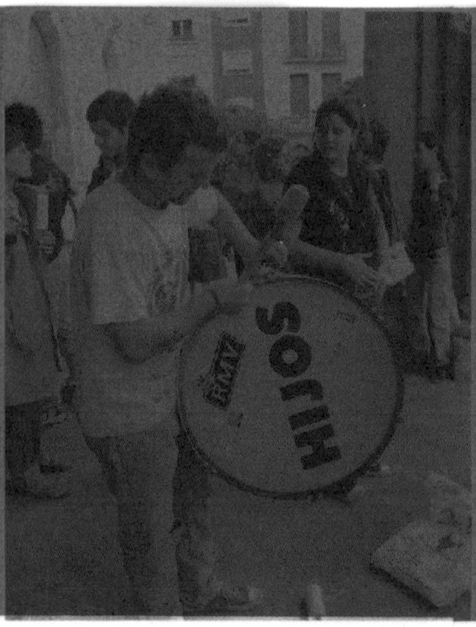

This action consisted of a street performance, re-enacting Ruiz's role in the child-snatchings, right in front of his cordoned-off villa. The performance was followed by a paint-attack on the house.

'Escraches' became well known as the spontanous protests of Argentina's middle class, which was robbed of their savings by a financial crisis. For months, pots and lids were banged against the closed blinds of banks in Buenos Aires.

'Escrache' bedeutet ans Licht bringen, markieren. Es ist die Antwort auf die Straflosigkeit argentinischer Junta-Täter. 'Escraches' werden eingesetzt, um die Anwesenheit der Verbrecher vor der Nachbarschaft zu denunzieren. Diese Taktik hat oft Erfolg: im Angesicht der Abscheu der Bewohner mussten die so markierten Personen mehrmals ihren Wohnsitz ändern.

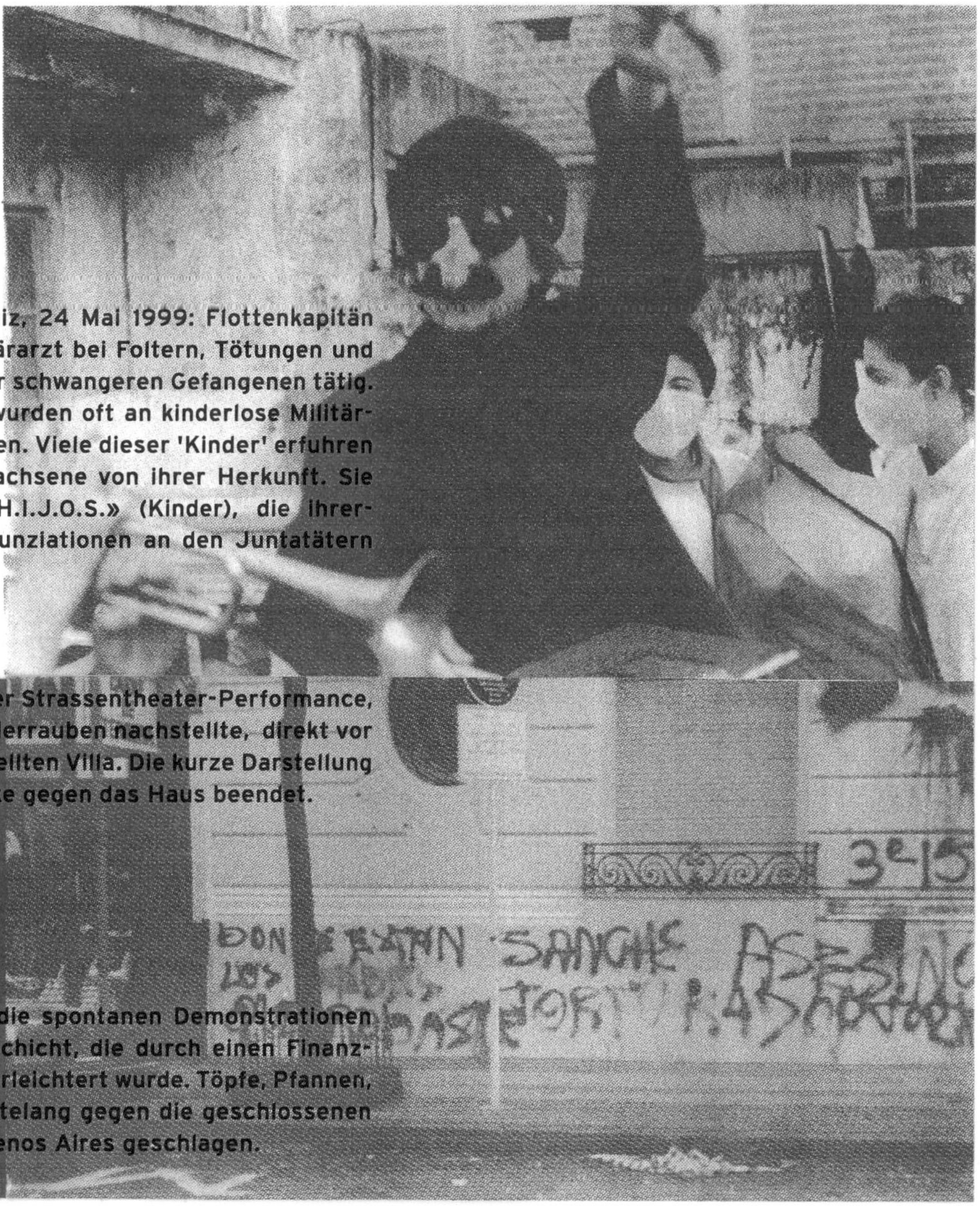

'Escrache' an Sánchez Ruiz, 24 Mai 1999: Flottenkapitän Ruiz war ab 1976 als Militärarzt bei Foltern, Tötungen und gezwungenen Geburten der schwangeren Gefangenen tätig. Die so geborenen Kinder wurden oft an kinderlose Militärpaare zur Adopition gegeben. Viele dieser 'Kinder' erfuhren durch Zufall erst als Erwachsene von ihrer Herkunft. Sie gründeten die Gruppe «H.I.J.O.S.» (Kinder), die ihrerseits 'escraches' und Denunziationen an den Juntatätern organisieren.

Die Aktion bestand aus einer Strassentheater-Performance, die Ruiz' Rolle bei den Kinderrauben nachstellte, direkt vor seiner von der Polizei umstellten Villa. Die kurze Darstellung wurde mit einer Farbattacke gegen das Haus beendet.

'Escraches' heissen auch die spontanen Demonstrationen der argentinischen Mittelschicht, die durch einen Finanzcrash um ihre Ersparnisse erleichtert wurde. Töpfe, Pfannen, Metalldeckel wurden monatelang gegen die geschlossenen Rolläden der Banken in Buenos Aires geschlagen.

Images: Etcétera, at the «Ex-Argentina» exhibition

«It's about half past eight on a Tuesday morning. Two uniformed officers ask a woman who leaves a hotel to show them her papers. They realize that the woman is a Nigerian refugee who has lost her fight for asylum. Their politeness becomes sternness. Ignoring her pleas and moans they lead her away. 'I don't want to go to Nigeria, please let me go. I don't want to die'.

A stewardess from KLM comes hurrying up and attempts to calm her. 'Please calm down madam, KLM will take care of your flight back home. You don't have to worry about anything. Perhaps you would like something to calm you down?'

The woman continues to struggle and is first hand-cuffed and then shoved on board of a KLM minibus. The bus starts its engine but the rear doors fly open and the woman jumps out, followed by the two officers. A police car that happens to be passing by skids to a halt to offer assistance. That does not appear to be neccesary. The woman is caught and once more dragged onto the minibus.

A second KLM bus arrives to pick up guests and take them to Schipol airport. The two buses leave and drive off towards Schipol one behind the other.

This scene took place in front of the Golden Tulip Barbazon Hotel, across the street from the Central Station in Amsterdam. It was repeated in front of various other hotels in Amsterdam. The «KLM – Your Deportation Agent» minibus spent the whole day driving either just behind or just in front of the official KLM airport shuttle bus and confronted guests and passersby with the role that KLM plays in the deportation of refugees.

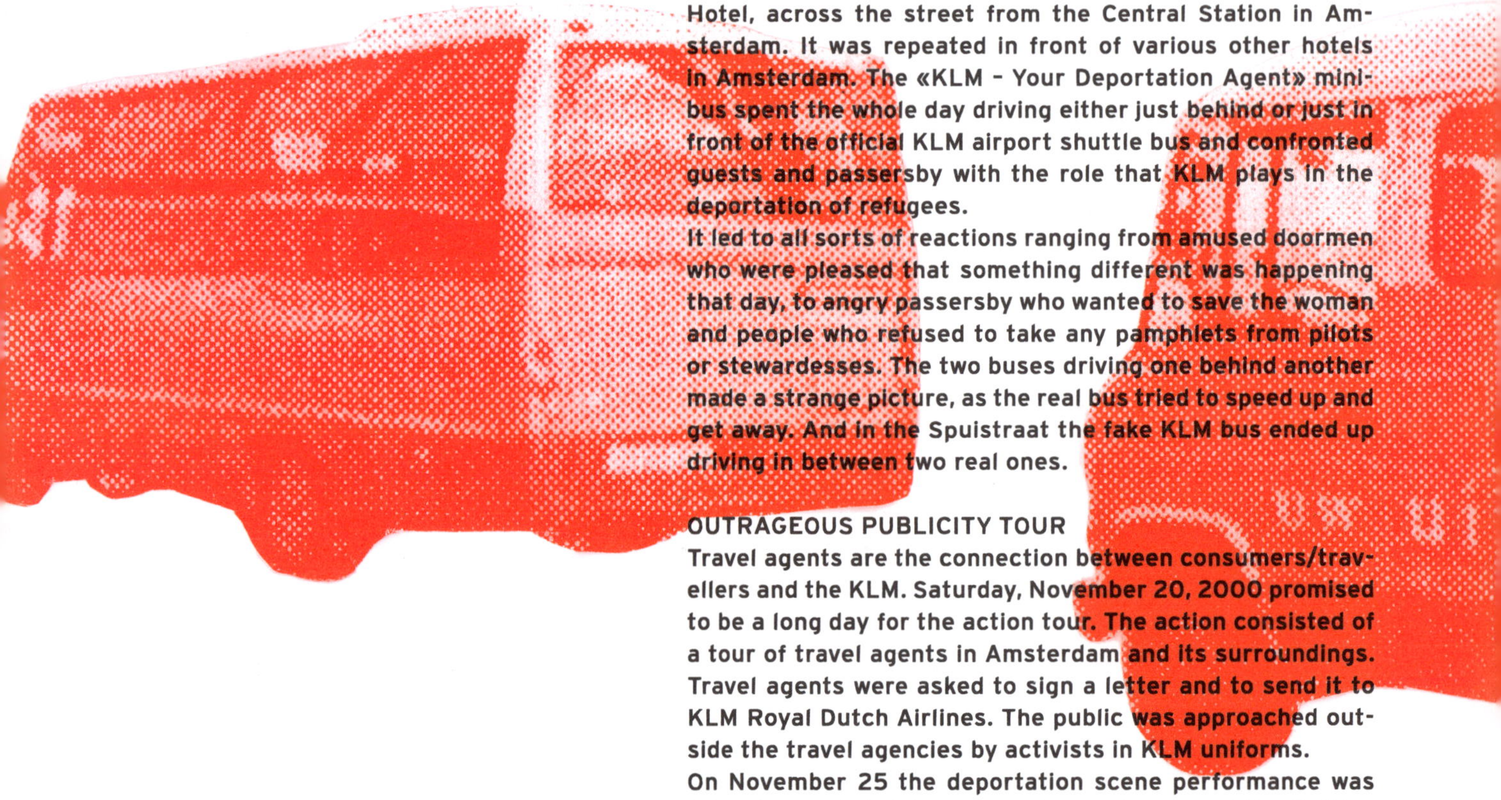

It led to all sorts of reactions ranging from amused doormen who were pleased that something different was happening that day, to angry passersby who wanted to save the woman and people who refused to take any pamphlets from pilots or stewardesses. The two buses driving one behind another made a strange picture, as the real bus tried to speed up and get away. And in the Spuistraat the fake KLM bus ended up driving in between two real ones.

OUTRAGEOUS PUBLICITY TOUR

Travel agents are the connection between consumers/travellers and the KLM. Saturday, November 20, 2000 promised to be a long day for the action tour. The action consisted of a tour of travel agents in Amsterdam and its surroundings. Travel agents were asked to sign a letter and to send it to KLM Royal Dutch Airlines. The public was approached outside the travel agencies by activists in KLM uniforms.

On November 25 the deportation scene performance was taken to the Dutch travel agents' conference at the Holiday 2000 Exhibition, along with leaflet-distributing 'KLM' stewardesses and pilots.

DEMONSTRATION AT THE HEADQUARTERS OF KLM

It was a piece of cake. As we approached the gates on the Amstelveenseweg, the security guard saw our minibus coming and waved us cheerfully through. Unloading our aeroplane model and setting it up in front of the entrance was a simple matter. One of us who was wearing a business suit took a handful of folders and went inside. It was 08.35.

Our man inside stood by the electric gates and waited for about fifteen minutes for the moment when everyone was looking the other way, at which point he vaulted over the gates and disappeared past the row of lifts. He was looking for the director's office. A few corridors further and he had found the right suite of offices. It was only as he attempted to enter the director's offices that he was stopped and asked who he was looking for. He handed over the information folders to a bewildered secretary and walked away calmly.

After finishing our action unchallenged and getting up to leave, we were approached by KLM's chief of security, who invited us to a meeting with the management. We accepted. (Actions and 'deportations' have been carried out at various official business dates.)

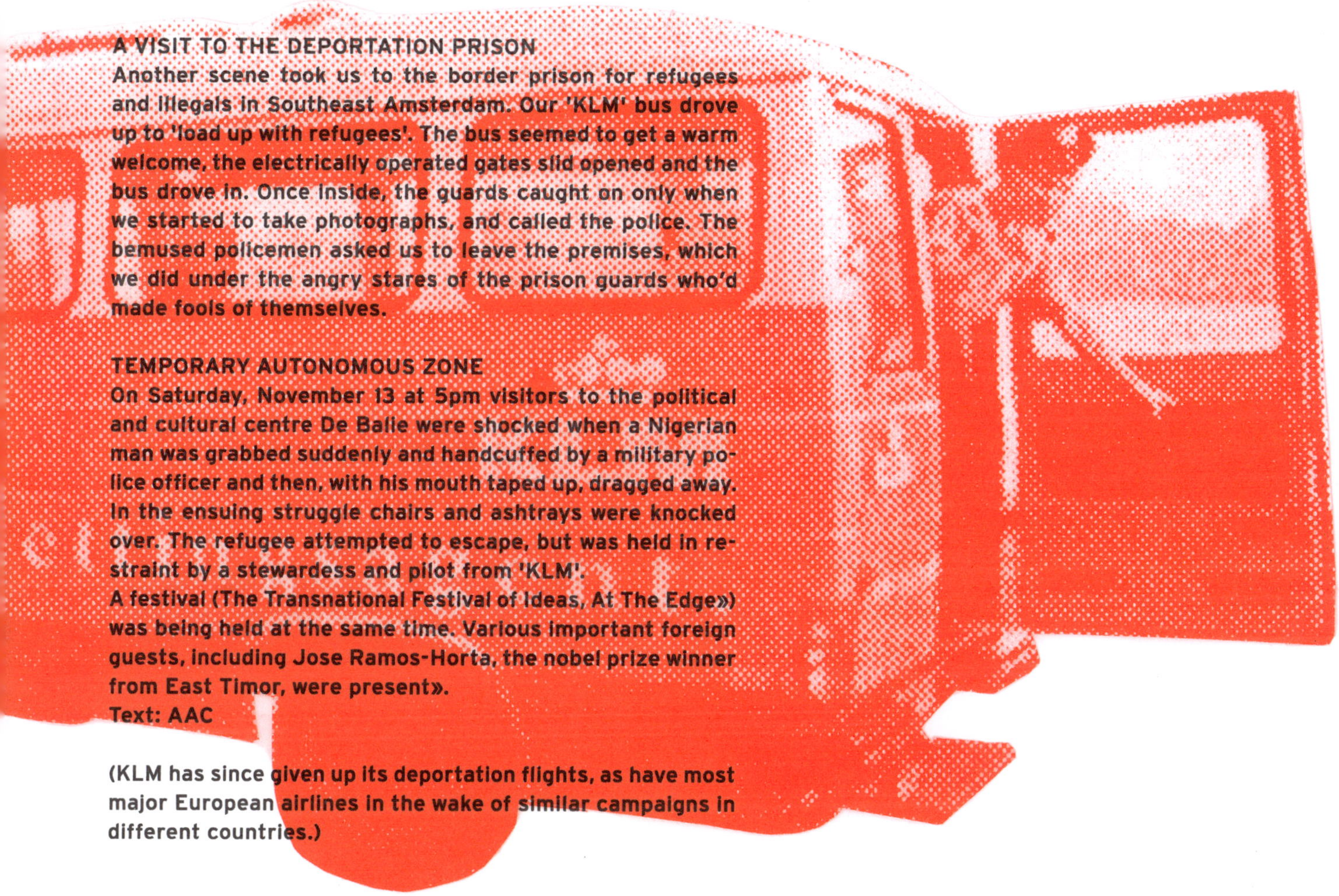

A VISIT TO THE DEPORTATION PRISON

Another scene took us to the border prison for refugees and illegals in Southeast Amsterdam. Our 'KLM' bus drove up to 'load up with refugees'. The bus seemed to get a warm welcome, the electrically operated gates slid opened and the bus drove in. Once inside, the guards caught on only when we started to take photographs, and called the police. The bemused policemen asked us to leave the premises, which we did under the angry stares of the prison guards who'd made fools of themselves.

TEMPORARY AUTONOMOUS ZONE

On Saturday, November 13 at 5pm visitors to the political and cultural centre De Balie were shocked when a Nigerian man was grabbed suddenly and handcuffed by a military police officer and then, with his mouth taped up, dragged away. In the ensuing struggle chairs and ashtrays were knocked over. The refugee attempted to escape, but was held in restraint by a stewardess and pilot from 'KLM'.

A festival (The Transnational Festival of Ideas, At The Edge») was being held at the same time. Various important foreign guests, including Jose Ramos-Horta, the nobel prize winner from East Timor, were present».

Text: AAC

(KLM has since given up its deportation flights, as have most major European airlines in the wake of similar campaigns in different countries.)

The Yes Men > 108-111, 119

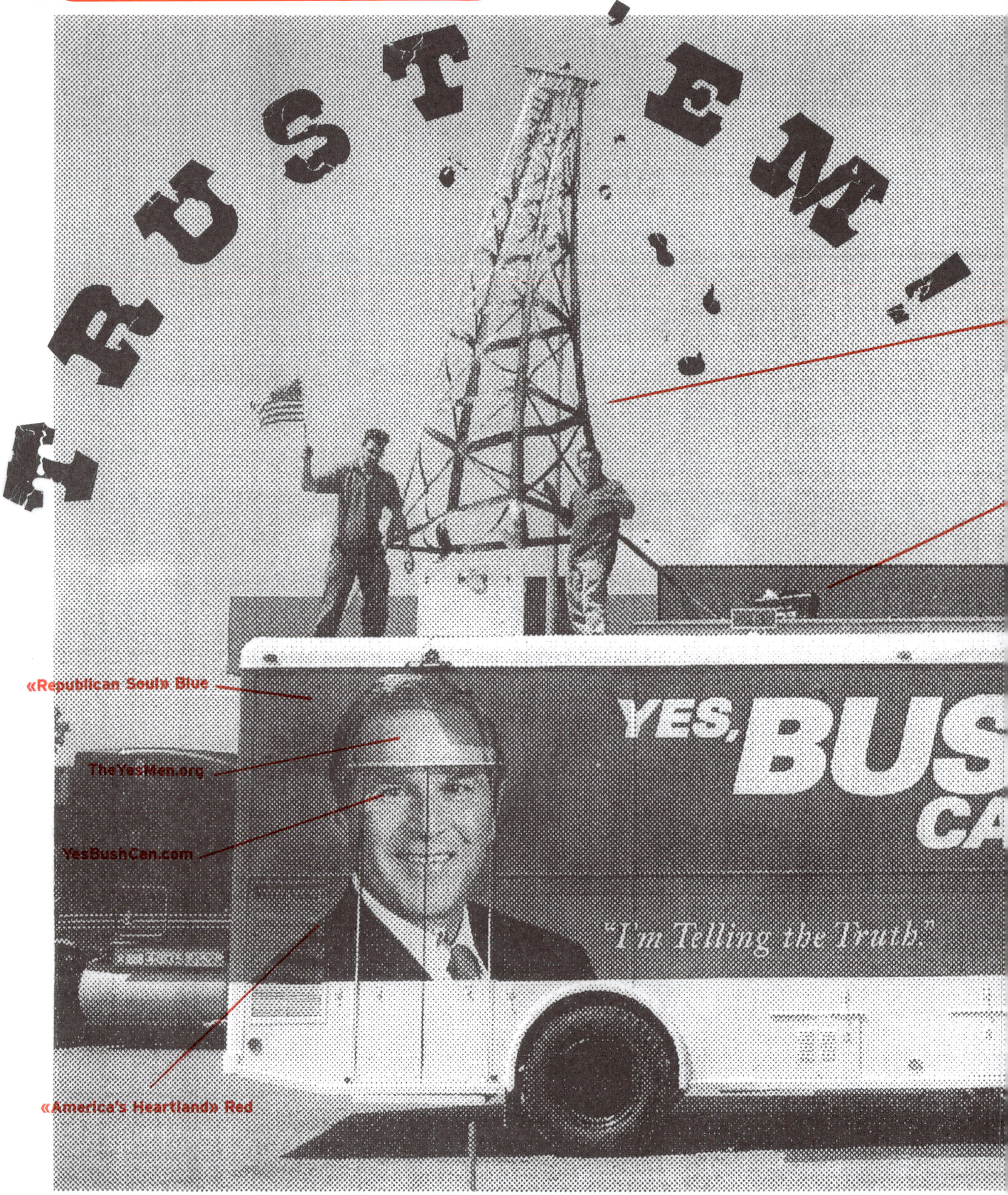

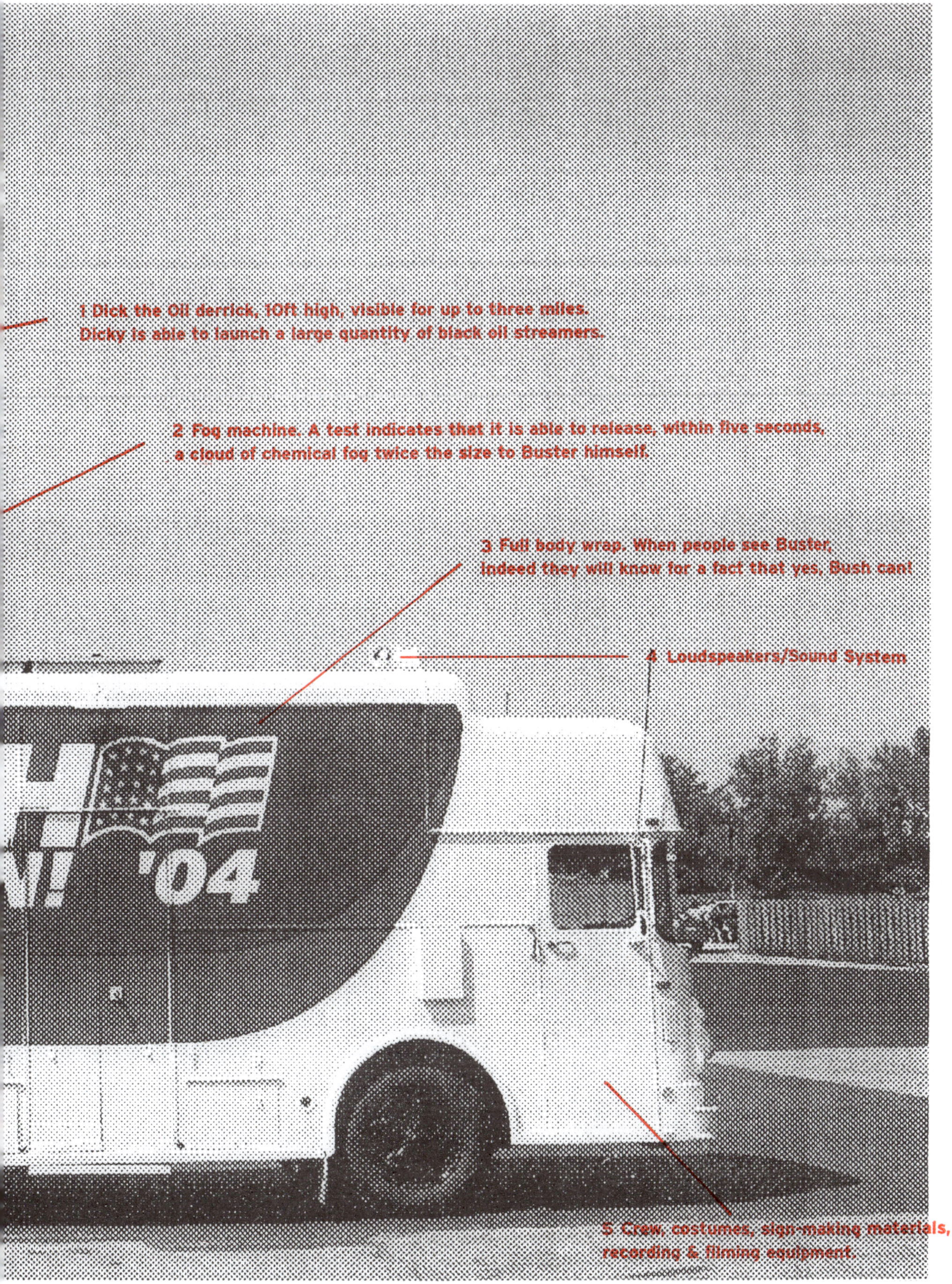
1 Dick the Oil derrick, 10ft high, visible for up to three miles.
Dicky is able to launch a large quantity of black oil streamers.
2 Fog machine. A test indicates that it is able to release, within five seconds,
a cloud of chemical fog twice the size to Buster himself.
3 Full body wrap. When people see Buster,
indeed they will know for a fact that yes, Bush can!
4 Loudspeakers/Sound System
'04
5 Crew, costumes, sign-making materials,
recording & filming equipment.

The Yes Men > 108-111, 119

LE TOUR

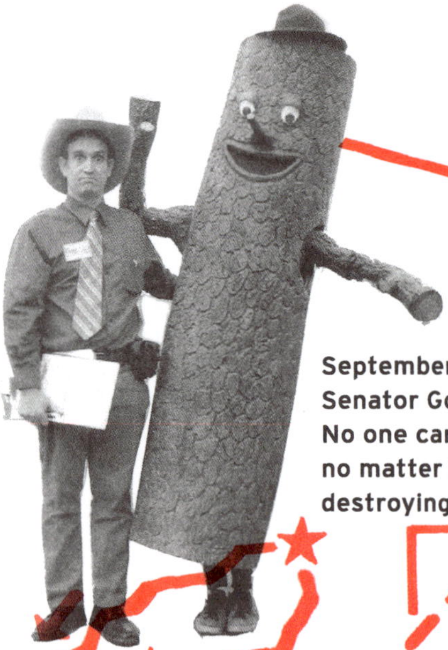

September 14: Portland.
Senator Gordon Smith's office.
No one can be dissuaded from signing, no matter how blatant the talk of destroying Yellowstone and Yosemite.

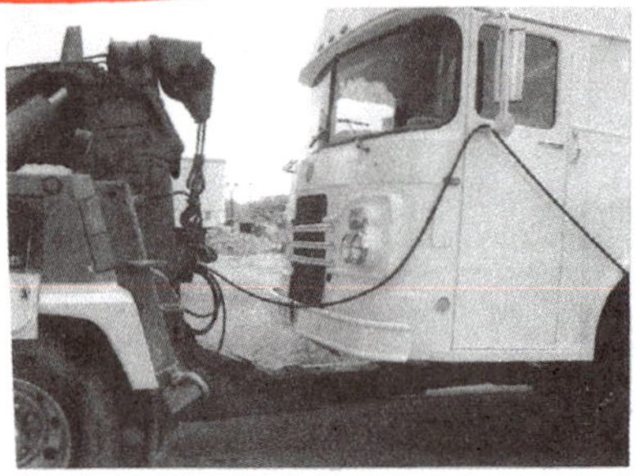

August 21: The engine is covered with oil: completely kaput. Tour is continued by other means of transport.

September 12: Only one fellow sees through our charade. Just like the one who saw through us in Cleveland, it turns out he's homeless and clearly «disturbed». What a country.

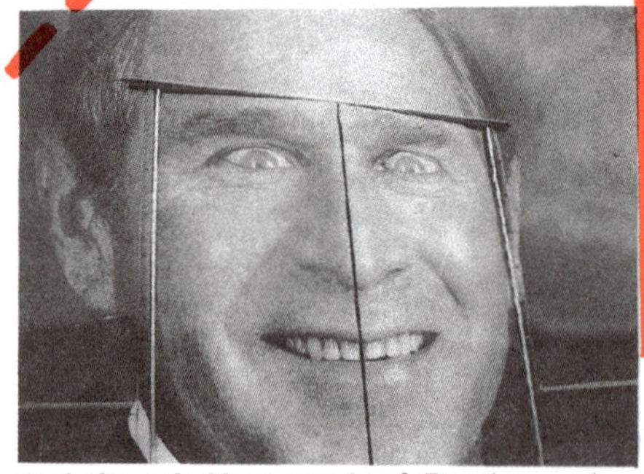

October 4: New engine! Buster gets new Magnetic Eyes.

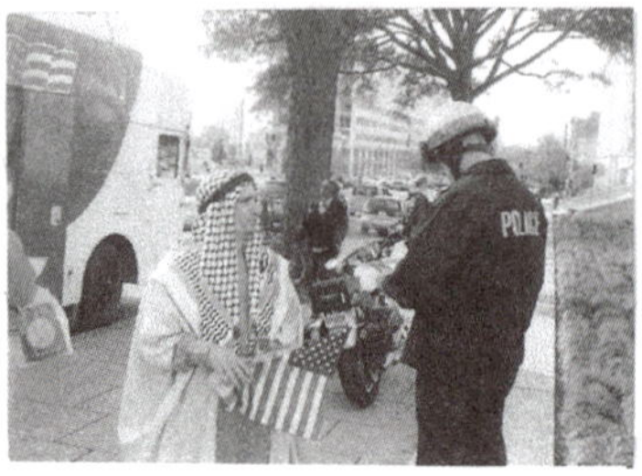

September 16: San Francisco.
Promoting gay divorce with a «Diversity Compassion Orangutan».

September 6: Hollywood!
Costumes borrowed from a friend.

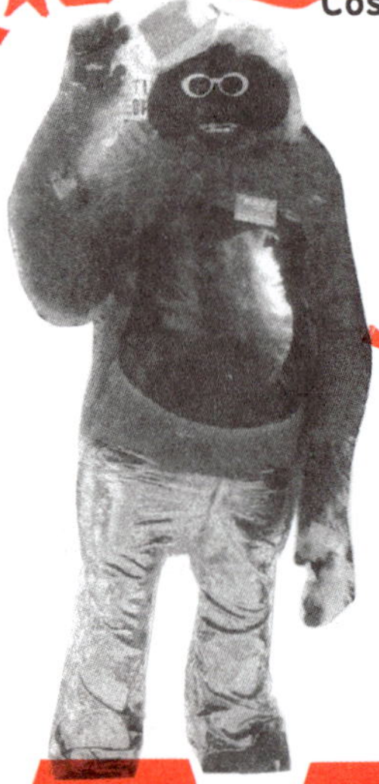

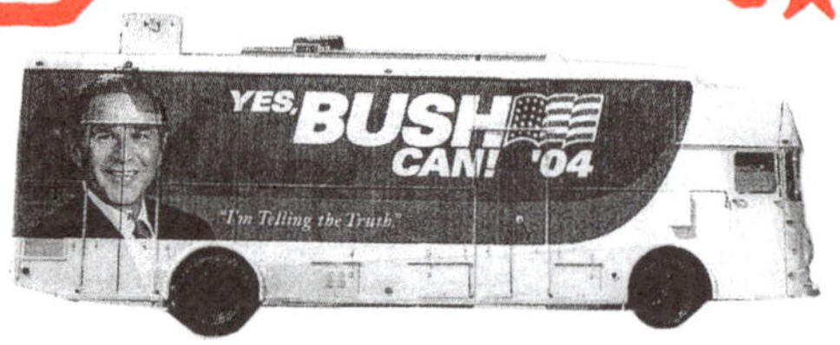

October 5: Cleveland: the VP debates.
We attract numerous Republicans.

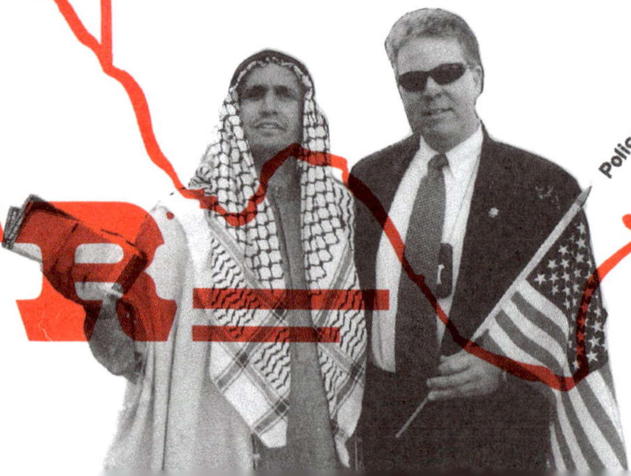

Police approve

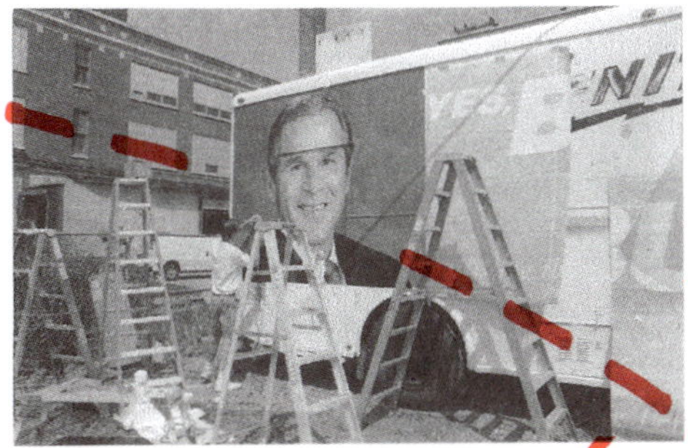

August 19, Chicago. Buster the Bush Bus(ter) is now in fighting shape.

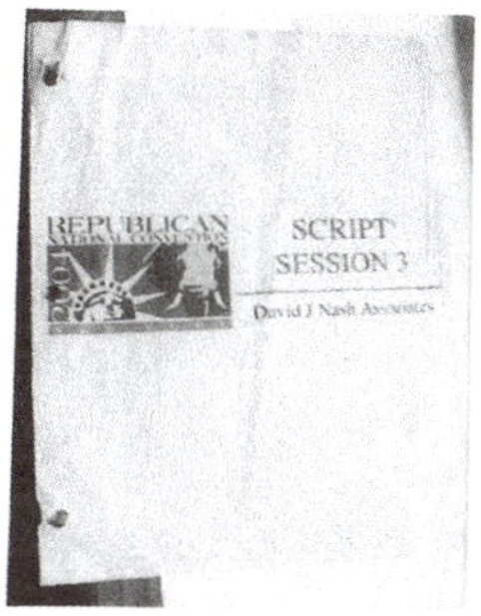

August 30: «Disaffected delegates» slip us their passes and we get to attend the Republican National Convention. USA Patriot Pledge brochures are distributed within the convention area.

August 31: NY. Still at the RNC, we find a 210-page document entitled «SCRIPT SESSION 3». Every word of today's session is here.

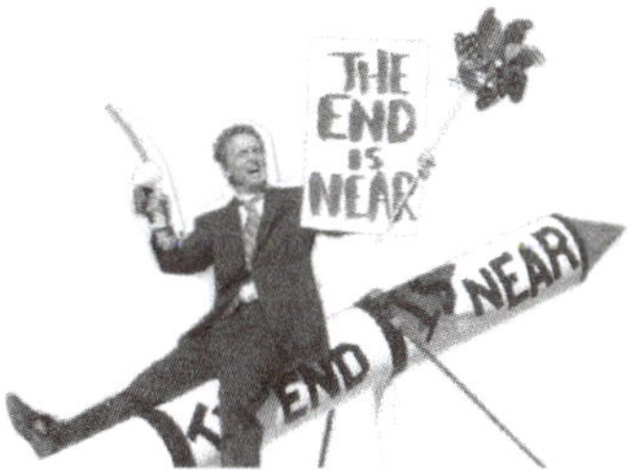

October 14: Washington, D.C. Buster clearly needs a big missile, since a lot of Republicans believe in Armageddon.

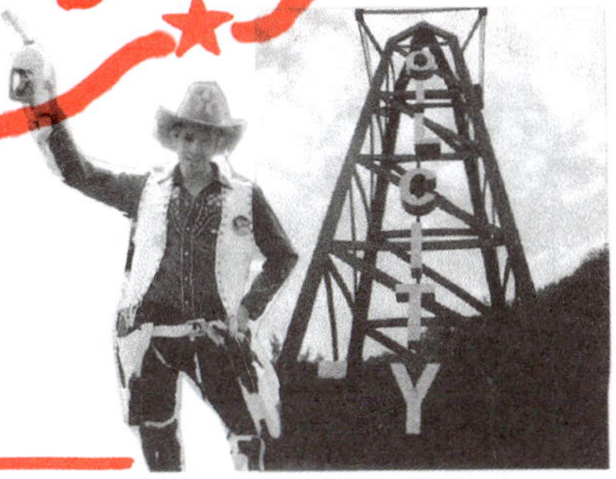

August 23: Oil City. Passing through Pennsylvania we pay tribute.

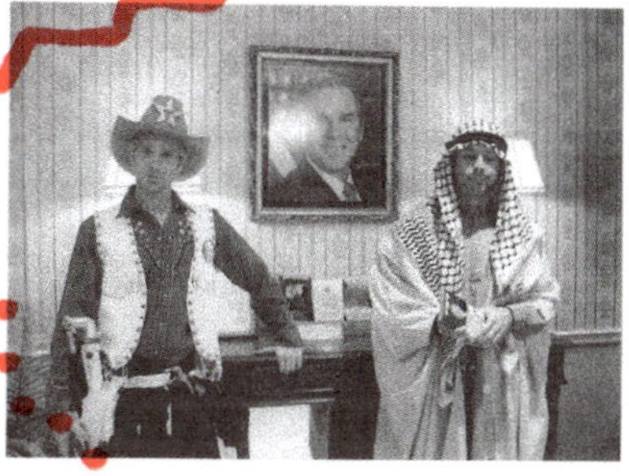

October 15: D.C., Republican National Committee and Club.

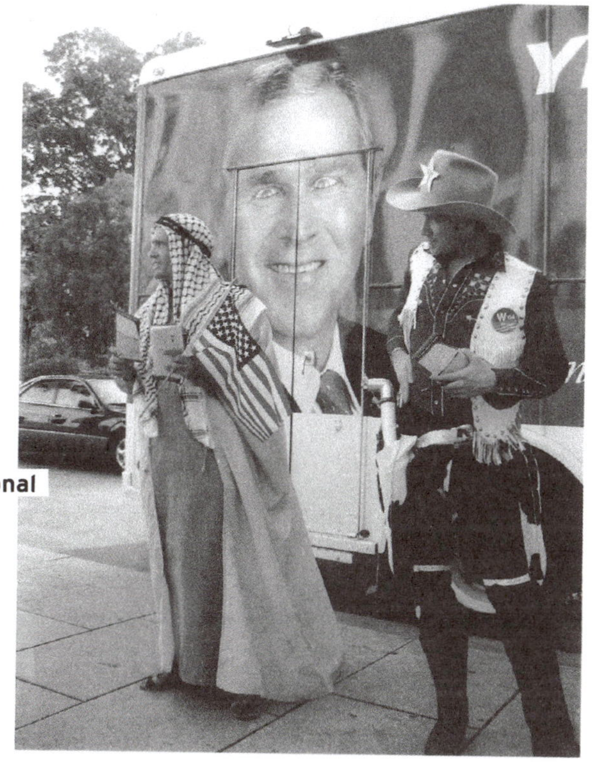

October 17: Even with the cowboy with gas-pump side arms, the orangutan, the Saudi prince, and assorted others cavorting around provocatively to unusual music, many Republicans don't get it.

October 21: Richmond, Virginia. Buster's second engine dies, a 3-inch hole in the engine block. Buster R.I.P.

Oct. 28: Florida. Holy Land Experience, a giant Christian theme park. Much of the bookstore focuses on the end of the world.

 The Yes Men > 108-111, 119

THE USA PATRIOT PLEDGE ★ THE USA PATRIOT PLEDGE

YES, BUSH CAN '04

The Environment

Liberals whine endlessly about global warming and other so-called dangers. But they never mention that while scientists forecast global warming catastrophes for Europe, Japan and China — *our main economic competitors* — North America is projected to emerge *relatively unscathed*. Only George W. Bush has had the political courage to **embrace global warming as a useful weapon in the trade wars** that will define our future economic well-being, and that of our children.

THE USA PATRIOT PLEDGE

- ☐ I volunteer to live with the relatively minor consequences of global warming if it will mean increased competitiveness for American industry.
- ☐ I volunteer to help generate *more* greenhouse gases if it results in a competitive edge for my country.

Family Values

The bedrock of everything that is great about our great country is Christian family values. Liberals cannot accept this fundamental truth, as they are dependent on the votes of homosexuals, adulterers, socialists, and the like. We invite you to let Washington know your commitment to the values we share.

THE USA PATRIOT PLEDGE

- ☐ I vow to never divorce, and to stay with my spouse until death do us part, no matter how incompatible we may be.
- ☐ I vow to remain celibate unless married.
- ☐ I vow to never have an abortion, even if I am raped, am the victim of sexual abuse or incest, or if medical tests show my unborn child to have serious congenital disease or deformities. *(Please skip this item if you are not a woman.)*
- ☐ I vow to never use drugs developed from stem cell research, and to not allow my dependents to do so, even if they are suffering from a life-threatening illness for which there is no alternative cure.

The Economy

In economic matters, President Bush has shown his leadership by taking necessary — but sometimes unpopular — steps. It would have been *easy* to invest the budget surplus left over by Clinton in Social Security or national health care. President George W. Bush chose the more difficult path of running a *"profit-smart deficit."* Tax cuts favoring the poor would have been *easy*; President Bush took the hard road of tax cuts favoring the elite, because it is the elite who drive our economy. On economic issues more than any others, Washington needs to hear that **USA patriots stand behind President Bush!**

THE USA PATRIOT PLEDGE

- ☐ I support tax cuts favoring the elite, and I volunteer to pay more than my share of taxes to allow the elite to invest their money in our country's economy. *(Please skip this item if your annual income exceeds $400,000.)*
- ☐ I commit my children to pay for the wars America is fighting to guarantee their security.

Child's Name: ______ Social Security Number: ______

- ☐ I volunteer to forfeit my social security checks when I retire in order to pay down the debt America is accruing.

Name: ______ Social Security Number: ______

On behalf of **President George W. Bush** and **Attorney General John Ashcroft**, we **thank you for your time, your patriotism, and your commitment to a great country and a great president.**

Filling out this form in no way substitutes for nor guarantees against present or future obligations toward parties public or private, including the United States government.

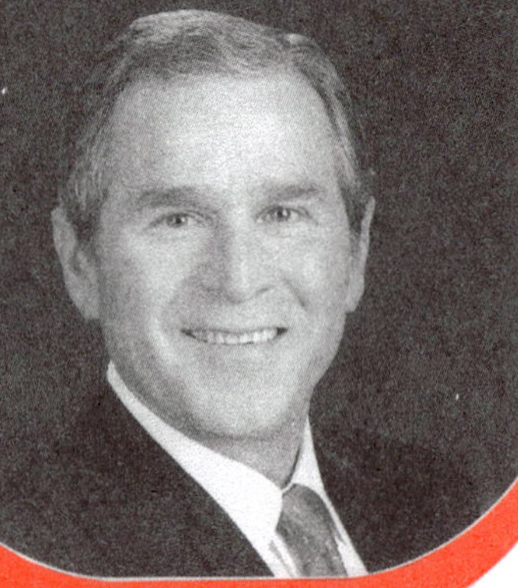

President George W. Bush

TAKE THE USA PATRIOT PLEDGE

An online version of this Pledge is available at **www.YesBushCan.com/pledge/**

Please mail completed Pledge to Yes, Bush Can!
PO Box 6245, Arlington, VA 22206

Fazit «3. November 2004: Eine gigantische Anzahl von Amerikanern hat gegen die Vernunft gestimmt.
Das sollte uns nicht überraschen. Wir hätten die tiefe Irrelevanz der Vernunft erkennen sollen, wenn Leute zufrieden und ehrlich Patriotengelöbnisse im Angesicht unserer 'Das Ende Ist Nahe' Rakete unterschrieben, oder Petitionen, die den Einsatz von Klimaerwärmung als Waffe forderten;

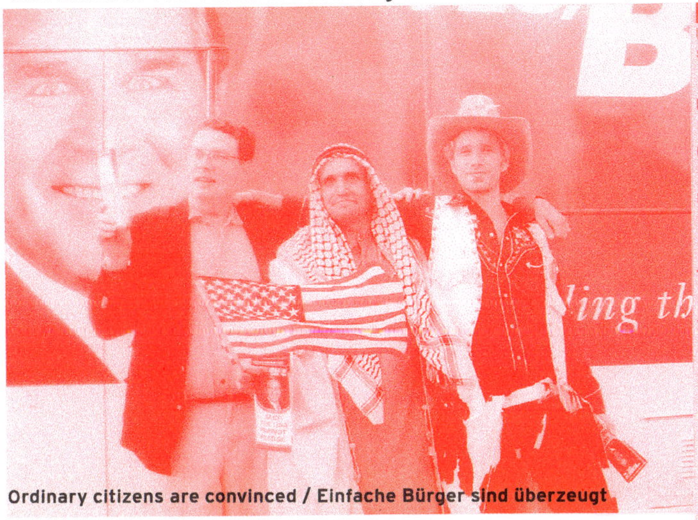

Ordinary citizens are convinced / Einfache Bürger sind überzeugt

THE USA PATRIOT PLEDGE

❑ I volunteer to give up *some* constitutional rights to support the war on terrorism, if this proves necessary.

Specifically:

❑ I volunteer to allow government agents to search my home without warrant, if necessary.

❑ I volunteer to have my phone tapped and my internet use monitored, if necessary.

❑ I volunteer to allow government agents access to my medical records, if necessary.
Doctor's Name and Address: ____________

Major Diseases/Illnesses: ____________

Medications: ____________

❑ I volunteer to allow government agents access to what I read at the library, if necessary.
Last books and magazines I have read: ____________

❑ I prefer TV.

❑ I volunteer to give up these additional rights (please specify): ____________

und als wir sahen, dass der Buchladen des 'Heiliges Land' Erlebnisparks mit Büchern über die Apokalypse gefüllt ist. Satire, wie auch Logik, sind nutzlos wenn Vernunft irrelevant wird». Texte: Yes Men

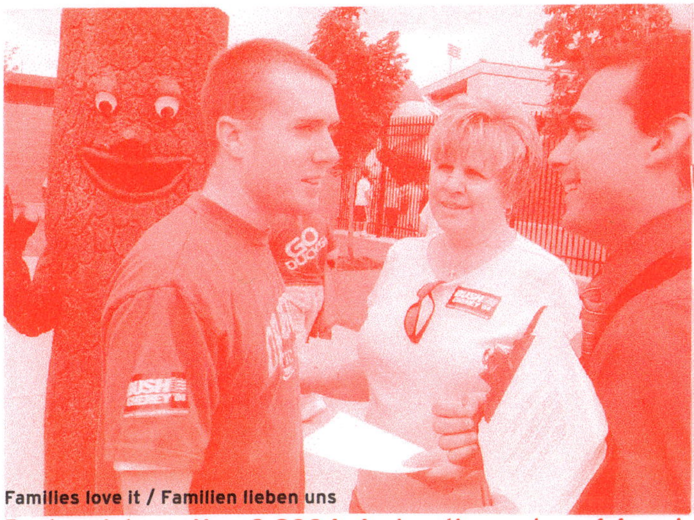

Families love it / Familien lieben uns

THE USA PATRIOT PLEDGE

❑ I volunteer to send my children to fight for America in Iraq, Afghanistan, Iran, Syria, North Korea, or anywhere else President George W. Bush deems necessary.
Name: ____________ Age: ______
Name: ____________ Age: ______
Preferred branch: ____________

THE USA PATRIOT PLEDGE

❑ I volunteer to allow a permanent nuclear waste storage facility to be built in my community, if such becomes necessary.

❑ I pledge to *actively lobby* local, state, and federal officials for a permanent nuclear waste storage facility in my community.

❑ I would personally feel more secure with America launching a new round of nuclear weapons development, even if this meant breaking current treaty obligations concerning nuclear weapons.

Post scriptum «Nov. 3 2004: A gigantic number of Americans have voted against Reason.
This shouldn't surprise us. We should have understood the profound irrelevance of Reason when people gladly and sincerely signed Patriot Pledges in front of our 'End is Near' missile, or signed petitions in favor of global warming as a weapon - or when the Holy Land Experience bookstore turned out to be filled with books about the Apocalypse.
Satire, like information and logic, is useless when Reason is irrelevant». Texts: Yes Men

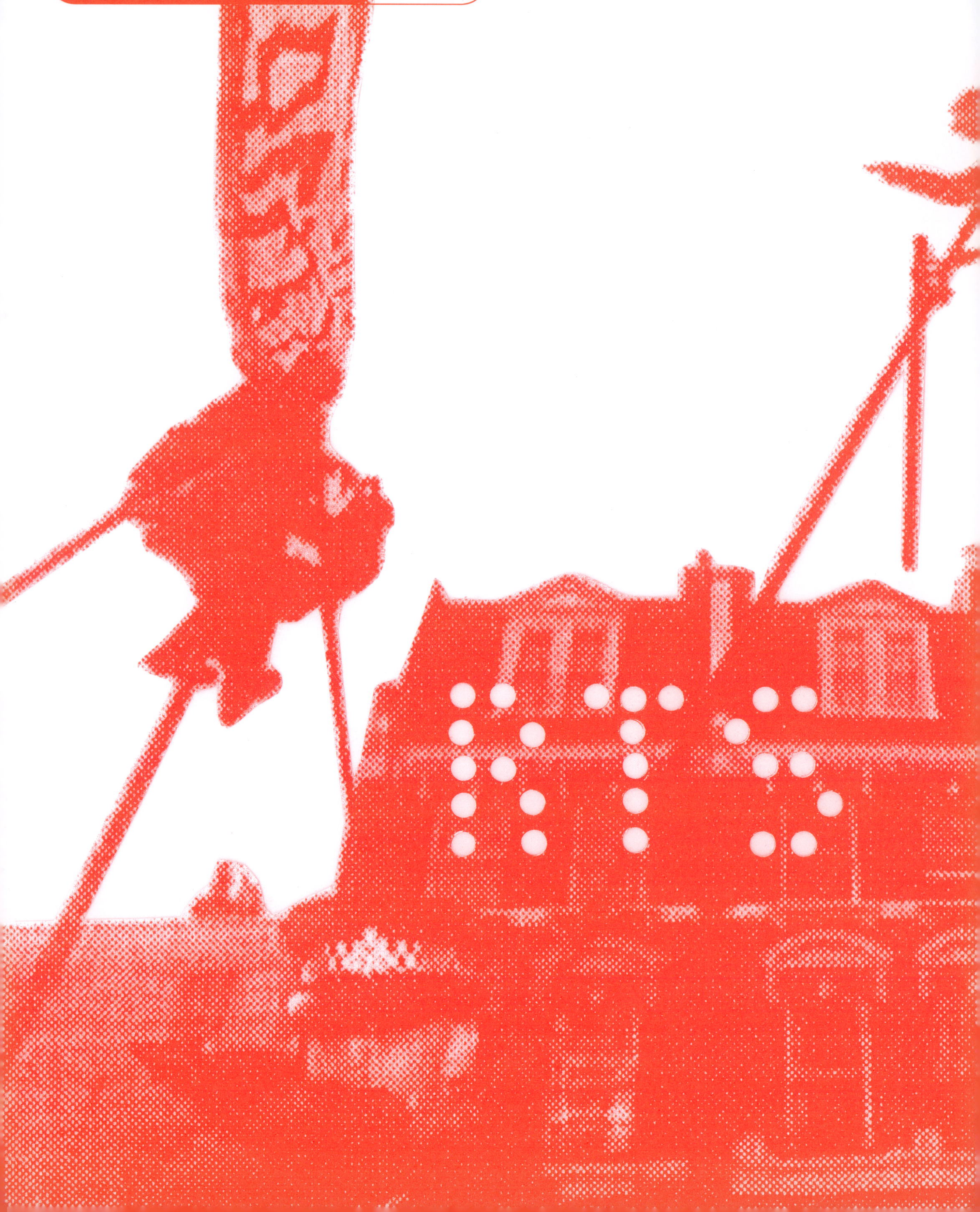
RTS

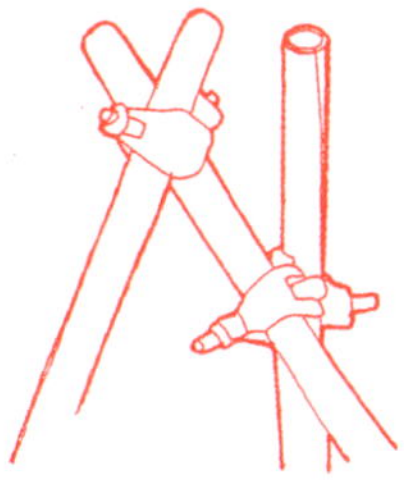

Scaffolding Tripod
Made out of 3 long tubes/ optional struts if more than one person climbs up/ two-way clamps/ rope to tie poles at the base

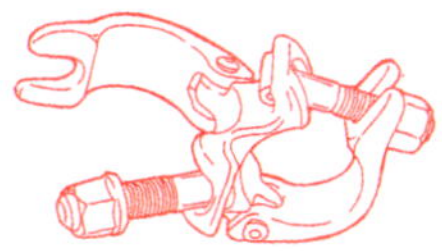

Assemble on ground, then raise/ min. 5 crew: two fix base of two support poles while they are being pushed up, starting from the tip/ 5th worker pulls on the remaining pole

«RTS was originally formed in London in Autumn 1991, around the dawn of the anti-roads movement. A small group of individuals got together to undertake direct action against the motor car. Their work was small-scale but effective, using surprise tactics which have moulded RTS's more recent activities. There was the trashed car on Park Lane symbolising the arrival of Car-mageddon, DIY cycle lanes painted overnight on London streets, disruption of the 1993 Earls Court Motor Show and subvertising actions on car adverts around the city.

However the onset of the «No M11 Link Road» Campaign presented the group with a specific local focus. The M11 Link Road campaign culminated in the symbolic and dramatic battle of Claremont Road. Eventually, police and security overpowered the barricades, lock-ons and the scaffold tower, but the war was only just beginning. ...

«RTS wurde 1991 an den Anfängen der Anti-Strassenbewegung in London gegründet. Am Anfang führte eine kleine Gruppe Aktionen gegen den Verkehr durch; ihre Arbeiten waren vereinzelt, aber überraschend und effektiv. Schrottautos wurden in der Innenstadt plaziert, nachts Radwege gezogen, Automessen gestört und Werbung subvertiert. Der Bau einer Verbindungstrasse zur M11 Autobahn in London gab der Gruppe ein spezifisches Ziel.

Die M11-Kampagne kulminierte in einer Schlacht um die Claremont Road. Letztenendes überrannten Polizei und private Wachdienste die Barrikaden, den Gerüstturm und die angeketteten Menschen, aber der Krieg hatte gerade erst begonnen. ...

rts.gn.apc.org, London (UK)

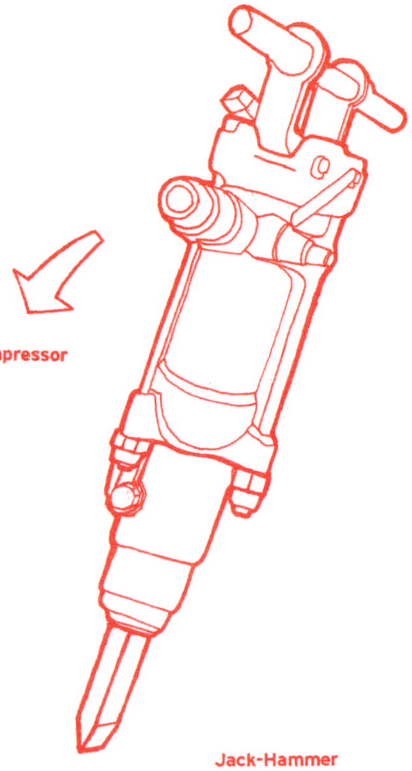

1995: Street Parties I and II and various other actions were pulled through. In July 1996 there was the massive success of the M41 Street Party, where for nine hours 8,000 people took control of the M41 motorway in West London and partied and enjoyed themselves, whilst some dug up the tarmac with jack-hammers and in its place planted trees that had been rescued from the construction path of the M11.

RTS is also about raising the larger questions behind the transport issue. Governments claim that 'roads are good for the economy'. It is all about increasing 'consumption', because that is an indicator of 'economic growth': the greedy, short-term exploitation of dwindling resources regardless of the immediate or long-term costs. Therefore RTS's attack on cars cannot be detached from a wider attack on capitalism itself.

More importantly, RTS is about encouraging more people to take part in direct action. Direct action is about destroying politicians' power and authority, and people taking responsibility for themselves. Direct action is not just a tactic; it is an end in itself. It is about enabling people to unite as individuals with a common aim, to change things directly by their own actions.» Text: RTS

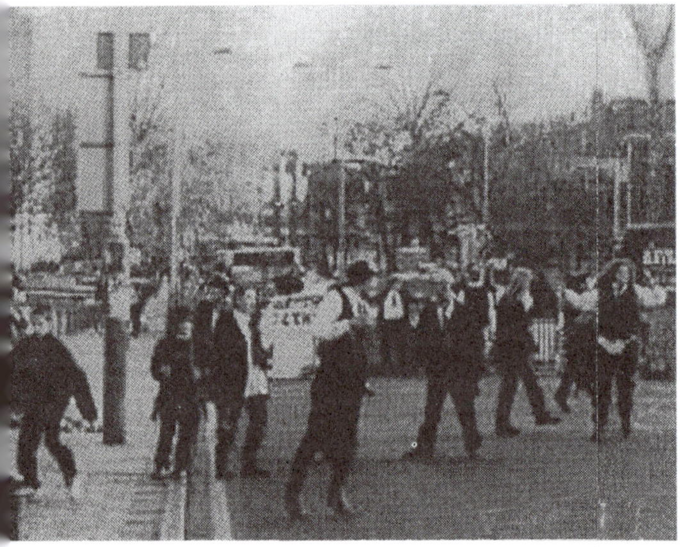

1995 wurden Strassenparties und Protestaktionen organisiert, 1996 wurde die M41-Autobahn in West London von 8000 Menschen neun Stunden lang besetzt. Währen die Party lief, bohrten andere, versteckt unter hohlen Skulpturen Löcher in den Asphalt und pflanzten Bäume, die vor dem M11-Ausbau ausgegraben worden waren.

RTS stellt die allgemeine Strassenbaupolitik der Regierung und ihre Argumentation infrage, welche lautet «Strassen dienen der Wirtschaft», weil sie «Konsum» antreiben der wiederum ein Indikator für Wirtschaftswachstum sei. Das ist sei gieriger, kurzzeitiger Raubbau schwindender Ressourcen ohne einen Gedanken an die langfristigen Folgen. RTS sieht seinen Angriff auf die Autos als eine Form von Kapitalismuskritik.

Entscheidend ist die Ermutigung zur Teilnahme an direkten Aktionen; diese stören die Macht und die Autorität der Politiker, Menschen übernehmen selbst die Verantwortung. Unmittelbare Aktionen sind deshalb nicht nur eine Taktik, sie sind ein Ziel in sich. «Es geht um die Ermöglichung von gemeinsam durchgeführten Aktionen mit einem gemeinsamen Ziel; darum, die Leute durch ihre eigenen Handlungen die Dinge verändern zu lassen.» Text: RTS

«The second Circle Line Party on the London underground was held on 14 March 2003, as an attempt to promote DIY culture in a closely monitored (public) space. A website was launched beforehand, with tips on how to stay out of trouble and survive a lap without arrests. Passengers arrived in small groups, a sound system, tequila bar and a pole dancing poduim were disguised as luggage.

«Die zweite Circle Line Party in der Londoner Metro fand am 14. März 2003 statt, als ein Versuch zur Verbreitung selbstgemachter Kultur in stark überwachten öffentlichen Zonen. Eine Webseite mit Tips zur Vermeidung einer vorzeitigen Entdeckung wurde ins Netz gestellt; Passagiere kamen in kleinen Gruppen, Verstärker, Instrumente, Bar und ein Tanzpodest wurden als Gepäck getarnt. Jeder sollte über seinen Partyklamotten als Pendler verkleidet sein.

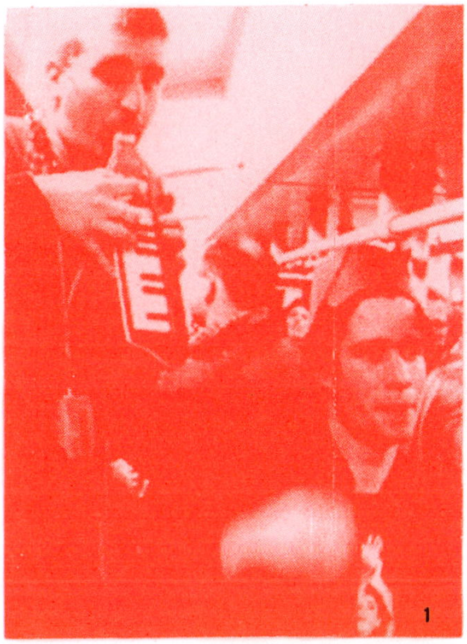

1

A street disco was started on May 1, 2003, midday, in the City of London, the heart of the capitalist machine.
The city was infiltrated by people wearing business clothes, the sound equipment again transported in luggage cases. The dancing was at first tolerated, but monitored closely by police that had arrived almost immediately. One participant was stopped and questioned under the prevention of terrorism act and the rest were given a police escort on the tube.» Text: Spacehijackers

Zwei Monate später, zum 1. Mai, brach die Disco in die City, das Herz des britischen Kapitalismus, ein. Während der Mittagspause versammelten sich die Spacehijackers/Businessleute vor der Bank of England. Das Sound-Equipment steckte in Stewardessenkoffern. Der Rave wurde von der sogleich eingetroffenen Polizei zunächst toleriert. Ein Teilnehmer wurde festgehalten und im Rahmen des Gesetzes zur Terrorismusabwehr befragt, der Rest zur nächsten U-Bahnstation eskortiert.» Text: Spacehijackers

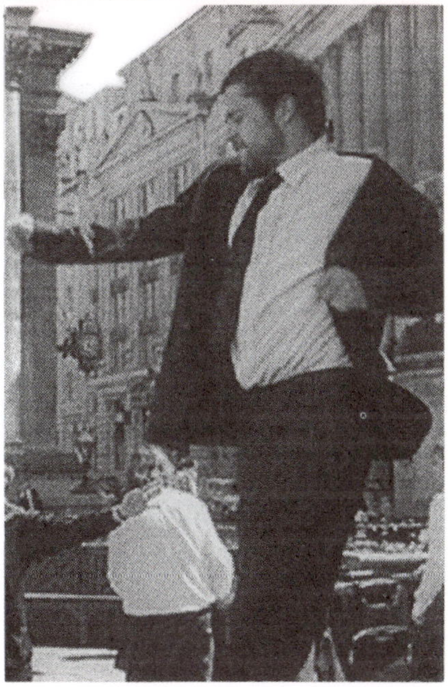

2

Christmas and the inflationary appeareance of commercial 'Santa Clauses' has been an inspiration for anarchist mobs of Santas, who, organizing themselves and sometimes going into the hundreds, invade cities and creat havoc in places where they appear. To participate contact The Cacophony Society, Santacon or one of their local branches.

Weihnachten und das inflationäre auftauchen von kommerziellen Weihnachtsmännern ist eine Inspiration für anarchistische Mobs von 'Stanta Clauses'. Sie organisieren sich per Internet um, manchmal zu hunderten, Chaosinvasionen zu veranstalten. Kontakt über The Cacophony Society, Santacon oder ihre lokalen Filialen.

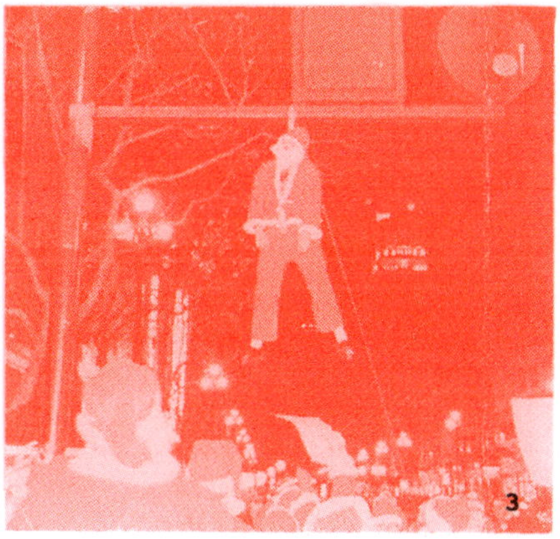

3

Remember the effect of Orson Welles' 1938 «War Of The Worlds» radio play? Set as a newscast, the play told the story of a Martian invasion of New York City and created panic among thousands of listeners.

So dress up smart, grab the pirate briefcase and take a stroll. Put in a CD with your broadcasts, messages or fake commercials. The more they sound like the real thing the better. Tune into different frequencies used by commercial stations and let the airwaves do the work. You can preach, you can seed mistrust through official-sounding newscasts, re-route traffic, create local disturbances – whatever you like. Such a radio transmits across a radius of roughly two miles. Care to build a pirate? Check the links below.

Erinnerst du dich an Orson Welles' Radiosendung «Krieg der Welten» im Jahre 1938? Welles vertonte die Romanvorlage einer Invasion vom Mars als Nachrichtensendung und versetzte ungewollt tausende New Yorker in Panik.

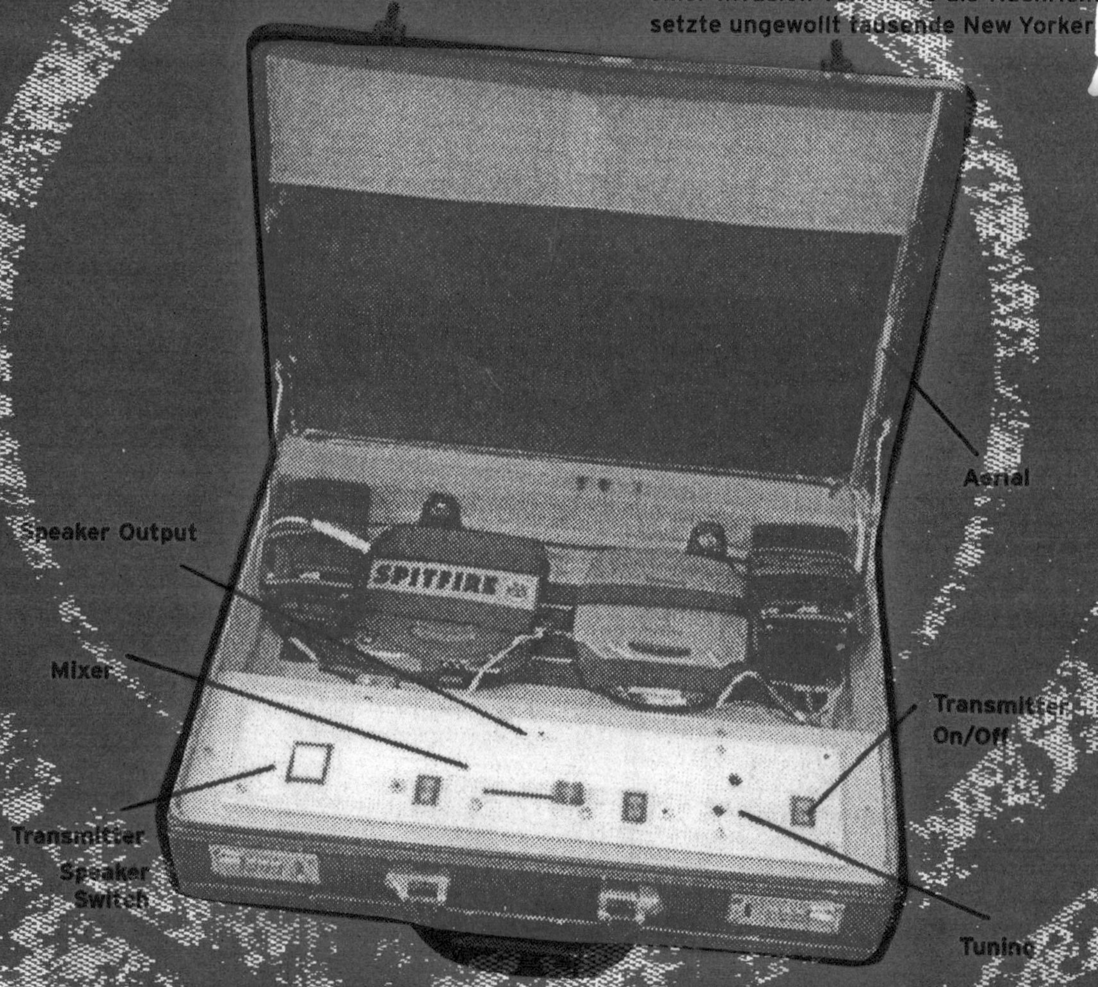

Also wirf dich in Schale, nimm den Aktenkoffer in die Hand und mach einen Spaziergang. Leg eine CD mit deinen Sendungen oder falschen Werbetextenen ein – je echter sie klingen, desto grösser die Wirkung. Der Koffer hat einen Senderadius von ungefähr 5 Kilometern. Willst du einen bauen? Geh auf die Links am Fusse der Seite.

<1> «Nomadic Broadcasts: easier to assemble but less protected; everybody'll get the direction of the broadcast when you pass on a bike with a small, but potent loudspeaker fixed under the saddle, or hidden under some cloth. The speaker is not visible, and your own speed will help get you out of reach before someone can react.»
Artistic performance by CAE and Paul Vanouse that included a number of nomads bradcasting fascist news items in Graz, Austria (2000). Quote: CAE

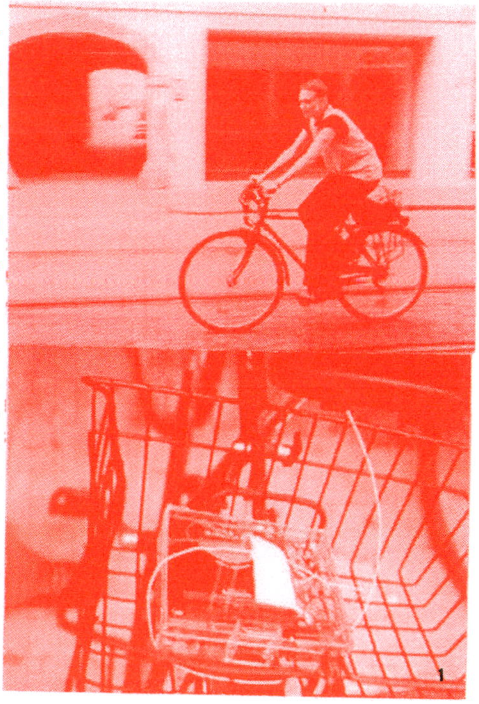
1

<1> «Nomadische Sendungen: einfacher zu bauen, dafür nicht so konspirativ – jeder wird die Richtung erahnen, aus der die Stimme kommt wenn du von einem Rad aus sendest. Montier einen kleinen, starken Lautsprecher unter den Sattel oder versteck ihn unter einem Kleidungsstück. Da er unsichtbar ist und du dich schnell bewegst, wirst du verschwunden sein ehe jemand reagieren kann.» Zitat: CAE
Solche Fahrräder waren Teil einer Kunstperformance der Gruppe CAE und Paul Vanouse in Graz, in deren Verlauf faschistische Nachrichtenbrocken ausgestrahlt wurden.

<2> Funded by RTMark, a netbased activist's hub, this pointed action was inspired by the classic Greek mathematician Archimedes. According to a legend, it was his idea to burn an attacking Roman fleet with giant mirrors.
Re-introduced in the 21st century, mirrors were supposed to blink as evidence of the people's presence to the G8 leaders who were to meet on warships in Genoa's harbour.
Plans were changed, and so the 1,000 handheld mirrors were used by protesters to temporarily blind police tanks, helicopters and attacking foot-soldiers.

<2> Der altgriechische Mathematiker Archimedes hatte Hohlspiegel benutzt, um eine römische Invasionsflotte abzubrennen, besagt die Legende. RTMark, ein internetbasiertes Projektforum, finanzierte ein comeback für die G8-Proteste in Genua (ursprünglich war geplant, die Konferenz auf Kriegsschiffen im Hafen durchzuführen).
Mit 1000 Spiegeln wollten Aktivisten ihre Anwesenheit hinüberblinken. Die Pläne wurden geändert, so dienten die Spiegel dazu, angreifende Polizisten, Fahrzeuge und Helikopter zeitweise zu blenden.

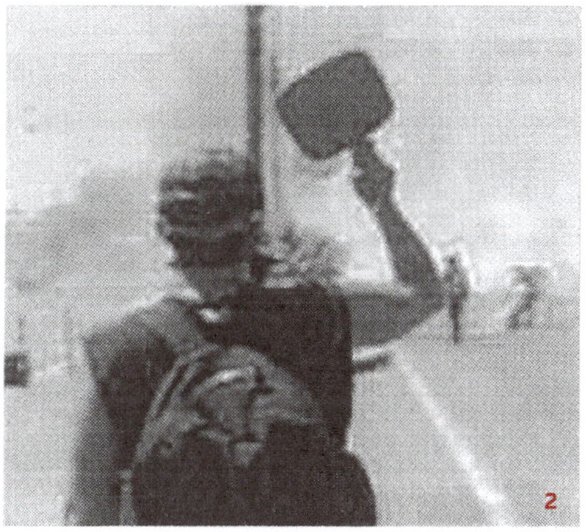
2

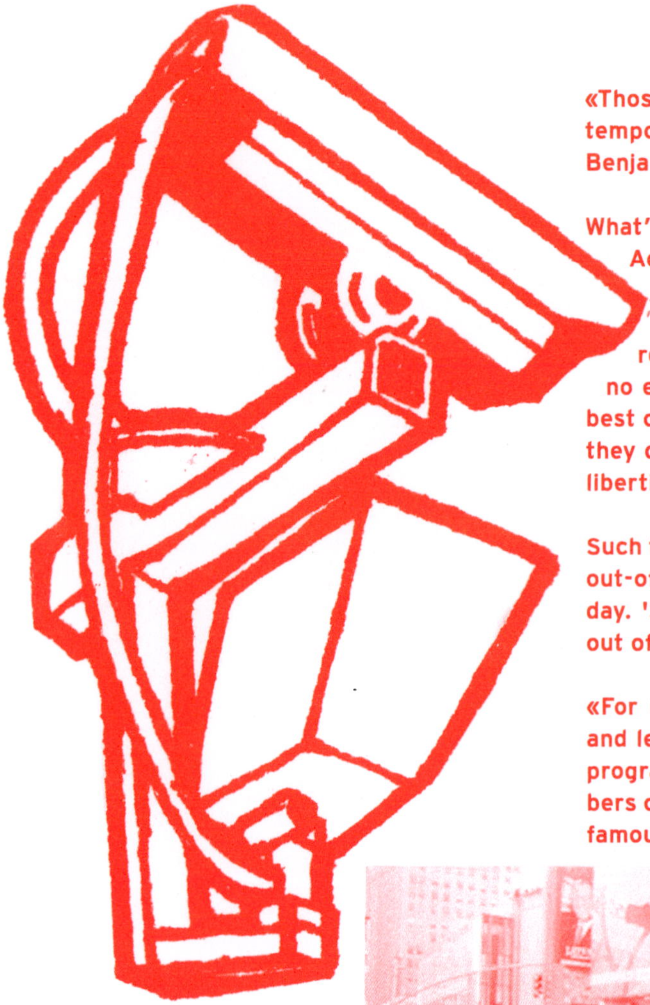

«Those that can give up essential liberty to obtain a little temporary safety deserve neither liberty nor safety.»
Benjamin Franklin, 1759

What's the use of closed-circuit television (CCTV) cameras? According to authorities and manufacturers they help prevent crime (and since 9-11, apparently terrorist attacks, too). In contrast, a British interior ministry report revealed that surveillance cameras had almost no effect on cutting crime rates. Many argue that in the best of cases they are a huge waste of time and money, but they can be used to trace dissent, too – thus violating civil liberties on the way.

Such thoughts apart, there is the human factor – the bored-out-of-their-mind surveillants facing their screens every day. 'Surveillance Camera Players' are keen to help them out of their misery:

«For untold numbers of police surveillants, there is less and less to watch every day. Answering the call of guerilla programming of video surveillance equipment, the members of the SCP have banded together to present a series of famous dramatic works for the entertainment and education

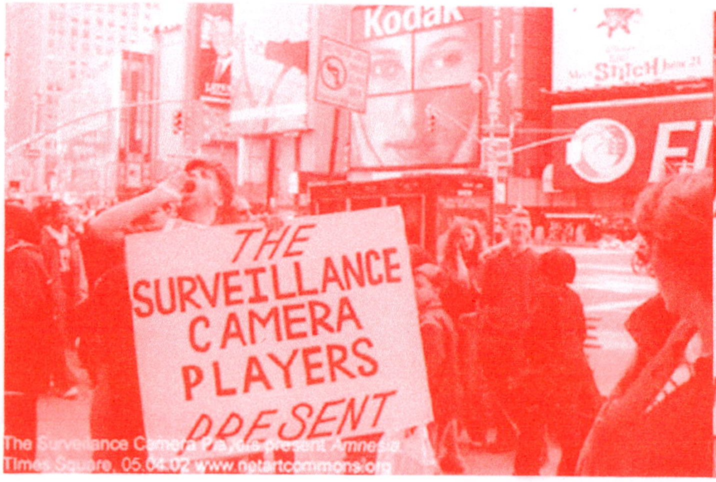

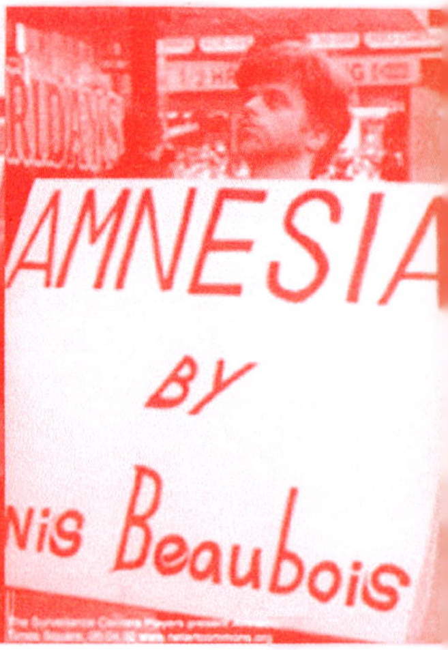

of members of the law enforcement community. The basic concept of guerilla programming is simple: create a scenario and act it out using the CCTV cameras as if they were your own, as if producing your own program.
This gives the opportunity to point out to the guardians that they are being studied, all the while making cameras visible for the general public». Quote: SCP

«Diejenigen, die notwendige Freiheiten aufgeben um temporäre Sicherheit zu erhalten verdienen weder Freiheit noch Sicherheit.» Benjamin Franklin, 1759

Welchem Zweck dienen die Überwachungskameras? Fragt man Hersteller und Behörden, helfen sie bei der Verbrechens- und Terrorbekämpfung (vor allem seit dem 11. September 2001). Dem entgegen stellt ein Bericht des britischen Innenministeriums fest, dass Kameras in den letzten 20 Jahren nicht die Verbrechensrate senken konnten.
Viele Menschen sind der Meinung, dass Überwachungskameras im besten Fall eine gigantische Geld- und Zeitverschwendung sind; im schlimmsten Fall könnten sie auch zur Verfolgung und Unterdrückung von Dissens benutzt werden und Freiheitsrechte einschränken.

Abgesehen von solchen Gedanken ist da noch der menschliche Faktor: die tödlich gelangweilten Überwacher die tagein, tagaus vor ihren Bildschirmen kleben. Die 'Surveillance Camera Players' sind bereit ihre Leiden zu erleichtern:

«Für Massen von Polizeiüberwachern gibt es täglich weniger zu sehen. Dem Ruf nach Guerrilla-Programmierung der Überwachungstechnik folgend, haben sich die Mitglieder der SCP zusammengeschlossen, um Gesetzeshüter durch die Aufführung berühmter Theaterstücke zu unterhalten und zu lehren. Das Konzept des Guerrilla-programmierens ist einfach: bereite ein Szenarium vor und führ es vor, so als ob

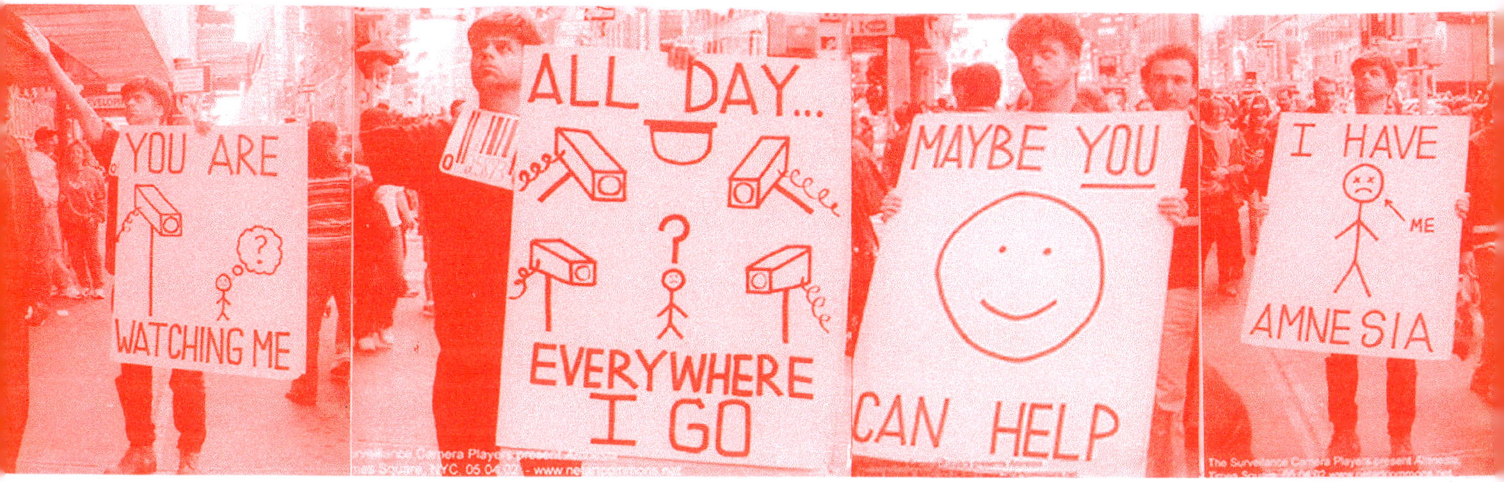

die Kamera dir gehörte, als ob du dein eigenes Programm machen würdest.
Dies zeigt den Wächtern, dass sie studiert werden und markiert die Kameras gegenüber der Öffentlichkeit.»
Zitat: SCP

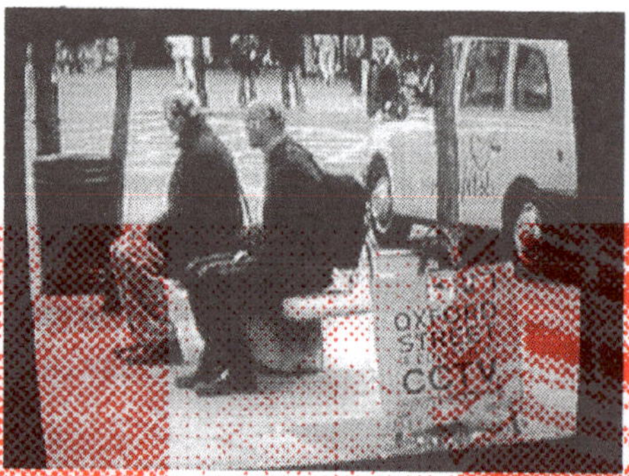

The average Londoner is caught on film about 300 times a day. «X-Heads kindly shaved their heads to the skin, leaving a highly visual X of hair, offering these new hairstyles as an idiot-proof and time saving alternative to face recognition software, to assist the surveillance workers, reduce the need to scan in faces, and thus save much needed capital.»

The record response time by the police to the haircuts was 45 seconds, which is how long it took for nine X-heads to exit a bus in central London before being questioned by two very skeptical policemen.

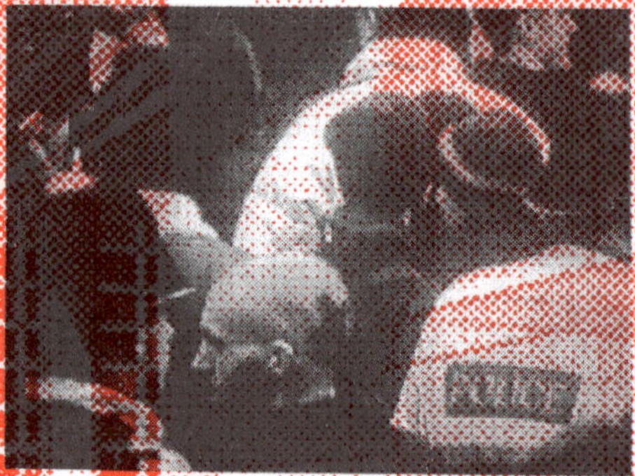

«The police must have been impressed by the proposed system as throughout the day the X-heads were photographed repeatedly.

Undoubtedly, Fanclub have proved that this cheaper alternative actually works, all that remains is for it to be enforced.» Quotes: Fanclub

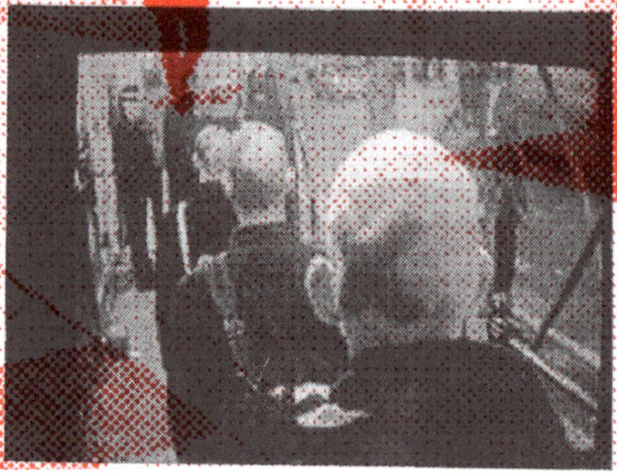

«iSee is a web-based application charting the locations of CCTV surveillance cameras in urban environments. With iSee, users can find routes that avoid these cameras – paths of least surveillance – allowing them to walk around their cities without fear of being «caught on tape» by unregulated security monitors. Text: IAA

It is worth pointing out that, according to a recent study, 40% of people that the police targeted in the UK were picked out «for no obvious reason» other than their ethnicity or apparent membership in various subcultural groups.
In other words, they were singled out not for what they were doing, but simply based on how they looked.

Ein durchschnittlicher Londoner wird ungefähr 300 mal am Tag aufgenommen. «Zuvorkommenderweise rasierten sich X-Heads die Köpfe zu einem grossen Haar-X. Dieser Style ist eine idiotensichere, zeitsparende Alternative zu Gesichtserkennungs-Software. Das scannen von Gesichtern ist jetzt nicht mehr nötig, Überwacher und Budgets werden entlastet.»

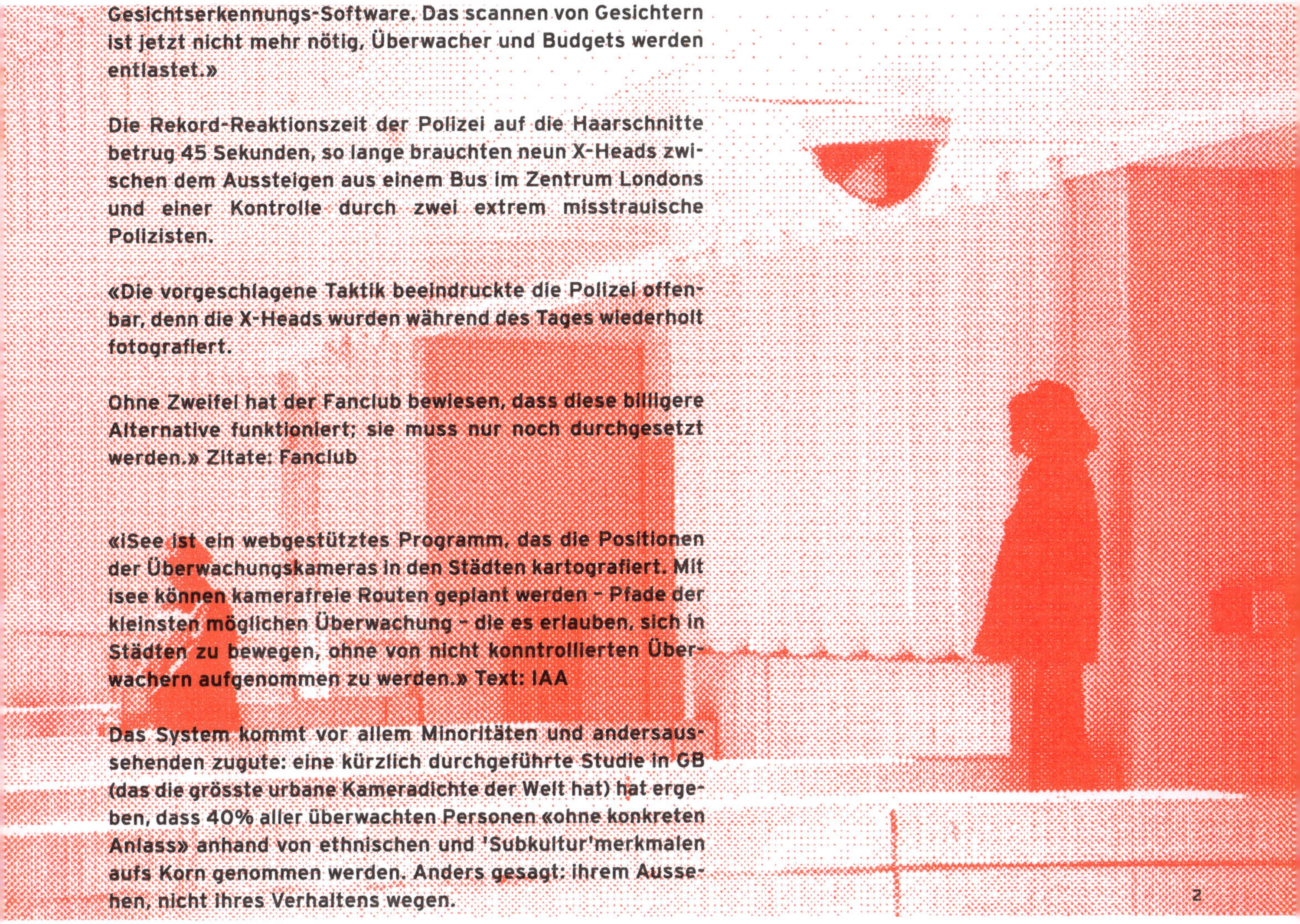

Die Rekord-Reaktionszeit der Polizei auf die Haarschnitte betrug 45 Sekunden, so lange brauchten neun X-Heads zwischen dem Aussteigen aus einem Bus im Zentrum Londons und einer Kontrolle durch zwei extrem misstrauische Polizisten.

«Die vorgeschlagene Taktik beeindruckte die Polizei offenbar, denn die X-Heads wurden während des Tages wiederholt fotografiert.

Ohne Zweifel hat der Fanclub bewiesen, dass diese billigere Alternative funktioniert; sie muss nur noch durchgesetzt werden.» Zitate: Fanclub

«iSee ist ein webgestütztes Programm, das die Positionen der Überwachungskameras in den Städten kartografiert. Mit isee können kamerafreie Routen geplant werden – Pfade der kleinsten möglichen Überwachung – die es erlauben, sich in Städten zu bewegen, ohne von nicht konntrollierten Überwachern aufgenommen zu werden.» Text: IAA

Das System kommt vor allem Minoritäten und andersaussehenden zugute: eine kürzlich durchgeführte Studie in GB (das die grösste urbane Kameradichte der Welt hat) hat ergeben, dass 40% aller überwachten Personen «ohne konkreten Anlass» anhand von ethnischen und 'Subkultur'merkmalen aufs Korn genommen werden. Anders gesagt: ihrem Aussehen, nicht ihres Verhaltens wegen.

2

Wenn du einen Machtmenschen angreifen willst ohne besondere Mittel zur Verfügung zu haben, gibt es ein exzellentes Mittel dafür: die öffentliche Demütigung. Zwei mögliche Taktiken sind: ein simulierter Anschlag mit einer Waffe – oder mit einer Ladung Sahne.

«Vielleicht haben einige vom kambodschanischen Studenten David Kang gehört, der in Australien einen Anschlag auf Prinz Charles simuliert hat. Charles wollte gerade zu einer Standardansprache ansetzen, als Kang über eine Absperrung sprang und Platzpatronen aus einer Pistole auf ihn abfeuerte.

Simulierst du nur den Tod eines Feindes, zeigst du dass du es ehrlich meinst, und erreichst wahrscheinlich mehr Aufmersamkeit für deine Bewegungsgründe. Die globalen Medien trennen ständig Gewaltakte von den Hintergründen, aber der Mut einer simulierten Ermordung und die totale Sicherheit für das Opfer lenken die Medien weg von sinnloser Gewalt hin zum Zweck hinter der Tat.

Ausserdem kann man nicht wegen eines Gewaltverbrechens angeklagt werden, da eine Simulation ohne Gewalt auskommt – es ist nur ihre Andeutung.»

Zitat: Jamie Miller, Time Bomb #2

If you want to knock a powerful person off his feet without having access to elaborate resources, there is an excellent way to do so: humiliate him publicly. Two possible tactics: simulated assassination with a weapon - or by a load of cream.

«Perhaps some of you may have heard about David Kang, the Cambodian student who simulated an assassination of England's Prince Charles while the royal twit was visiting Australia. Charles was about to give a droll little speech when Kang leapt over a barricade and fired blanks from a pistol at him.

By simulating the murder of your enemy, you demonstrate your sincerity and you will probably have more attention paid to your demands. The global media consistently divorce terrorist actions from their original purpose, but the boldness and complete safety of simulated assassination could circumvent the media's focus from mindless violence and attract attention to your cause instead.

Plus: one cannot be seriously charged with any violent crime, since there is nothing violent whatsoever about simulation; it's only a suggestion that violence is possible.»

Quotes from: Jamie Miller, Time Bomb #2

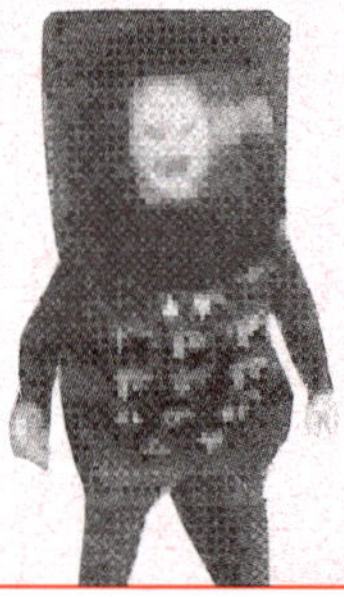

Du würdest gerne mehr Zeit fürs Lauftraining haben, aber das Telefon klingelt ständig? Hilfe > phonebashing.com

Want to have more spare time for running exercises, but the mobile is ringing all the time? > phonebashing.com

Jamie Miller, Time Bomb #2 / featured in: history.louisvillehardcore.com

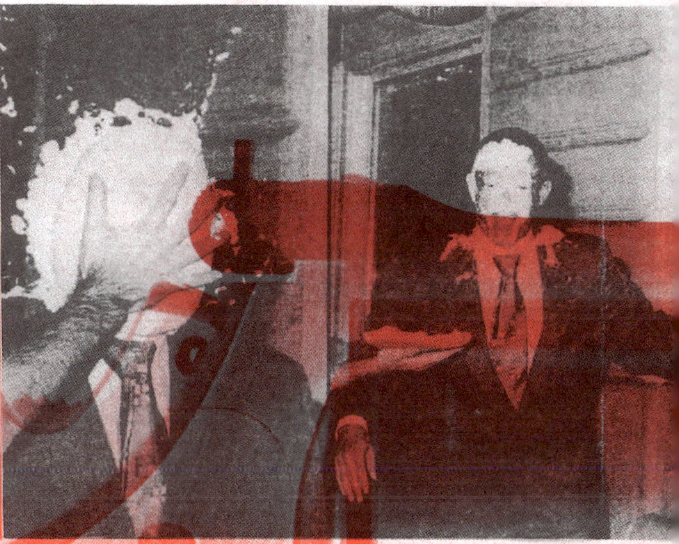

«No Pastry, No Peace! As multinational corporations accelerate the plunder of our world, a militant resistance has formed in response. Since the GPU began in the late 20th century, dozens of prominent corporate executives, politicians, economists, and sellout non-governmental organization 'leaders' have received their just desserts for crimes against people and the land.
The Biotic Baking Brigade (BBB) builds on just that. Under neo-liberalism, we all can throw a pie in the face of economic fascism. No bosses, offices, foundation grants, or neverending consensus meetings are needed. As the Nike corporation says, 'Just Do It!'.
Pie-throwing enjoys an illustrious history... It's as American as apple pie. Satire has always been one of the last weapons of the dispossessed, as the widespread public support for this brand of pielitical pressure shows.»
Quote: The Biotic Baking Brigade

«Während multinationale Konzerne die Welt aussaugen, hat sich ein militanter Widerstand geformt: von der GPU im späten 20.Jh. begonnen, haben Dutzende Prominenter, Politiker und Wirtschaftsführer ihren gerechten Dessert für Verbrechen gegen die Menschen und die Erde bekommen.
Die Biotische BackBrigade (BBB) fundiert darauf; im Neoliberalismus kann man dem kommerziellen Faschismus nur eine Torte ins Gesicht werfen. Keine Chefs, Büros, Finanzierungsstipendien, nicht endende Besprechungen. Wie der Nike Konzern sagt, 'Just Do It!'.
Tortenwerfen hat eine illustre Tradition... es ist so amerikanisch wie Apfelkuchen. Satire war schon immer die letzte Waffe der Enteigneten, wie die breite Unterstützung der Tortenpolitik zeigt.» Zitat: The Biotic Baking Brigade

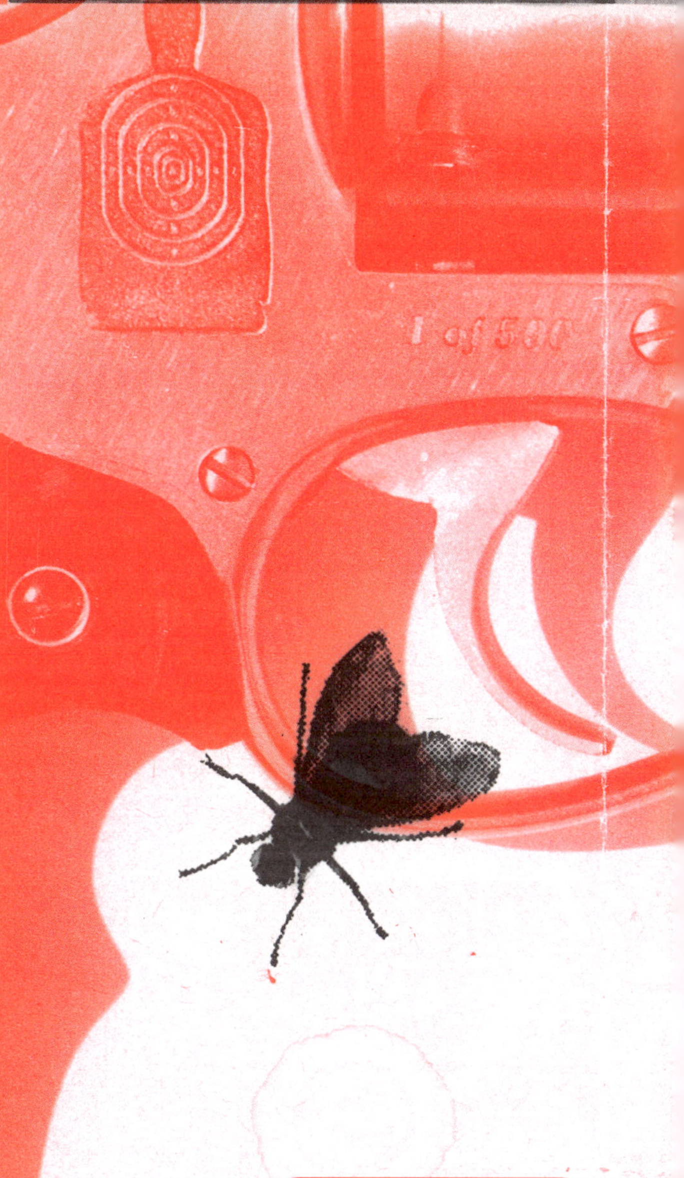

Inspirationen für weitere Formen biologischer Sabotage liefern Critical Art Ensemble in ihrem Pamphlet «The Molecular Invasion». Sie propagieren die Nutzung von Naturkräften, wie die Züchtung und Freilassung von exotischen Fliegenschwärmen in der Nähe von Forschungsinstituten für Biotechnik, oder das Aussetzen von kornfressenden Nagern in Felder mit genetisch manipulierten Pflanzen.
Weitere Details unter: critical-art.net

Inspirations for other forms of biological sabotage can be found in the Critical Art Ensemble's article «The Molecular Invasion». They propose using nature's power, such as breeding and releasing hoards of exotic flies close to biotech reaserch institutes, or infiltrating genetically modified fields with cropeating rodents.
For further details see: critical-art.net

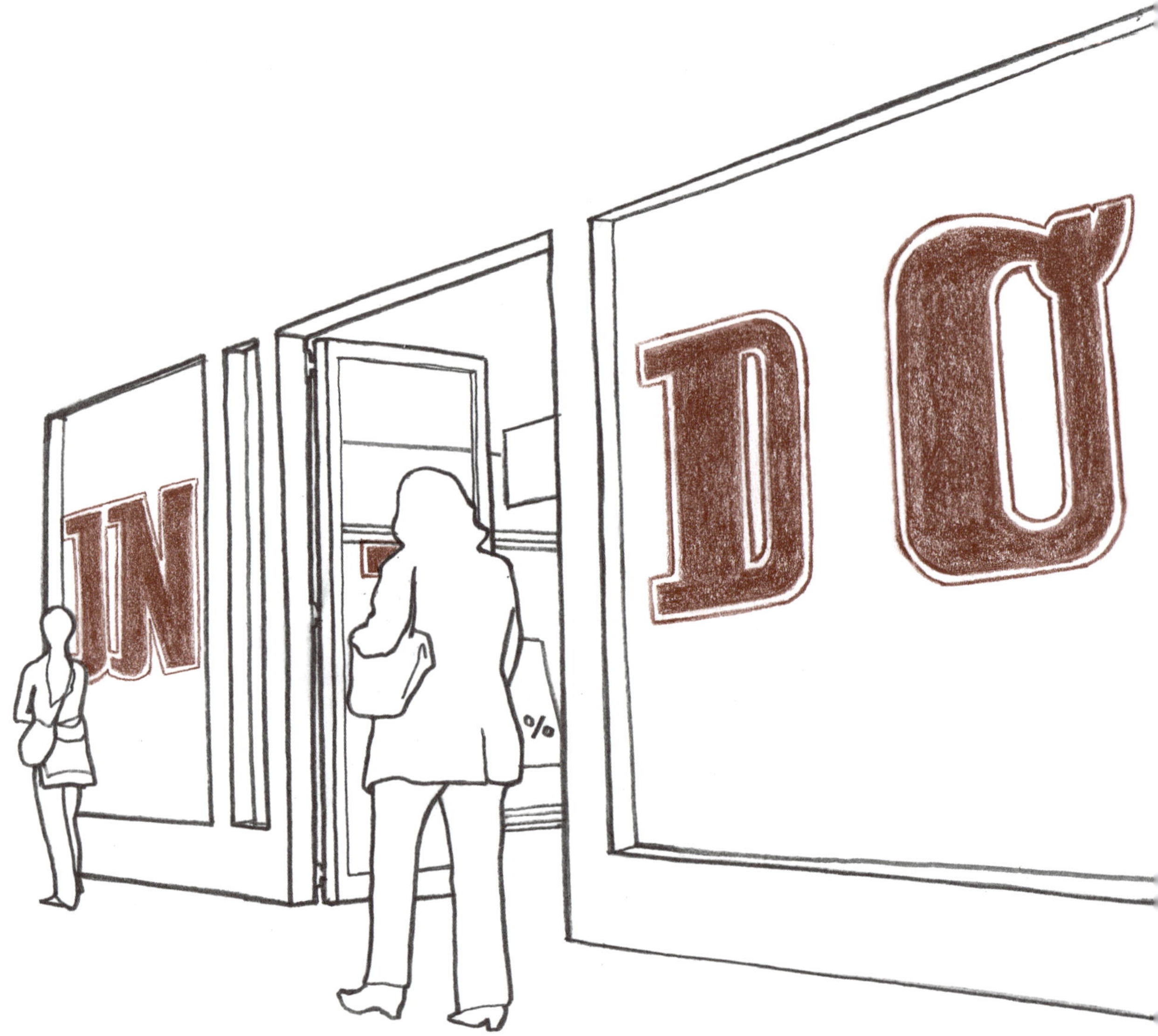
UN
DƠ

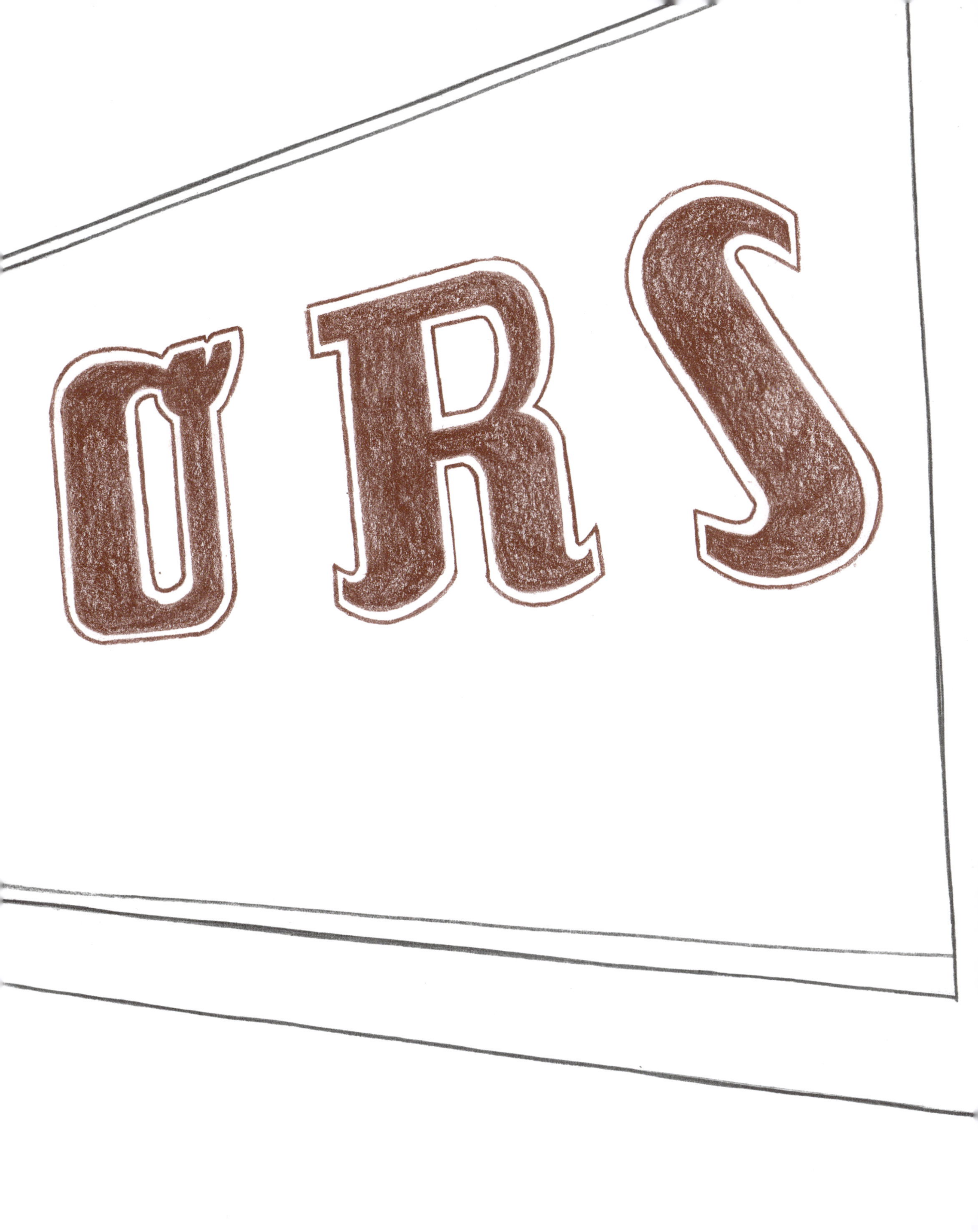
URS

NO SHOPPING RITUALS

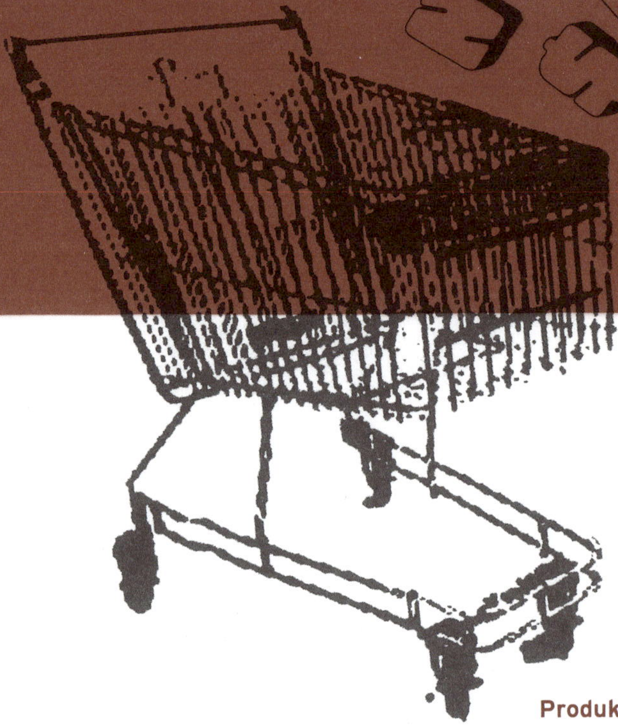

Produkte anbeten: Einkaufszentren sind moderne Tempel des Konsums – warum nicht dort beten, und dem eintönigen Alltag der anderen einen surrealen Moment schenken?

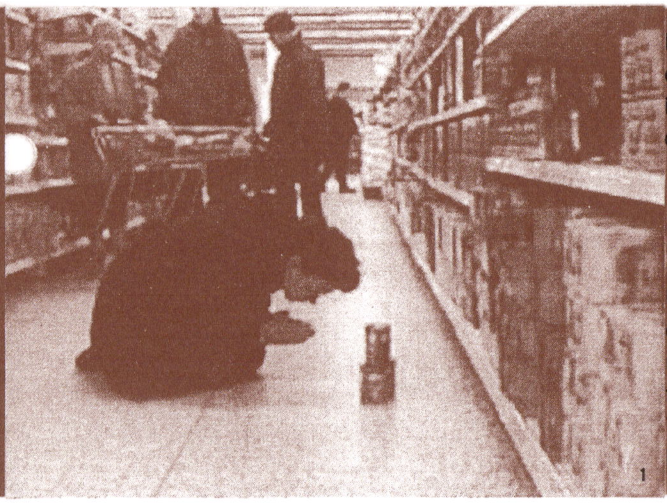

1

Prayers to products: since malls are already modern temples of consumption, why not go there to pray? Such acts of poetic terrorism give a surreal touch to your peers' repetitious daily routines.

Useful Cristmas presents: on Dec 24, 2002 in Rome at a Virgin Megastore a Santa Claus hands out pirated bestselling music albums, complete with a recorded statement saying that the music industry's pricepushing forced him to do so. The package includes pirating software and instructions for its use in the booklet.

Nützliche Weihnachtsgeschenke: am 24. Dez 2002 verteilt ein Santa Claus in der römischen Virgin-Filiale kopierte Musik CD's, komplett mit einem eingespieltem Statement zur Preispolitik der Musikindustrie, Kopiersoftware und Anleitung im Booklet.

«WHIRL-MART is an anti-shopping ritual in which a local troupe gathers and silently pushes empty shopping carts through the aisles of a local superstore. The point is not to protest outright the emptiness of material consumption, but to call attention to it through an absurdist mirroring of the shopping process.» It took about 45 minutes for the staff to lose their composure and put an end to the performance.

«WHIRL-MART ist ein anti-Einkaufsritual, bei dem eine Gruppe leere Einkaufswagen wortlos durch ihren lokalen Hypermarkt schiebt. Es geht nicht um einen direkten Konsumprotest, sondern um die Schaffung einer absurd verzerrten Kopie des Einkaufs, die zum nachdenken zwingt.»
Es dauerte ca. 45 Minuten, bis dem Personal die Geduld riss und sie die Runden unterbrachen.

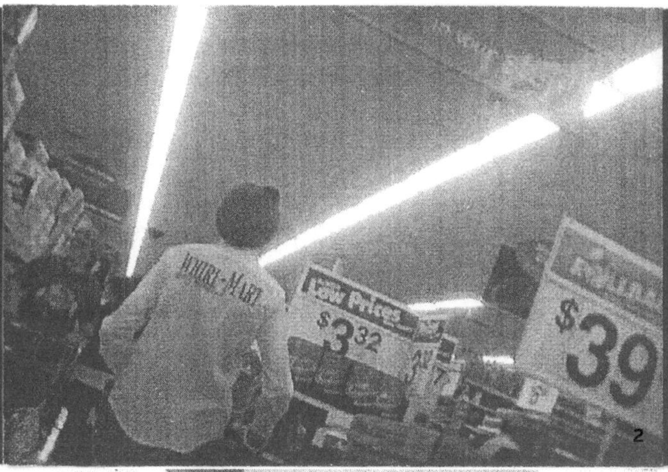

2

«Spucks aus für die moderne Kunst. Das Museum of Contemporary Arts in Chicago (USA) wird von Phillip Morris dotiert. Während ihrer Putzaktion schnorrte der Vacuum Cleaner Zigaretten bei den Besuchern. Teil einer Putzkampagne in den USA und GB. Hinter dem Kapitalismus aufräumen - ihre Teppiche staubsaugend.»

«Coughing up for modern art. The Museum of Contemporary Arts, Chicago (USA), receives funding from Phillip Morris; the Vacuum Cleaners cleaned their floors whilst asking visitors if they had a spare smoke. Part of a cleaning campaign in the US and UK. Cleaning up after capitalism – vacuuming their carpets.»

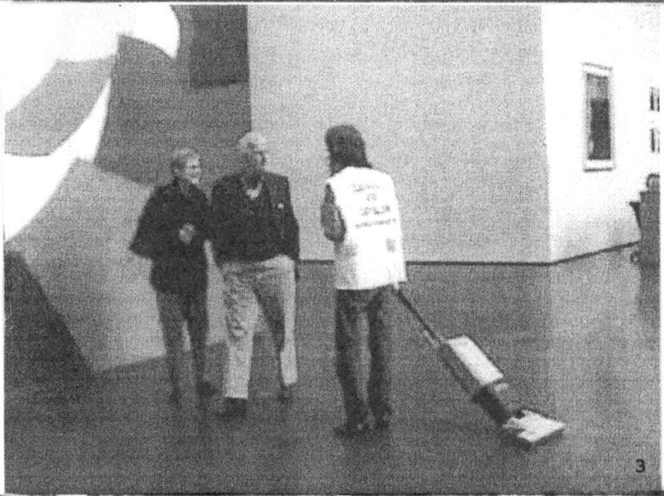
3

Invading the Borders bookstore in Chicago. «In collaboration with My Dad's Strip Club and students from the school of the Art Institute of Chicago, a group of 10 entered a Borders and meandered silently through the store displaying selected book covers.» The group spent 30 minutes traveling around the three floors in a silent takeover /poetic protest.
Quotes: My Dads Strip Club & WHIRL-MART

Invasion der Buchhandlung Borders in Chicago. «Zusamen mit Mitgliedern von My Dad's Strip Club und Kunststudenten rearrangierte eine Gruppe von 10 Leuten die Bücher in den Regalen, neue Zusammenhänge schaffend. Diese wurden in einer stummen Prozession durch die Stockwerke getragen.»
Zitate: My Dads Strip Club & WHIRL-MART

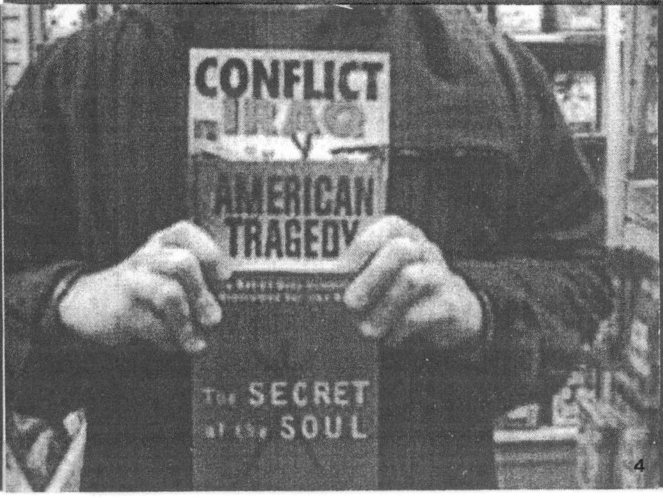

4

Die anti-kommerzielle Institution und Zeitschrift «Adbusters» propagiert jährlich einen «Buy Nothing Day» und «TV Turnoff Day» zur Entwöhnung für den industrialisierten Menschen. The critical Vancouver-based institution and magazine «Adbusters» promotes a yearly «Buy Nothing Day» as a weaning cure for the inhabitant of an industrialized nation (they offer a «TV Turnoff Day», too).

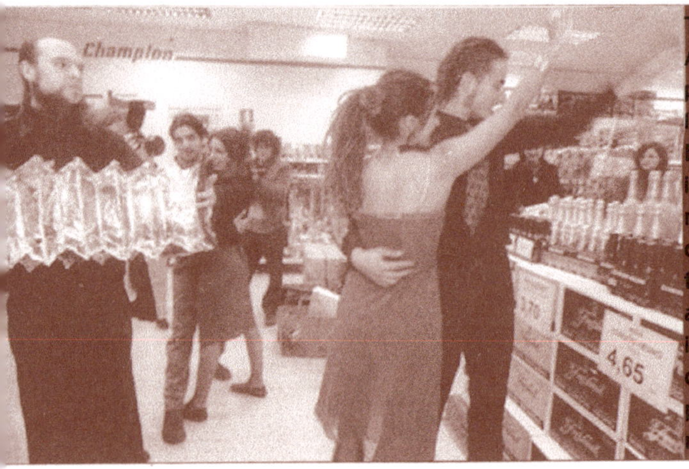

To celebrate the one-year anniversary of protests in Argentina in 2002, YOMANGOtango went Christmas unshopping: a multitude of tango dancers passed the surprised police protecting the Champion/Carrefour hypermarket in Barcelona, shed their regular client clothes and began dancing around the shelves to the rhythm of a techno-tango remix. Using the most elegant of moves, they snatched champagne bottles, passed the cashiers and placed them in the YOMANGO Christmas basket. The next day 'cacerolazos' and concentrations were held in front of bank headquarters in the center of town. YOMANGOtango penetrated into Banco Santander, uncorked the bottles and toasted for the people of Argentina, shouting «Que se vayan todos! (They all must go!)», under a rain of champagne.

Das einjährige Jubiläum der Proteste in Argentinien wurde 2002 von YOMANGO durch ein Weihnachts-Unshopping-Tango gefeiert. Eine Gruppe von Tänzern, verkleidet als Einkäufer, infiltrierte den Carrefour-Hypermarkt in Barcelona. Drinnen begannen sie, begleitet von einem Harmonikaspieler, durch den Supermarkt zu kreisen.

NO

Tanzend und mit graziösen Bewegungen klauten sie Champagner und tanzten an den Kassen vorbei Richtung Tür. Der Champagner musste am richtigen Ort getrunken werden; YOMANGOtango penetrierten die Banco Santander, tanzten, liessen die Korken schiessen und stiessen mit dem Ruf «Que se vayan todos! (Alle (Kapitalisten) müssen verschwinden!)» auf die Menschen in Argentinien an.

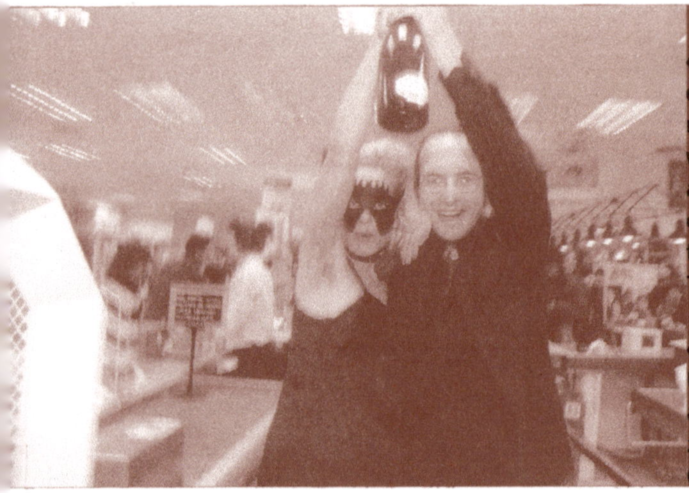

«Money is a code: to have money/not to have money. This difference is what operates the repetition machine we call reality. The violence of currency excludes and demands work. Free money, on the other hand, blocks this code and attacks reality. If reality has gone mad we must invent delirious concepts. Free money doesn't belong to us: it belongs to everyone and, at the same time, to no-one.»
Text: El Dinero Gratis

«Geld ist ein Code: Geld haben/kein Geld haben. Dieser Unterschied lässt die Wiederholungsmaschine, genannt Realität, funktionieren. Die Gewalt des Geldes schließt aus und zwingt zur Arbeit. Das Gratisgeld dagegen blockiert diesen Code und greift die Realität an. Wenn die Realität verrückt geworden ist, müssen wir wahnsinnige Konzepte erfinden. Das Gratisgeld gehört uns nicht: es ist allen und gleichzeitig niemandem.» Text: El Dinero Gratis

«Las Agencias provide responses to a new reality.» They do organisational work, through direct actions and subvertisements or design lines of demonstration fashion/protection wear. One highlight is a turtleneck with an integrated ski mask.

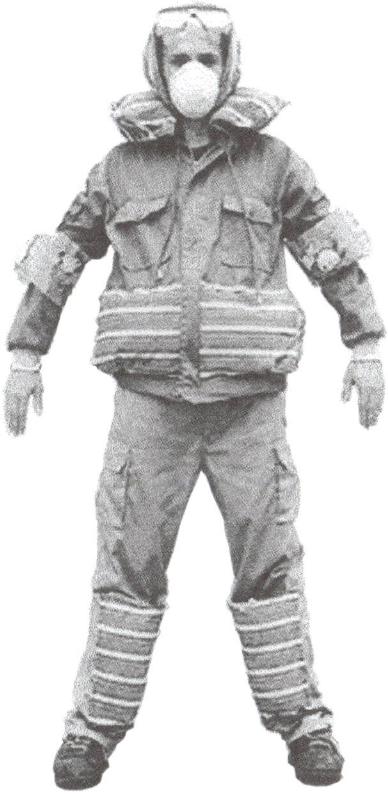

1

«Las Agencias stellen Lösungen für eine neuer Realität bereit.» Sie arbeiten organisatorisch, mit Aktionen, Kampagnen oder angewandt; z.B. durch die Herstellung eine Linie von Demonstrations/Mode/Schutzkleidung. Ein Highlight ist ein Pullover mit eingebauter Skimaske im Rolli.

«Suited for Subversion ist ein Projekt zur Herstellung eines Schutzanzugs für Massenproteste. Der Anzug überwacht ausserdem den Puls seines Trägers und strahlt den verstärkten Herzschlag über einen Brustlautsprecher aus. Somit ist mein Anzug zugleich Rüstung und Entwaffnung in einem; zugleich schützend wie auch provozierend».
Text: Ralph Borland

«Suited for Subversion is a project to create a suit that protects the wearer at large-scale street protests. The suit also monitors the wearer's pulse and projects an amplified heartbeat out of a speaker in the chest of the suit. As much as my suit is armour, it is also disarming; as much provocation as protection.» Text: Ralph Borland

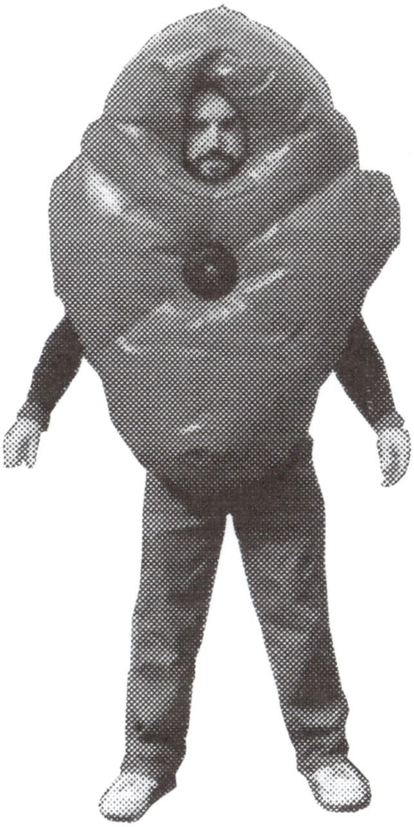

2

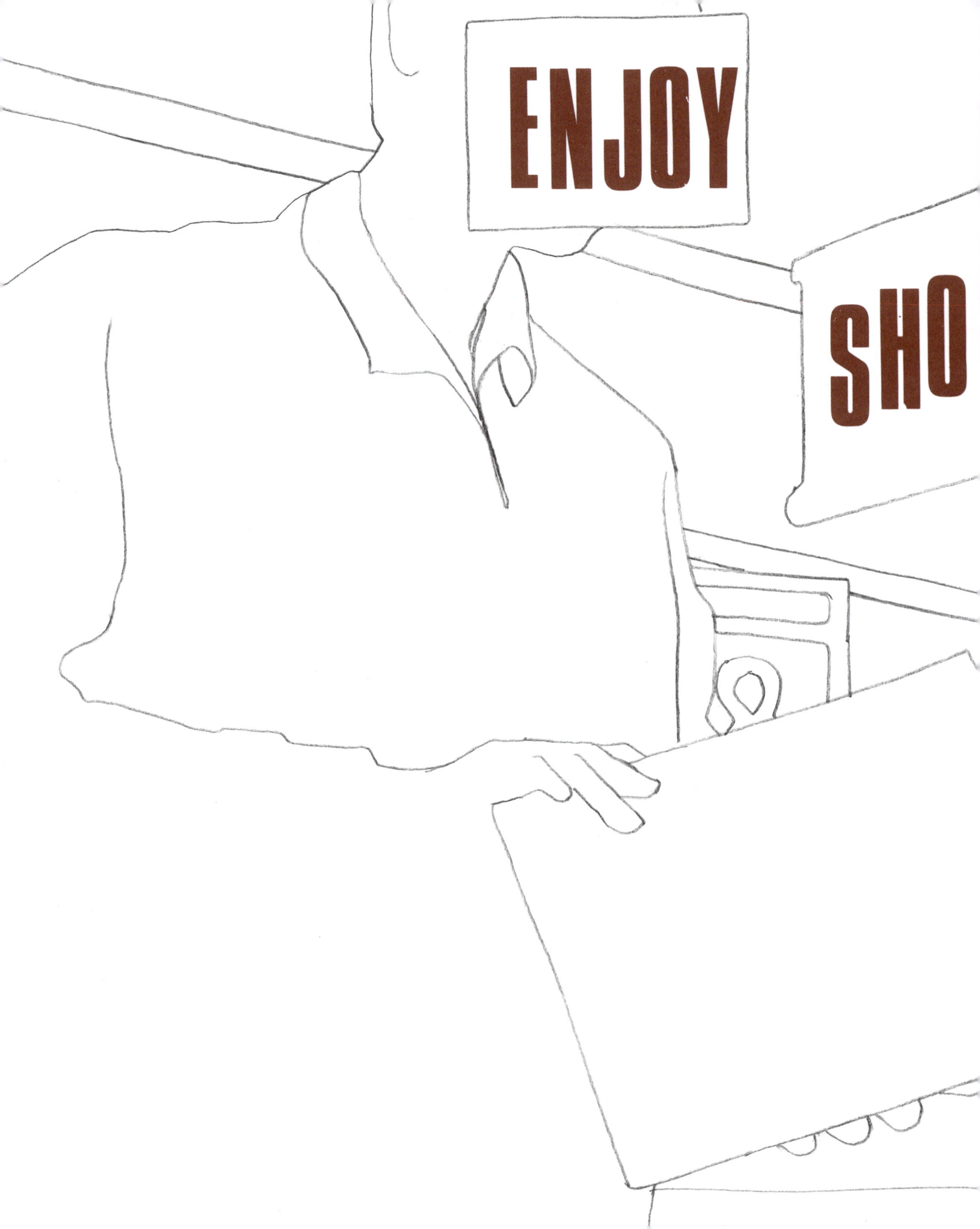
ENJOY
SHO

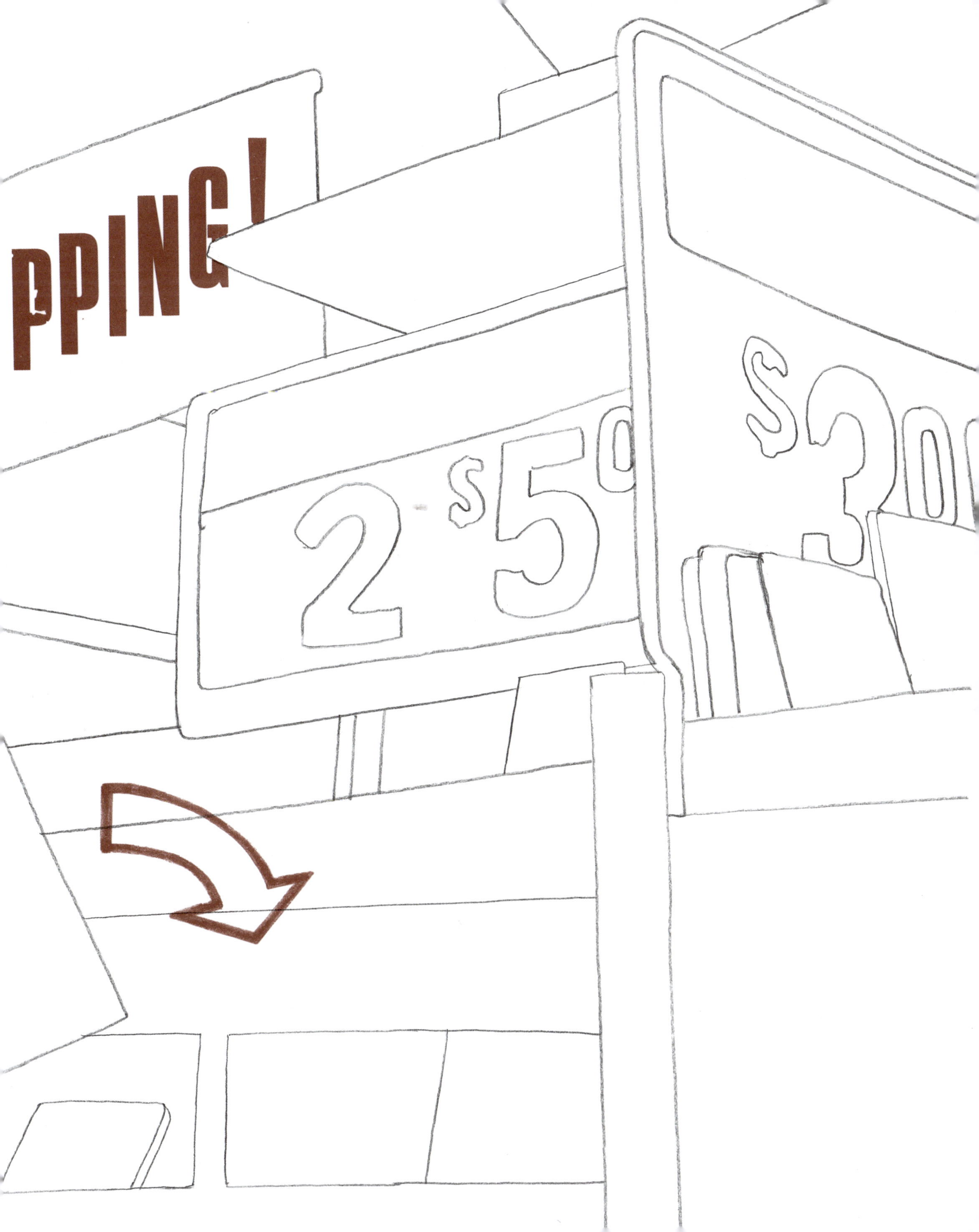
PPING!
2 $5
$3

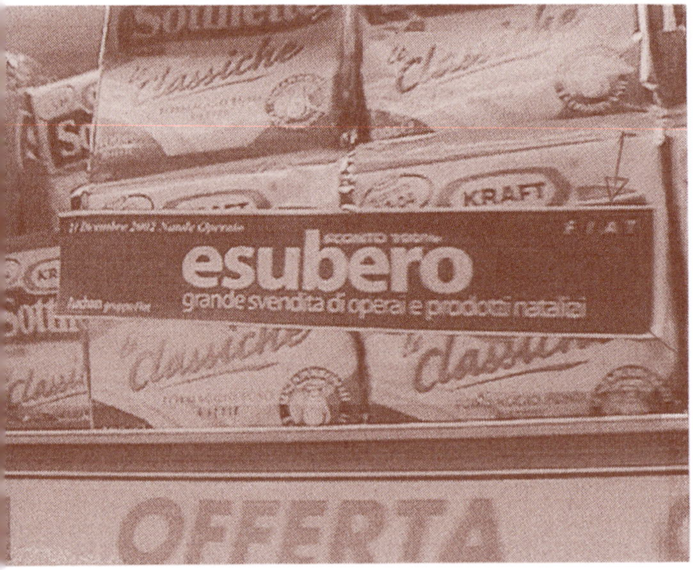

Outright nicking or «YOMANGOing» of goods is one way. But there's also the 'giving' approach, as opposed to the «taking» one, in which hidden, poetic (or radical) interventions are prepared and left for the next one passing by, to liven up his everyday-numbed-down brain.

Direktes klauen oder «YOMANGOing» von Gütern ist eine Möglichkeit. Aber im Gegensatz zu diesem 'nehmenden' gibt auch einen 'gebenden' Ansatz. Diesem zufolge werden versteckte poetische (oder radikale) Interventionen vorbereitet und als Belebung für die vom Alltag abgestumpften Geister hinterlassen.

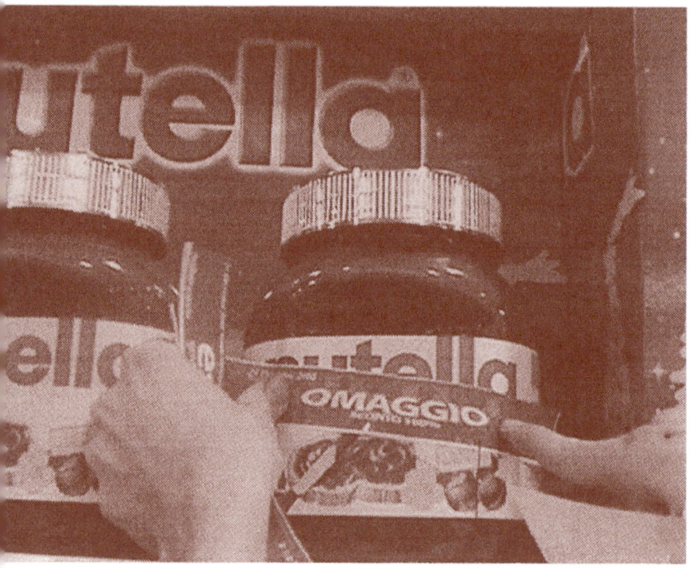

These small stickers are designed to look like any other piece of commercial graphics abundant in Italian supermarkets. Just like the 'official' ones, these scream Sale and Free, and stick on various goods. It's only when you grab the product that you notice the small text which offers varius discounts on «Goods and Workers», related to massive layoffs at the car maker FIAT.

Diese kleinen Aufkleber sehen aus wie all die anderen kommerziellen Grafiken, die die italienischen Supermärkte vollstopfen. Wie die 'offiziellen' Versionen schreien auch diese Ausverkauf und Gratis und sind auf verschiedenen Produkten zu finden. Erst wenn du nach der Packung greifst, entzifferst du den kleingeschriebenen Text, der diverse Discounts auf «Weichnachtsartikel und Arbeiter» offeriert, auf massive Entlassungen bei FIAT schielend.

Peter Coffin produced this piece of public art for the NY Free Biennal. You could download the barcode stickers, print them onto standard sticker labels, then apply to consumer products. When scanned codes will generate words instead of prices.

Peter Coffin produzierte diese poetische Subversion für die New Yorker Free Biennal. Die Aufkleber konnte man herunterladen, ausdrucken und auf Produkte kleben. Beim scannen generieren die Codes Worte statt Preise.

Have Keep

Give Want

Take Need

Lose

1

For a strictly consumer-oriented re-use of bar codes please leaf forward to «Re-Code.com».

Eine unmittelbar konsumorientierte Umnutzung von Barcodes bot «Re-Code.com» an (im nächsten Kapitel).

IDIOM, masters of miniature camouflage subversions, have travelled to the US Library of Congress to improve the American history books, with the help of a simple printing alphabet.

IDIOM, die Meister getarnter Mini-Subversionen, machten sich die Mühe einer Reise zur US – Kongressbibliothek, um deren Geschichtsbücher mittels eines überall erhältlichen Stempel-ABCs zu verbessern.

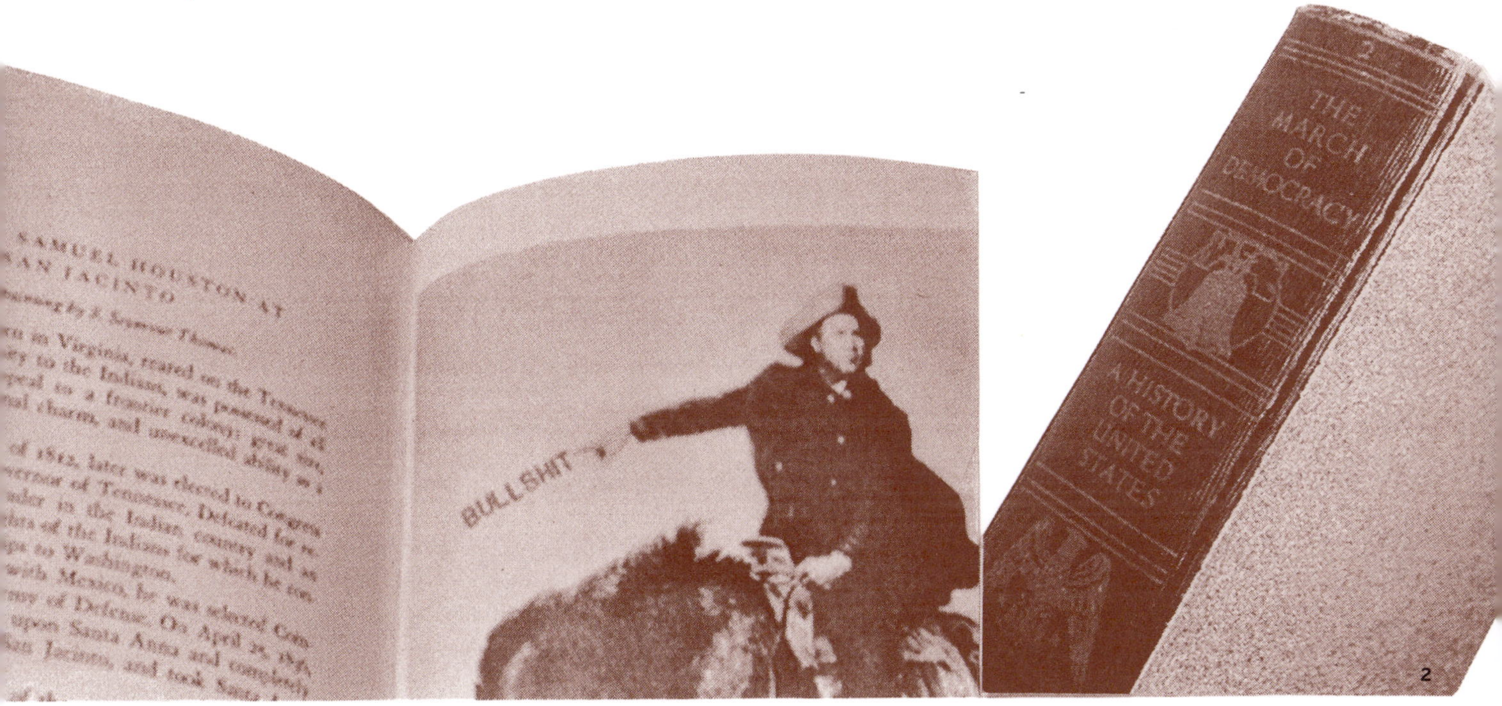

2

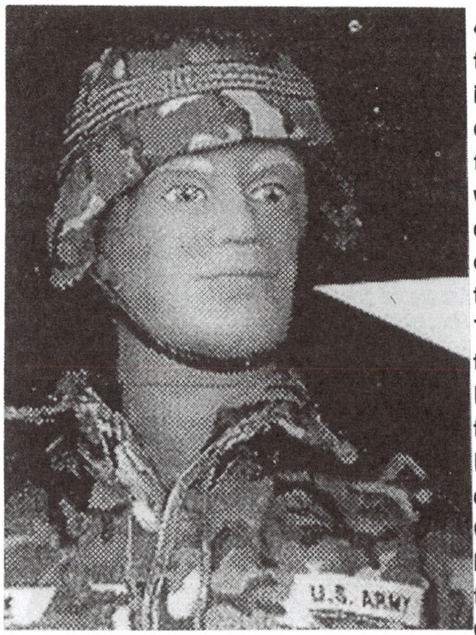

«People who were already upset at Barbie couldn't believe their ears when Barbie's electric voice box giggled: 'Math is hard!/I love shopping!' and 'Will we ever have enough clothes?' In 1989 the Barbie Liberation Organization was formed. Taking advantage of similarities in the voice hardware of 'Teen Talk Barbie' and the 'Talking Duke G.I. Joe' doll, er, action figure, they absconded with several hundred of each and performed a stereotype-change operation on the lot.

The surgery was no simple matter – circuit boards had to be trimmed, a capacitor moved, and a switch reengineered. The BLO returned the altered dolls to the toy store shelves, who then resold them to children who had to invent scenarios for Barbies who yelled 'Vengeance is mine!' and G.I. Joes who day-dreamed 'Let's plan our dream wedding!'.

Cleverly placed 'Call your local TV news' stickers on the back ensured that the media would have genuine recipients to interview as soon as the news broke.

One BLO member counted up the many benefits of their program: 'The storekeepers make money twice, we stimulate the economy – the consumer gets a better product – and our message gets heard'.» Text: BLO

The BLO received funding from ®TMark (see next chapter).

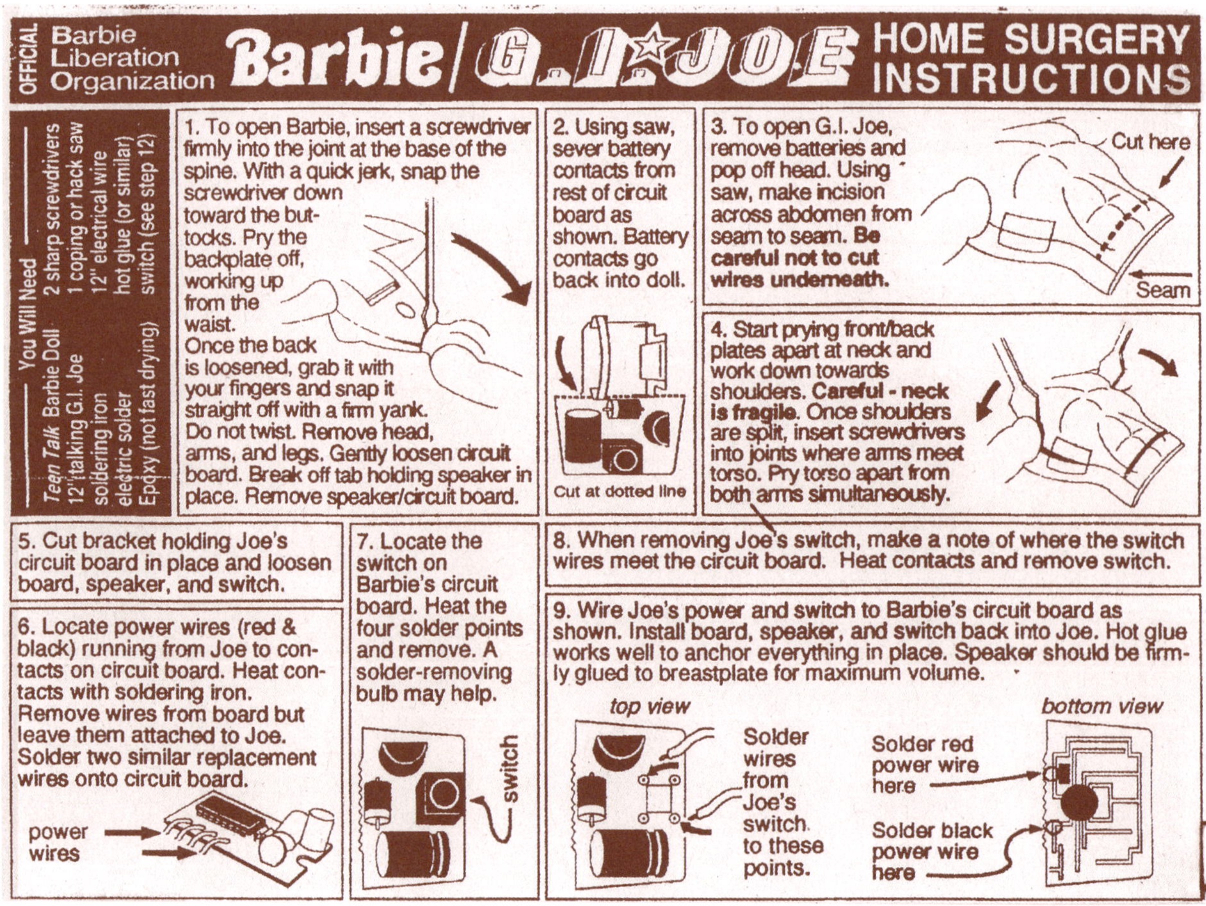

«Leute, die sowieso schon den Hals voll von Barbie hatten, trauten ihren Ohren nicht, als Barbie mit elektronischer Stimme zu kichern begann: 'Mathe ist schwer!/Ich liebe einkaufen!' und 'Werden wir jemals genug Kleider haben?'

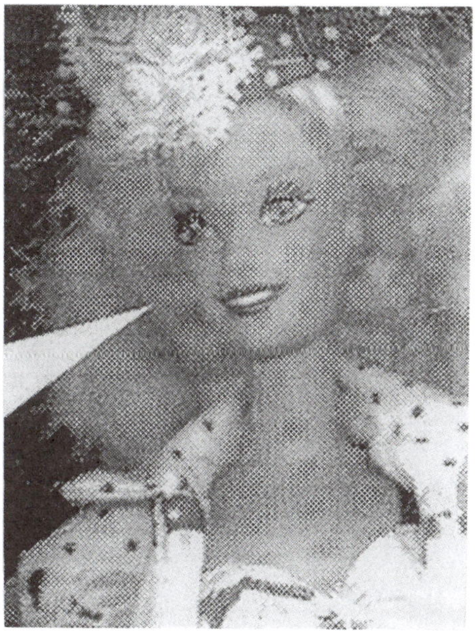

1989 wurde die Barbie Liberation Organization gegründet. Die Ähnlichkeiten der Stimmelektronik von 'Teen Talk Barbie' und 'Talking Duke G.I. Joe' nutzend, machten sie sich mit hunderten der Puppen (bzw. 'Action-Figuren') davon, um an ihnen einen Stereotypenwechsel vorzunehmen.
Die Operation war nicht einfach. Die BLO brachte die veränderten Puppen in die Ladenregale zurück, aus denen sie wieder an Kinder verkauft wurden, die nun neue Szenarios erfinden mussten für Barbies, die 'Rache ist mein!' schrien und G.I. Joes, die seufzten 'Lass uns unsere Traumhochzeit planen!'
Auf den Verpackungen wurden 'Ruf Deinen lokalen TV-Sender an' Aufkleber plaziert, um sicherzustellen dass die Medien echte Puppenkäufer an die Strippe bekamen, sobald die Geschichte platzen würde.
Die vielen Vorteile des BLO-Programms: 'Ladenbesitzer verdienen doppelt, wir stimulieren die Wirtschaft – der Konsument erhält ein besseres Produkt – und unsere Message wird gehört' Text: BLO

Die BLO wurde von ®TMark co-finanziert (siehe nächstes Kapitel).

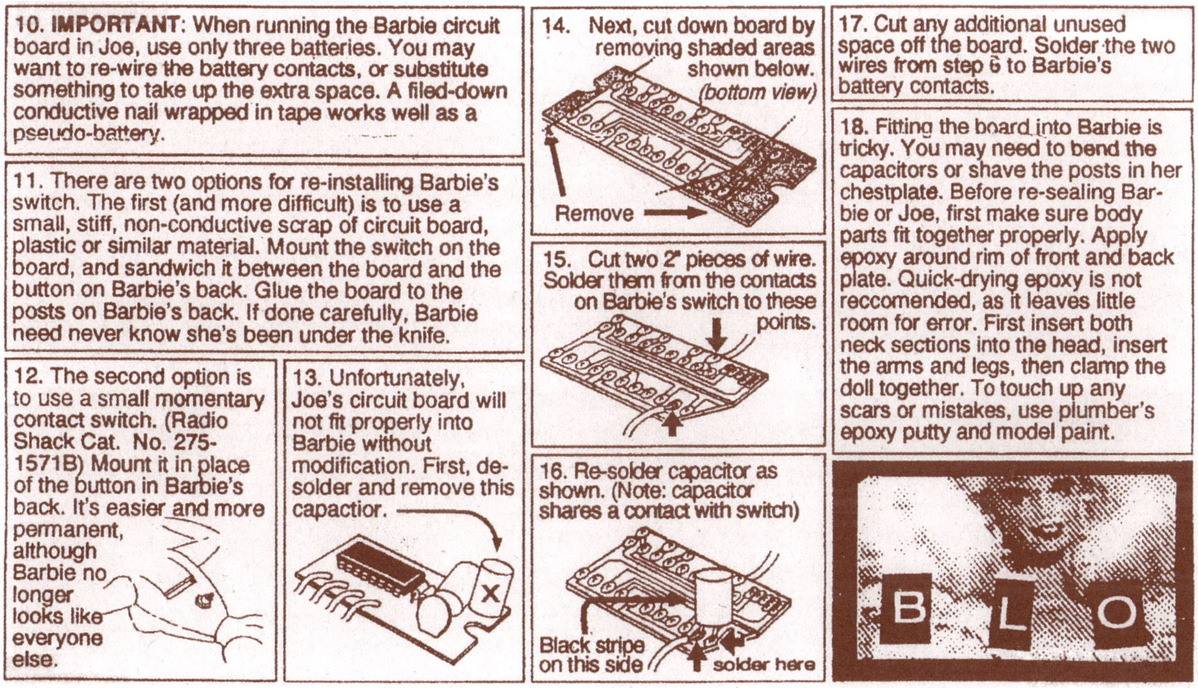

10. **IMPORTANT**: When running the Barbie circuit board in Joe, use only three batteries. You may want to re-wire the battery contacts, or substitute something to take up the extra space. A filed-down conductive nail wrapped in tape works well as a pseudo-battery.

11. There are two options for re-installing Barbie's switch. The first (and more difficult) is to use a small, stiff, non-conductive scrap of circuit board, plastic or similar material. Mount the switch on the board, and sandwich it between the board and the button on Barbie's back. Glue the board to the posts on Barbie's back. If done carefully, Barbie need never know she's been under the knife.

12. The second option is to use a small momentary contact switch. (Radio Shack Cat. No. 275-1571B) Mount it in place of the button in Barbie's back. It's easier and more permanent, although Barbie no longer looks like everyone else.

13. Unfortunately, Joe's circuit board will not fit properly into Barbie without modification. First, de-solder and remove this capactior.

14. Next, cut down board by removing shaded areas shown below. *(bottom view)*
Remove

15. Cut two 2" pieces of wire. Solder them from the contacts on Barbie's switch to these points.

16. Re-solder capacitor as shown. (Note: capacitor shares a contact with switch)
Black stripe on this side
solder here

17. Cut any additional unused space off the board. Solder the two wires from step 6 to Barbie's battery contacts.

18. Fitting the board into Barbie is tricky. You may need to bend the capacitors or shave the posts in her chestplate. Before re-sealing Barbie or Joe, first make sure body parts fit together properly. Apply epoxy around rim of front and back plate. Quick-drying epoxy is not reccomended, as it leaves little room for error. First insert both neck sections into the head, insert the arms and legs, then clamp the doll together. To touch up any scars or mistakes, use plumber's epoxy putty and model paint.

B L O

<1,3> «The Centennial Society is a hand-made product line that was installed covertly in Wal-Marts around western New York and Minnesota from 1998–2000. Each product addresses negative trends in Wal-Mart's business practice. Most of these trends are common practice for any large retail chain. Wal-Mart is the largest grossing corporation in the world. There are Wal-Marts all over the world and its influence is expanding. The implications of this are staggering». Text: Packard Jennings

<2> «Child as an audience, 2001. This package, designed primarly for teenage boys, offers a host of radical software, instructions on how to hack a GameBoy, a hardcore CD, and a pamphlet on the oppression of youth.»
Placed in record stores. Quote: CAE, Carbon Defense League, and Creation is Crucifixion

<4> The US company behind action figure «Invisible Jim» says it encourages children to use their imaginations and doesn't take up any space. The figure boasts a «lack of darting eyes» and «realistic fake hair». It costs 5p to make, is on sale in the UK for £ 1.99 – and sells well. The packaging states: «Invisible Jim. As not seen on TV. Warning: Small parts may ruin your sex life. Batteries not included. A gripping hand would be nice. Camouflage suit sold separately.» It is made by the «What-if-Atlas-Got-An-Itchy-Bum Company», whose mission is «to save the world from crap dolls».

<1,3> «Die Centennial Society ist eine handgefertigte Produktserie, die 1998–2000 in Wal-Mart Hypermärkten plaziert wurde. Jedes Produkt spricht negative Aspekte der Wal-Mart Geschäftspolitik an (die jedoch auch von den meisten anderen Einzelhandelsketten praktiziert werden). Wal-Mart ist die grösste Handelskette der Welt, die Filialen sind überall; die Folgen sind verheerend.» Text: Packard Jennings

<2> «Kind als Publikum, 2001. Die Packung wurde für Jungs entworfen, beinhaltet eine Sammlung radikaler Software, Instruktionen zum Hacken eines GameBoy, eine Hardcore CD und ein Pamphlet über die Unterdrückung der Jugend.» Platziert in Plattenläden. Zitat: CAE, Carbon Defense League, und Creation is Crucifixion
<4> Der US-Hersteller der Aktionsfigur «Invisible Jim» behauptet sie ermutige Kinder zur Benutzung ihrer Fantasie zudem nehme sie keinen Platz weg. Die Herstellungskosten liegen bei 5 Pence, der Ladenpreis ist 1,99 Pfund – und sie verkauft sich gut. Packungstext: «Invisible Jim. Nicht im Fernsehen gesehen. Warnung: Kleinteile können Ihr Sexleben ruinieren. Batterien nicht vorhanden. Eine Greifhand wäre schön. Tarnanzug wird separat verkauft.» Produzent ist die «What-if-Atlas-Got-An-Itchy-Bum Company», Auftrag: «Die Welt von miesen Puppen befreien».

1

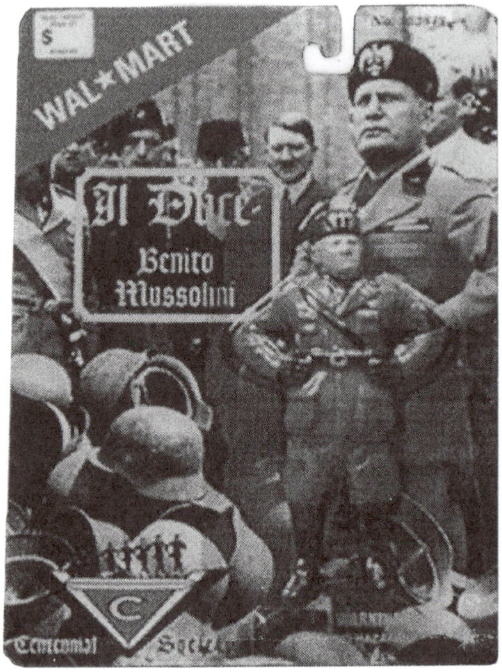

1,3 centennialsociety.com (Oakland, USA)

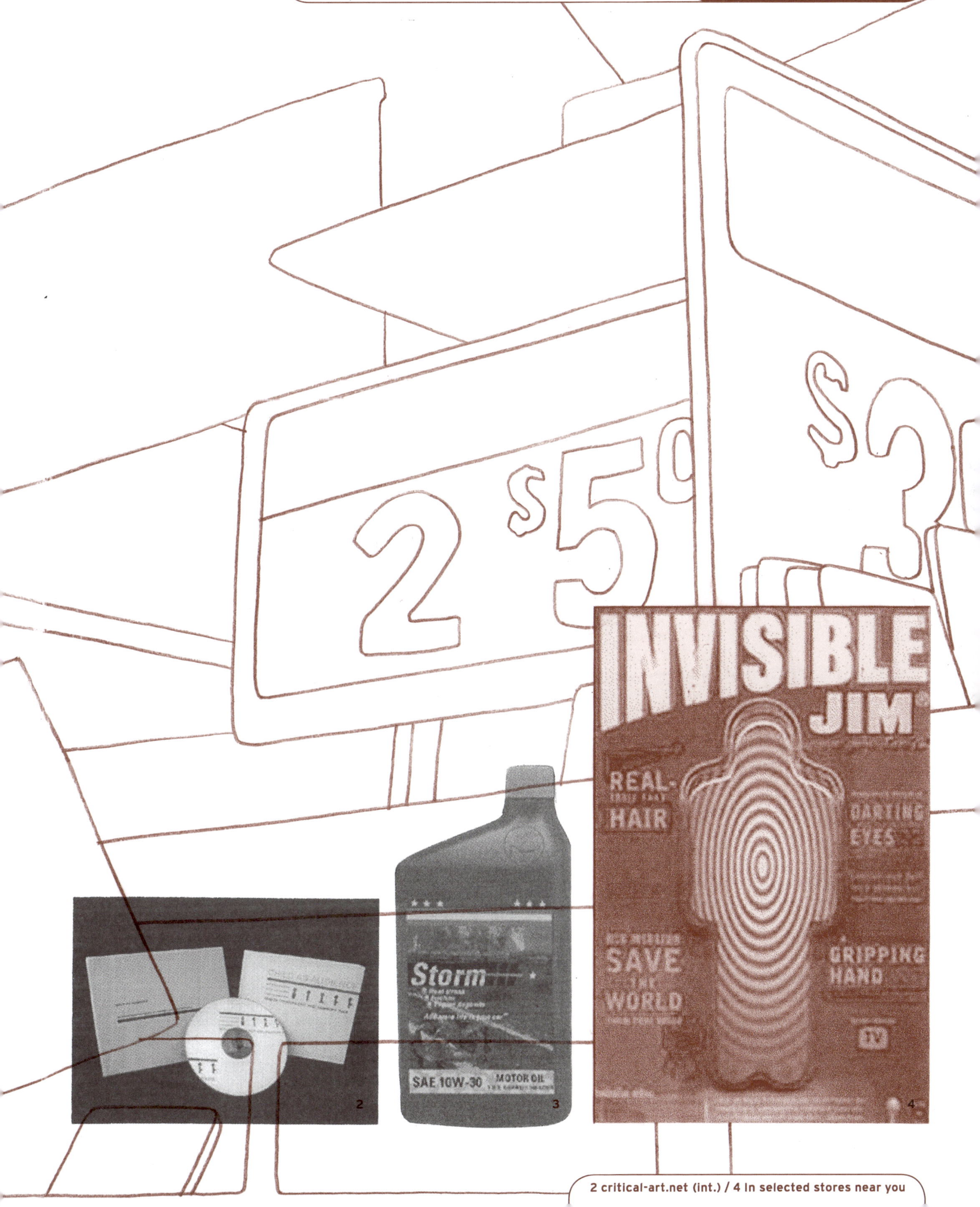
Storm
SAE 10W-30
MOTOR OIL
INVISIBLE
JIM
REAL-
HAIR
DARTING
EYES
SAVE
WORLD
GRIPPING
HAND
2
3
4

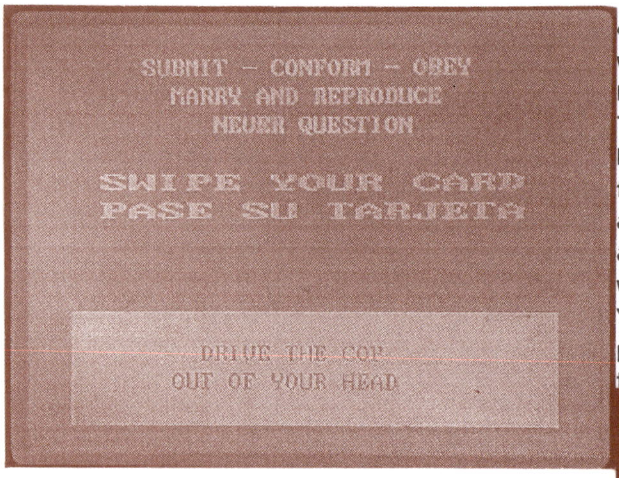

«We have a cash machine inside the club DNA Lounge and when reading the manual for the machine, I was pleased to learn that one can customize many of the messages on it! There is a small area at the top of the screen plus a 'billboard' area at the bottom of the screen that cycles through four settable messages. The manual encourages you to sell advertising in these spaces. I chose different ones.» (see images) «Additionally, the heading of the paper receipt begins with 'SHOPPING IS NOT CREATING – YOU ARE NOT WHAT YOU OWN'. This last one is my favorite, because people will probably only notice it after they've gotten home and fish the receipt out of their pockets!» Text: DNA Lounge

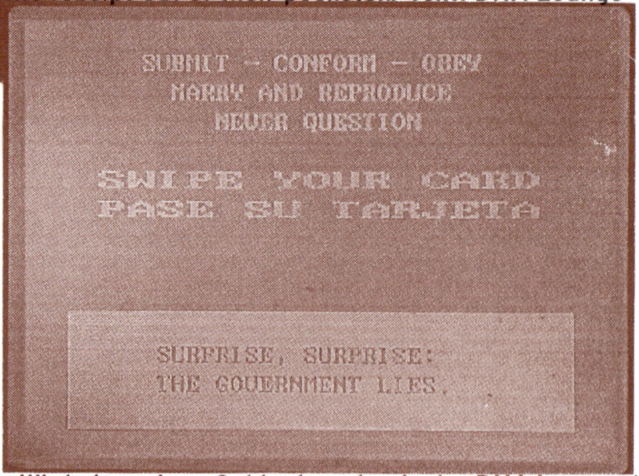

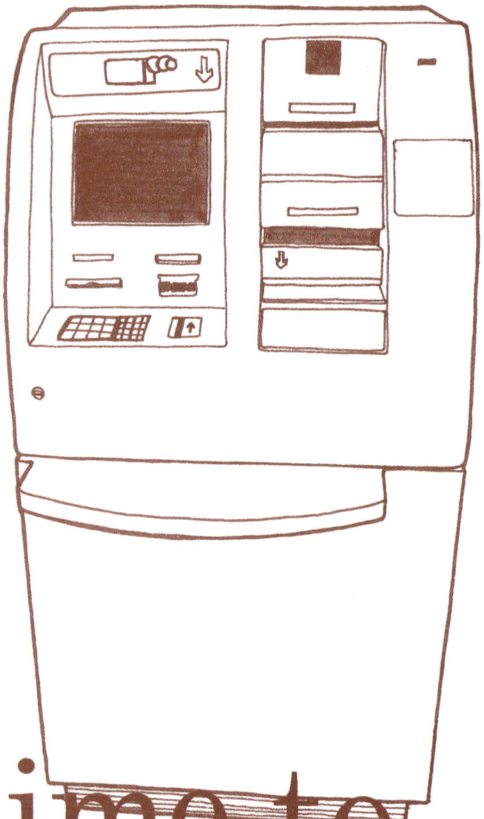

«Wir haben einen Geldautomaten in der DNA Lounge (einem Club); als ich seine Bedienungsanleitung las, merkte ich, dass man die Texte auf dem Bildschirm selbst programmieren kann! Es gibt zwei freie Felder, oben ein kleineres und unten ein grosses, auf dem bis zu vier Texte abwechselnd erscheinen. Die Anleitung schlägt vor, dort bezahlte Werbung unterzubringen. Ich wählte andere Botschaften.» (siehe Abb.) «Auf die Quittung wird dieser Text gedruckt: 'EINKAUFEN IST NICHT ERSCHAFFEN – DU BIST NICHT, WAS DU BESITZT'. Das ist mein Favorit, weil die meisten den Text erst bemerken wenn sie den Zettel zu Hause aus der Tasche fischen!» Text: DNA Lounge

time to pay up...

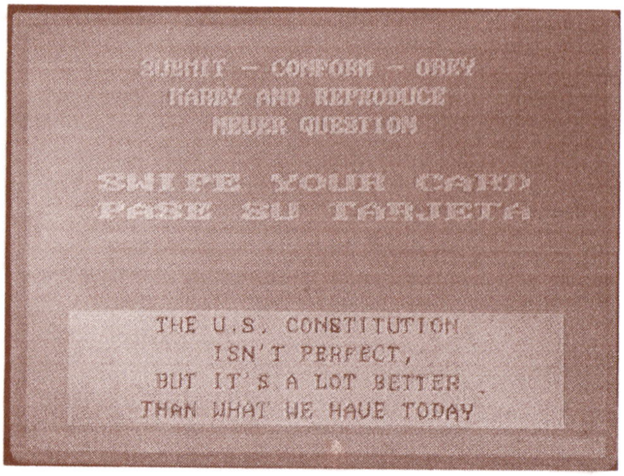

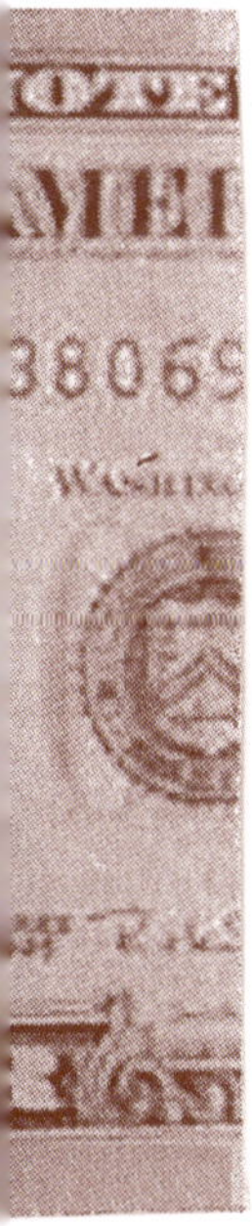

BUT WHAT IF THE MONEY'S MARKED?

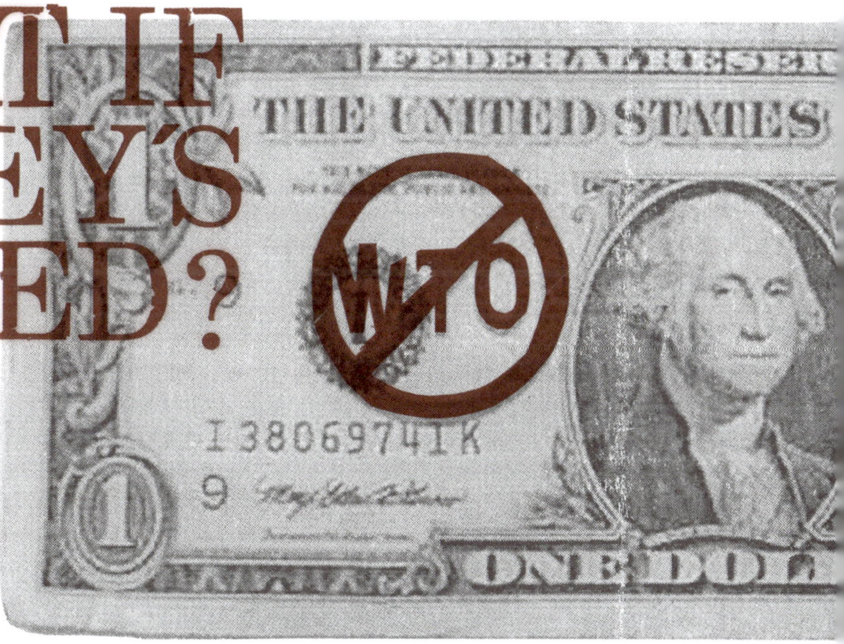

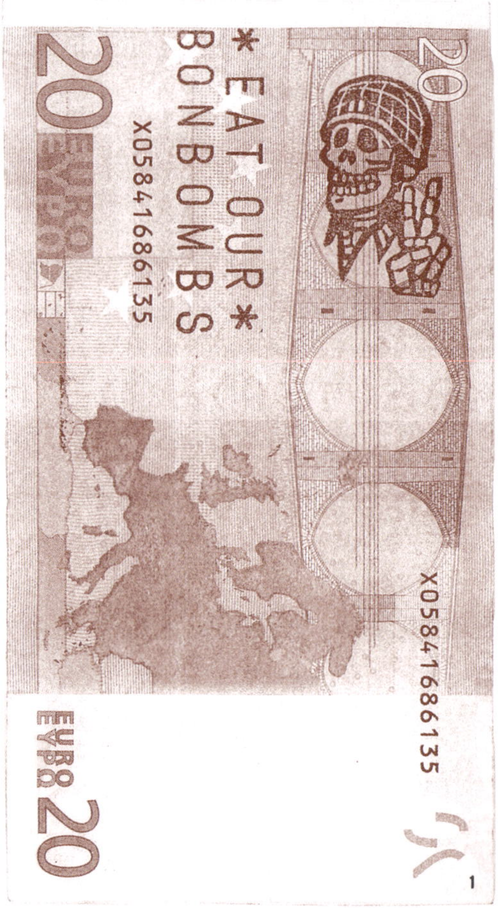

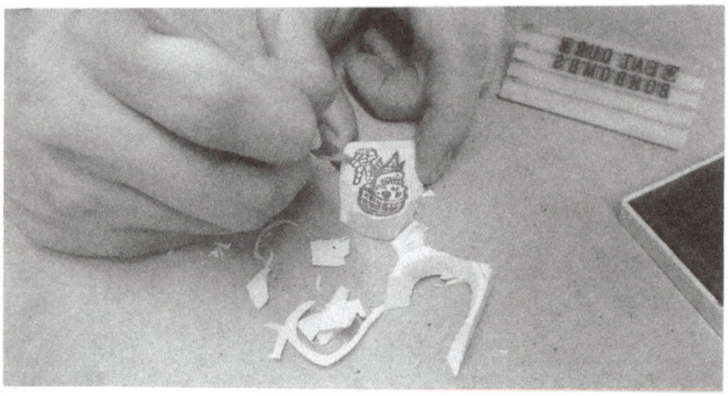

Money Speaks! It passes from hand to hand and around the country (sometimes the world) / everybody has to use it / a target market and distribution beyond the wildest dreams of any PR company! And: paying with message-bills gives some additional sense to spending, apart from emptying your account.

Making a stamp is simple. Using a pointed scalpel, I cut images out of cancelling gums; they are elastic but firm enough for details and last forever.
You can transfer an image by tracing it with a pencil on transparent paper, then rubbing the lines onto a (white) gum, but remember to cut a mirrored image!

The text can be assembled with a stamp alphabet. You can have one made industrially, too. A 1:1 image or print-out is all you need. Text: Vito Focaccia

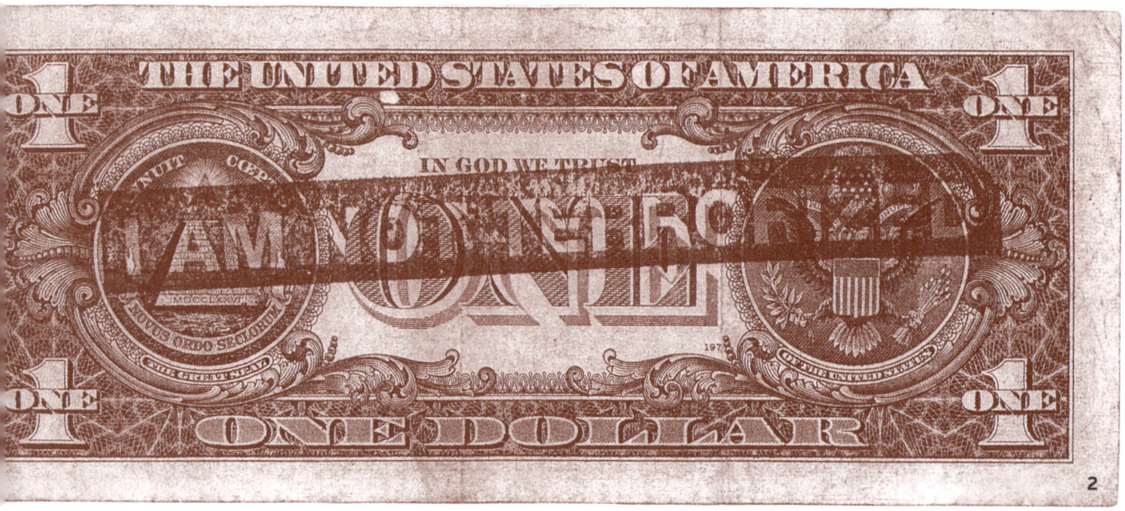

<1> Vito's skeleton G.I. offers a sobering diet
<2> Dollar from NY (USA), shortly after 911. Harth's messages became much less patriotic after the Iraq Invasion.
<3> right: commenting on a news story about children from developing countries being literally 'bought' by Italian pro soccer clubs
<4> Then Italy's prime minister Berluscouni and his habit of showing off rude signs during press shootings

Geld spricht! Es geht von Hand zu Hand durchs Land (und manchmal die Welt) / jeder muss es benutzen / Distribution und Zielgruppe, wie es keine PR-Agentur erträumen kann! Und: bezahlen mit Geld(Botschaften) gibt dem bezahlen einen zusätzlichen Sinn, ausser dem leeren deines Kontos.

Einen Stempel zu machen ist zu einfach. Ich schneide das Bild mit einem spitzen Skalpell aus einem Radiergummi; sie sind weich, aber fest genug für Details und halten lange.

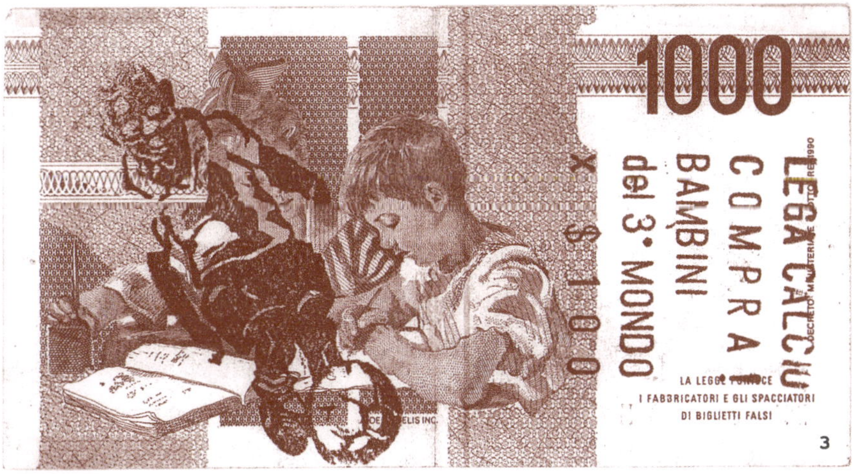

Ein Bild kann auch mit Bleistift auf Transparentpapier nachgezeichnet werden, die Linien dann auf einen (weissen) Radiergummi durch Andruck transferiert werden.
Pass auf: der Stempel wird beim Drucken gespiegelt!

<1> Vito's Skelett-G.I. bietet eine einseitige Diät an
<2> Dollar aus NY (USA), kurz nach dem 11.Sept. Harth's Inhalte blieben nicht lange patriotisch
<3> Verpflichtung talentierter Kinder aus der '3.Welt' durch italienische Fussballclubs
<4> Silvio Berlusconi's Vorliebe für rüde Gesten bei offiziellen Anlässen

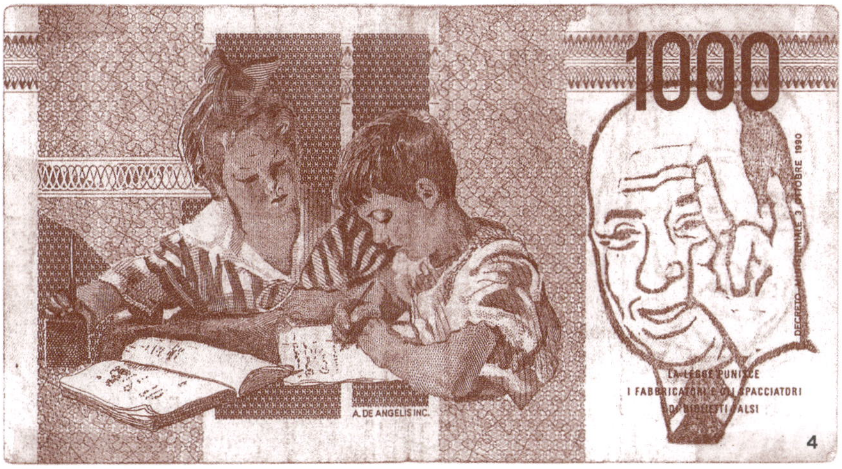

Texte können mit einem einfachen Stempel-ABC gesetzt werden. Du kannst dir auch innerhalb weniger Tage einen industriellen Stempel fertigen lassen. Eine 1:1 Bildvorlage ist alles was du brauchst. Text: Vito Focaccia

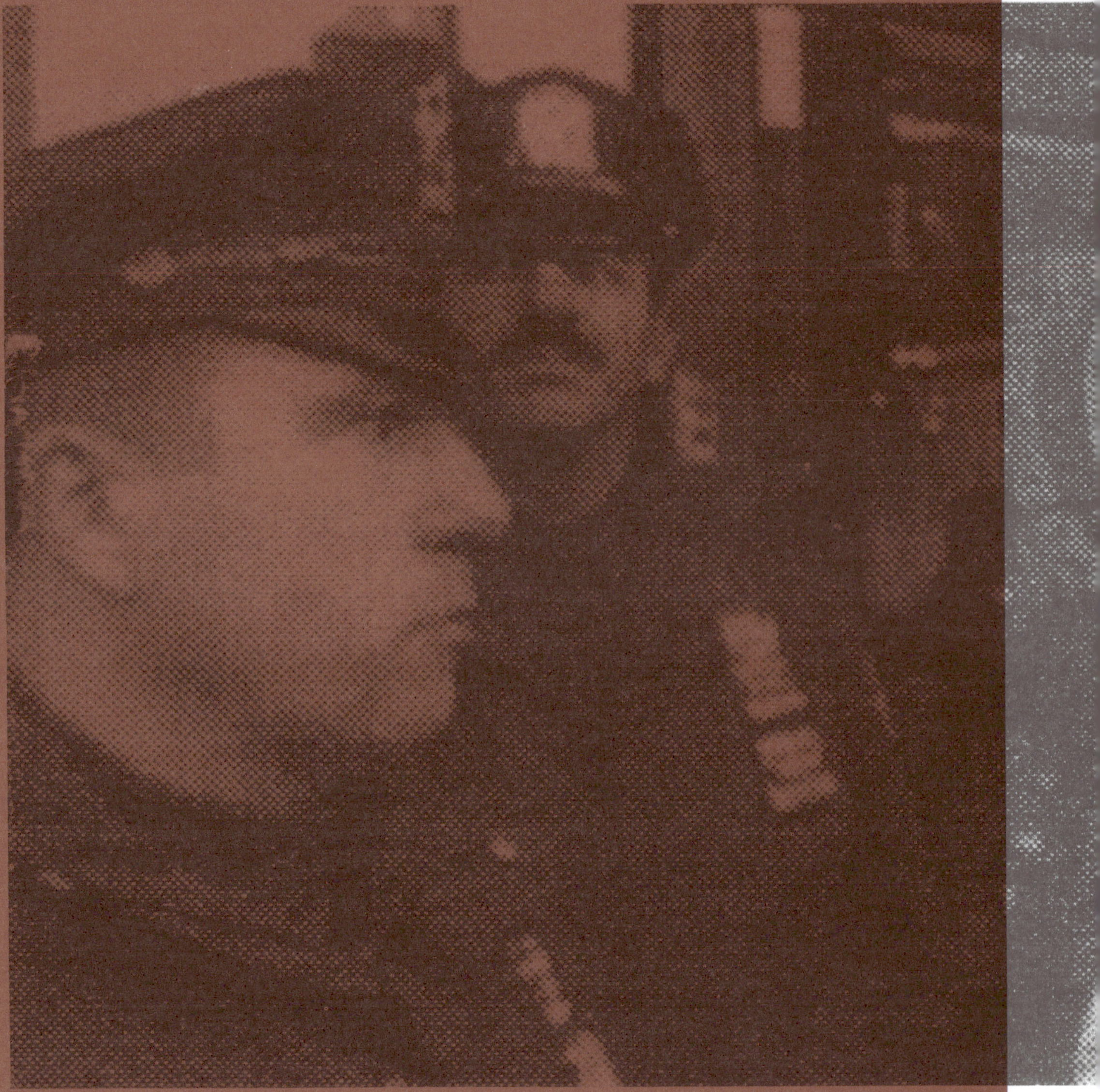

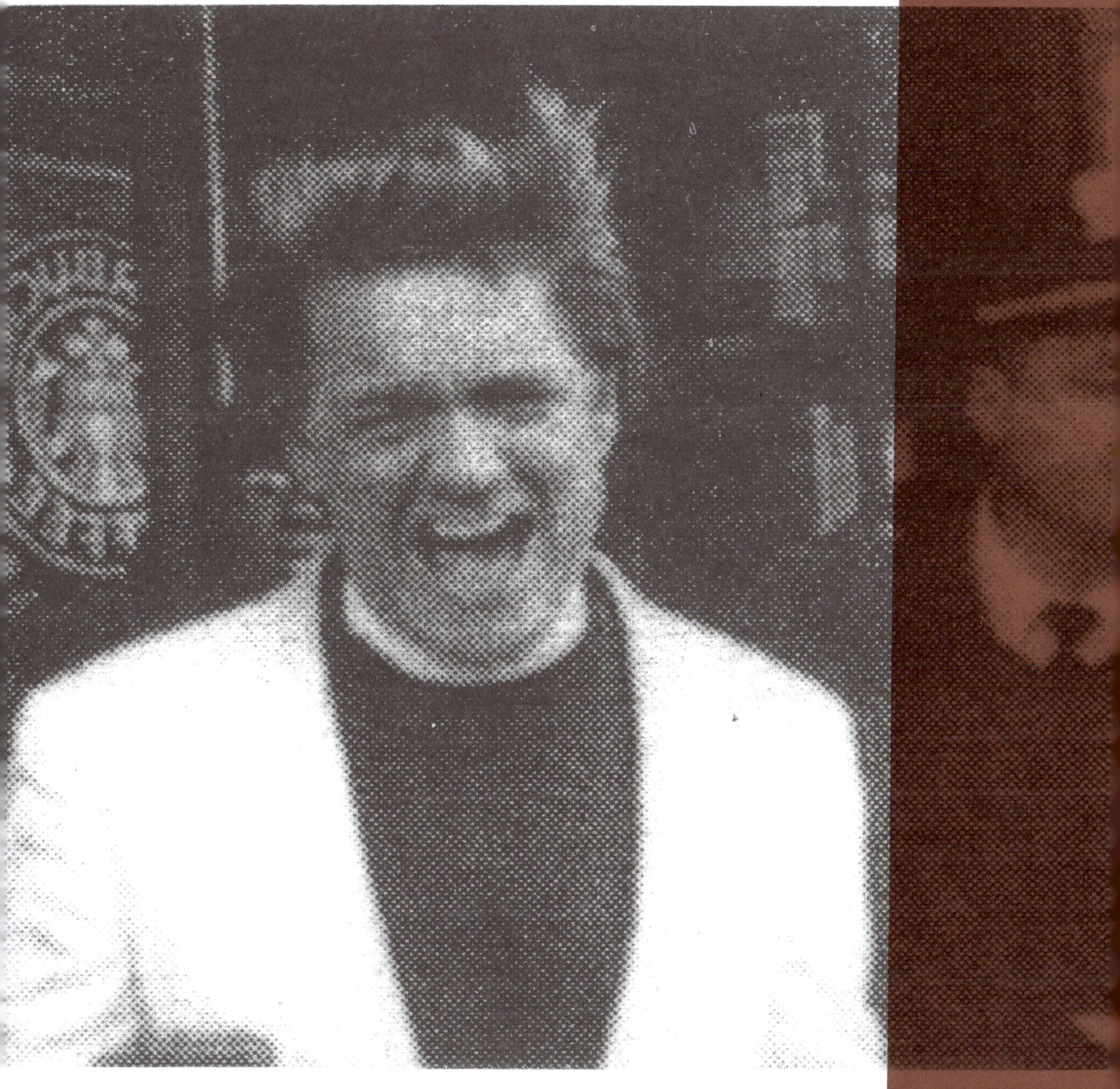

(Rev. Billy)

Seit seinem Umzug in den späten 1990er Jahren aus San Francisco nach New York City verwandelt Reverend Billy Einzelhandelsketten in Bühnen für dramatische Proteste.
In deren Verlauf predigt er gegen das Übel der Massenmedien und Wirtschaftskonglomerate, und gegen die von diesen Seiten begünstigte «Kultur der Bequemlichkeit».

Seine Aktionen beschwören die Stimmung einer US-amerikanischen Fernsehpredigt herauf. In ihrem Verlauf 'segnet' der Reverend nichtsahnende Kunden zunächst um sich sodann in eine heilige Empörung hineinzusteigern.
Er beschwört die Anwesenden dazu, sich Gedanken zu machen über die Herkunft der Produkte die sie gerade konsumieren, sowie über diejenigen die diese Waren hergestellt haben - und zu welchem Preis.

Die erste Bühne des Reverend war der Disney-Megastore am Times Square (NYC), 1998. Die denkwürdige Performance bestand aus einer 'Telefonoper': 'Kunden'-Aktivisten bewegten sich durch den Laden und sprachen dabei in ihre Mobiltelefone, dabei sagten sie Dinge wie: «Liebling, ich glaube nicht, dass wir ihm das schenken sollen, die Sachen werden von Sklavenarbeitern hergestellt!»
Der Protest wurde schliesslich von der Polizei unterbrochen, doch nicht bevor der Reverend erschien und verkündete, Mickey Mouse sei der Antichrist.

Auch die Läden der Kaffeehauskette Starbucks bieten ihm häufig die Bühne für Proteste. Der Reverend betritt die Läden und mahnt die Milchkaffee geniessenden Kunden dazu nachzudenken, wie Handelsketten lokale Gemeinschaften und Läden zugrunde richten, vor allem wenn es sich um eine Kette wie Starbucks handelt (üblicherweise eröffnet die Firma reihenweise Filialen auf engem Raum und schöpft so eine Mehrzahl der Kunden ab. Meist können sich unabhängige Cafés nicht lange gegen die billige Konkurrenz durchsetzen).

Rev. Billy's spirituelles Heim ist Manhattan's Lower East Side, doch seine Botschaft und seine Herangehensweise haben sich mittlerweile weit herumgesprochen.

Quelle: revbilly.com

After moving from San Francisco to New York City in the late 1990s, Reverend Billy and the 'Church of Stop Shopping' have been transforming retail chain stores into stages for dramatic protests that preach against the ills of mass media and corporate conglomerates that breed a uniform «culture of convenience.»

His activism evokes the mood of TV evangelism, both in how he 'blesses' unknowing customers and whips himself up into a fury, exhorting anyone that listens to consider where the products they are consuming come from, who makes them, and at what cost.

The Disney Store in Times Square (NYC) was one of his first stages. In 1998, Revered Billy organized a 'cell phone opera,' during which activists moved through the Disney Store speaking into their mobiles, saying things like, «Oh, I don't think we should buy him that, honey. They use sweatshops to make this stuff!»
The police eventually disrupted the protest, but not before Reverend Billy declared that Mickey Mouse was the Antichrist.

Stores of the coffee chain Starbucks have also been the scene for many of Reverend Billy's protests. He urges consumers enjoying their lattes to think about how chain stores break apart communities and small businesses, especially with a chain like Starbucks that opens stores in neighbourhoods that already have independent cafés, that are soon to be pushed out of business by the low-wage coffee giant.

The Reverend's spiritual home is Manhattan's Lower East Side, but his message and approach have traveled far and wide.

Source: revbilly.com

1.ST AID

In 2001 the Berlin-owned bank broke down amid illegal transactions. The accumulated debt (almost 22 billion Euro) forced the city to cut drasticlly its culture, education, social and public services budgets. The city's culture workers wanted to do even more: ...

2001 brach die Berliner Bankgesellschaft aufgrund spekulativer Geschäfte zusammen. Um die Schulden von 22 Milliarden Euro begleichen zu können beschloss die Stadt drastische Sparmassnahmen in ihren Kultur-, Bildungs-, Sozial- und Versorgungssektoren. Berliner Kulturschaffende wollten noch mehr beisteuern: ...

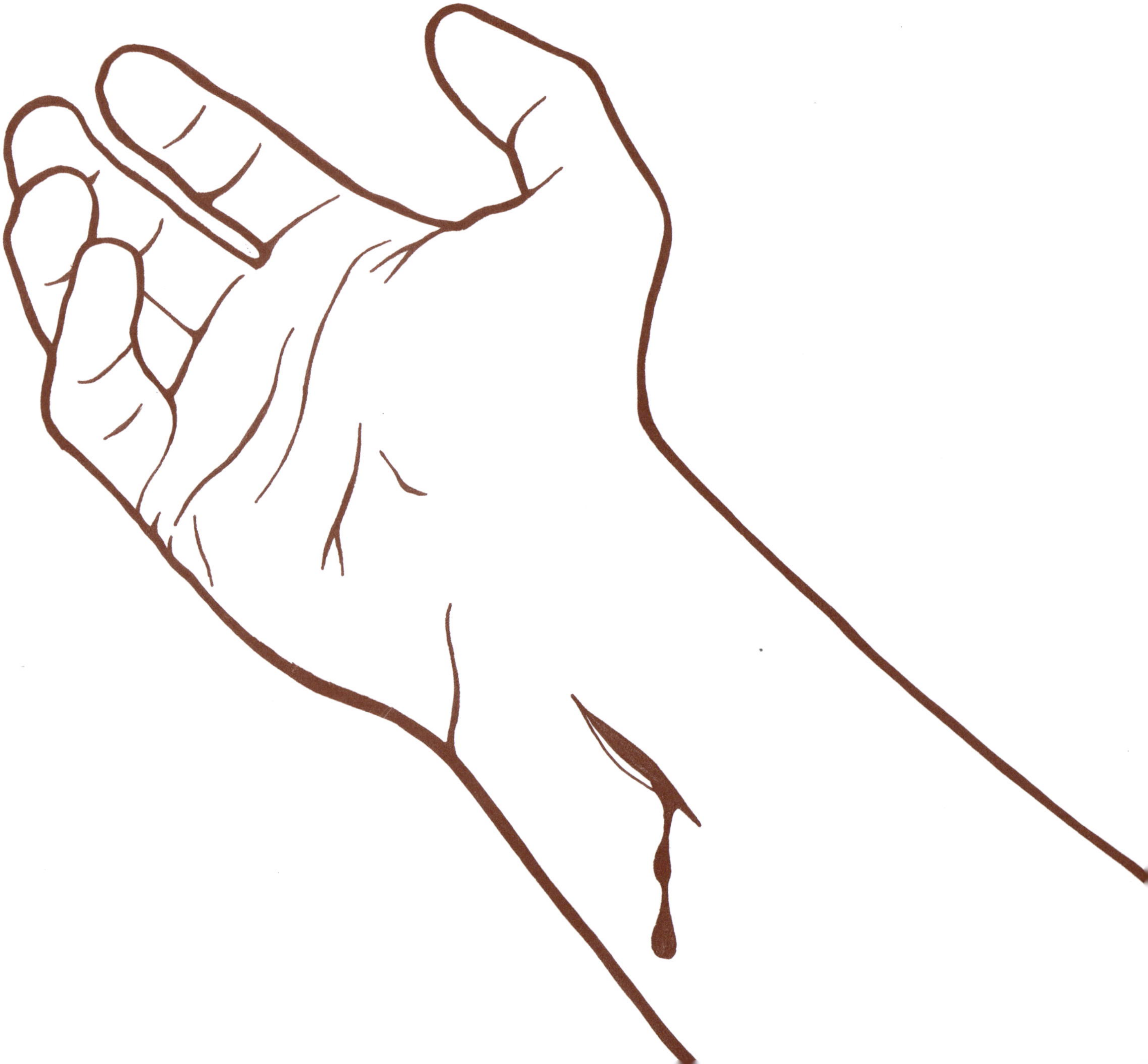

«BLOOD BANK: Charity for the Bank of Berlin (politico-medical proceedings).
On June 27, 2002, the city council will pass next year's budget. Facing the council chambers, we'll run a mobile blood donation station. Between midday and 5 pm the city's artists will give blood in half-hour intervals; the blood packs will go to the Charité hospital, the donors' compensation of 20 Euro will be transformed into a fund for the benefit of the bankrupt bank. First aid in a time of need.»

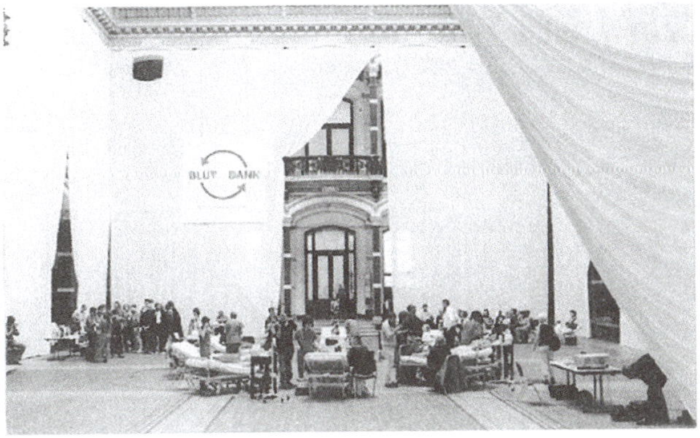

At the end of the day, 2.180 Euro had been collected – the bank refused the donation. But people had given their blood, and the mission had to be fulfilled. The curators had an idea: they simply opened an account with the Bank of Berlin and paid the sum in cash – since then, the bank is slowly using up the money through its own fees. A «permanent infusion», medically speaking.
Quote: Blutbank Benefiz

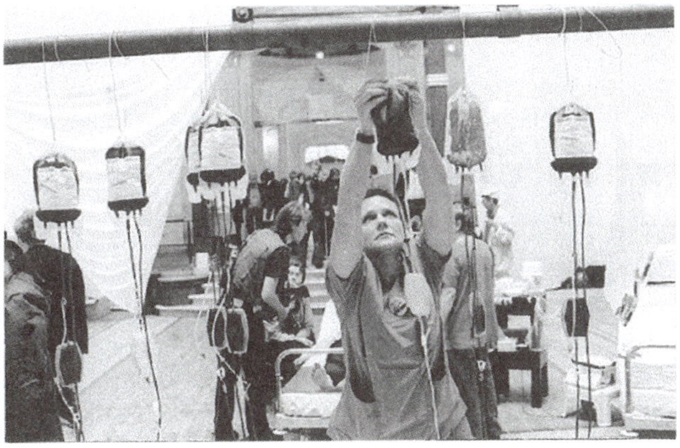

«BLUTBANK: Benefiz für die Bankgesellschaft Berlin (ein medizinisch-politischer Vorgang).
Am 27. Juni 2002 verabschiedet das Berliner Abgeordnetenhaus den Haushalt. (Gegenüber) schlagen wir an diesem Tag eine ambulante Blutspendestation auf, und von 12 bis 17 Uhr spenden im Halbstundenrhythmus Berliner Künstler ihr Blut für den Transfusionsdienst der Charité. Ihre Aufwandsentschädigungen in Höhe von jeweils 20 Euro spenden sie für die Sanierung der Bankgesellschaft Berlin. Erste Hilfe in schwerer Zeit.»

2180 Euro kamen zusammen – die Spende wurde abgelehnt. Doch Menschen hatten geblutet, der Auftrag musste erfüllt werden. Die Kuratoren hatten eine Idee; ein Konto bei der Bankgesellschaft wurde eröffnet, die Summe bar einbezahlt. Seitdem bedient sich die Bank über ihre eigenen Kontogebühren selbst – eine «Dauerinfusion».
Zitat: Blutbank Benefiz

«In 1999, just before the big protests in Seattle, Mike and Andy set up a parody of the WTO website at the domain GATT.org. Some people mistook it for the real thing and Mike and Andy found themselves invited to conferences to speak as the organization they opposed. They scrounged up their savings, bought plane tickets, and went.

January 2001: «Textiles of the Future» conference in Tampere, Finland send an e-mail to GATT.org asking for a WTO representative to deliver their keynote address. This time, Mike and Andy decide to cook up more drastic fare: Andy describes how the US Civil War (fought over the textile, cotton) was a great waste of money, because slavery would have been replaced by its infinitely more efficient version: remote sweatshop labor, such as we have today.
The only problem still remaining with the efficiency of today's sweatshops, Andy continues, is a lack of control over workers. But there is a technological answer. He spreads his arms out, and Mike rips off Andy's breakaway business suit to reveal the management solution of the future: a shimmering golden leotard – which, when Andy pulls a rip-cord in his crotch, sports a three-foot-long golden phallus.

we say:

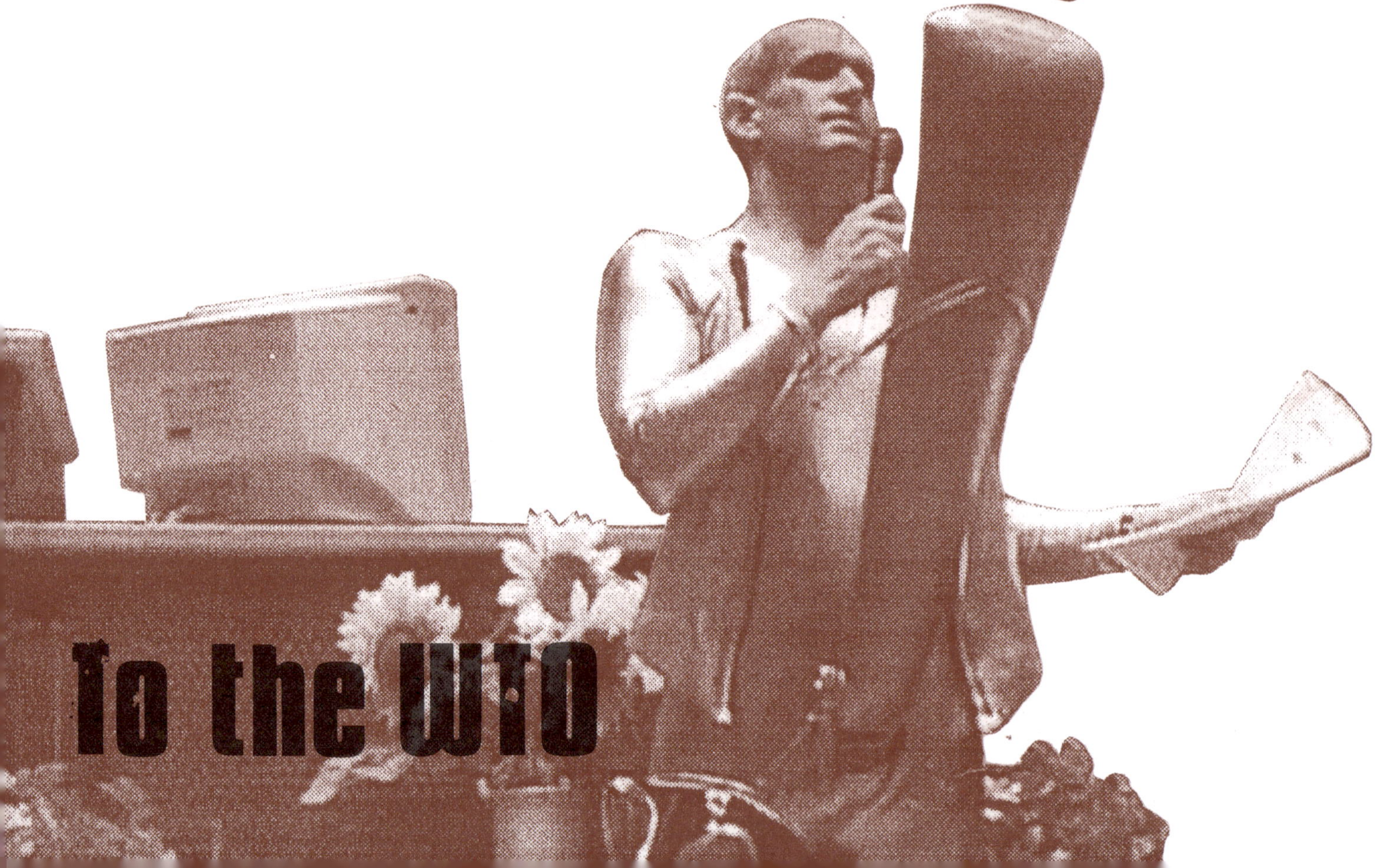

To the WTO

Andy explains that this tool, the «Employee Visualization Appendage», will allow the manager of the future to watch, control (and punish by electric shocks) workers, while managers engage in healthful leisure activities.
A healthy round of applause, no questions. A reporter takes photos. The conference leader thanks the WTO for its presentation three times in public, and seats Andy at the table of honor. All day, in fact, Mike and Andy come up again and again against a blank wall: no one is bothered by the content of the speech, including when they're reminded about the slavery issue. Finally they find one woman who admits being terribly offended – because Andy's «Appendage» implies that only men can be factory managers.»
Text: Yes Men

«1999, kurz vor den grossen Protesten in Seattle, stellten Mike und Andy eine WTO-ähnliche Satire-Homepage unter der Domain GATT.org. Manche verwechseln sie mit der echten, und Mike und Andy finden sich auf den Einladungslisten von Wirtschaftskonferenzen wieder, als Sprecher der Organisation, die sie ablehnen. Sie kratzen ihre Ersparnisse zusammen und kaufen die Flugtickets.
01-2001, die «Textiles of the Future» Konferenz in Tampere (Finnland), schickt eine Einladung für die Eröffnungsansprache an GATT.org. Dieses Mal wollen Mike und Andy härtere Seiten aufziehen. Andy erklärt, dass der amerikanische Bürgerkrieg eine Zeit- und Geldverschwendung war, weil die Sklaverei sowieso von einem unvergleichlich effizienteren System ersetzt worden wäre, der Sweatshop-Produktion der Entwicklungsländer.
Das einzige Problem dabei ist, dass ein Manager schwer die Effizienz der Arbeiter kontrollieren kann – doch es gibt eine technologische Lösung: er öffnet seine Arme und Mike, sein Assistent, reisst seinen präparierten Anzug ab – ein goldener Gymnastikanzug kommt zum Vorschein. Andy zieht an einer Zugschnur im Schritt und ein gold-ener Phallus schwillt stolz auf einen Meter Länge.
Dieser «Arbeiter-Visualisierungs-Anhang», erklärt Andy, erlaubt es dem Manager der Zukunft, seine fernen Arbeitermassen auch in der Freizeit zu überwachen (und per Elektroschock zu bestrafen).
Applaus. Keine Fragen, ein Reporter macht Fotos. Der Konferenzveranstalter dankt der WTO drei Mal in der Öffentlichkeit für ihre Präsentation und Andy bekommt einen Ehrenplatz am Tisch. Den ganzen Tag laufen die beiden gegen eine Wand: Niemand stört sich an der Rede, auch nicht wegen den Sklaven. Endlich finden sie jemanden, der zugibt, gekränkt zu sein: eine Frau beschwert sich, Andy's 'Anhang' impliziere, dass nur Männer Fabrikmanager werden können.»
Text: Yes Men

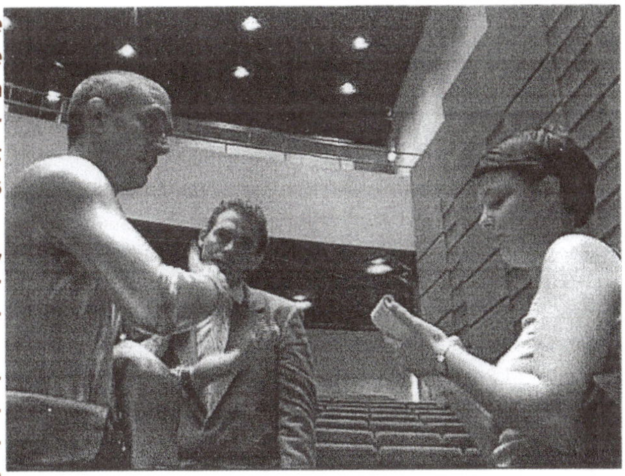

The Yes Men > 66-71, 108-109, 119

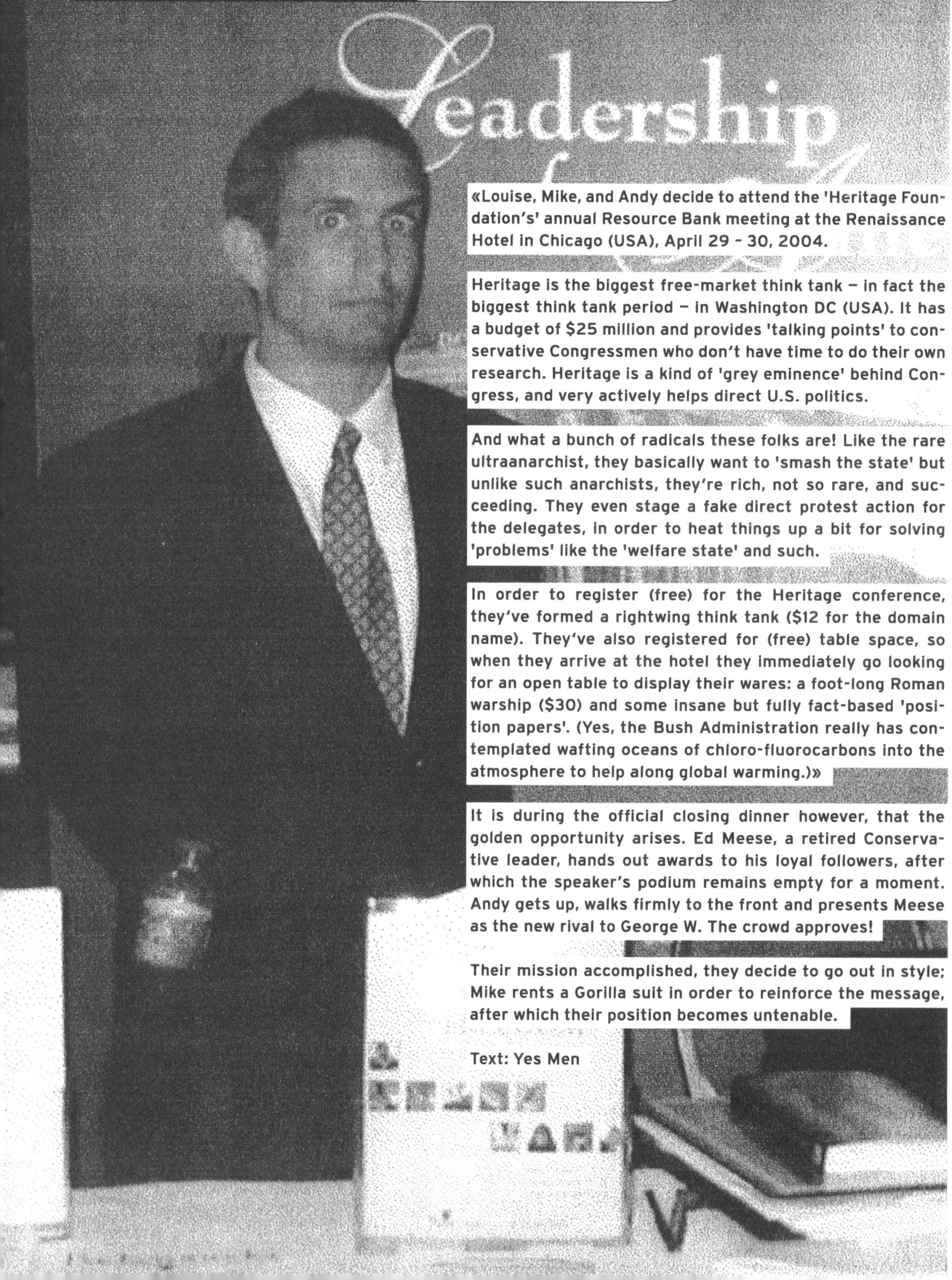

«Louise, Mike, and Andy decide to attend the 'Heritage Foundation's' annual Resource Bank meeting at the Renaissance Hotel in Chicago (USA), April 29 – 30, 2004.

Heritage is the biggest free-market think tank – in fact the biggest think tank period – in Washington DC (USA). It has a budget of $25 million and provides 'talking points' to conservative Congressmen who don't have time to do their own research. Heritage is a kind of 'grey eminence' behind Congress, and very actively helps direct U.S. politics.

And what a bunch of radicals these folks are! Like the rare ultraanarchist, they basically want to 'smash the state' but unlike such anarchists, they're rich, not so rare, and succeeding. They even stage a fake direct protest action for the delegates, in order to heat things up a bit for solving 'problems' like the 'welfare state' and such.

In order to register (free) for the Heritage conference, they've formed a rightwing think tank ($12 for the domain name). They've also registered for (free) table space, so when they arrive at the hotel they immediately go looking for an open table to display their wares: a foot-long Roman warship ($30) and some insane but fully fact-based 'position papers'. (Yes, the Bush Administration really has contemplated wafting oceans of chloro-fluorocarbons into the atmosphere to help along global warming.)»

It is during the official closing dinner however, that the golden opportunity arises. Ed Meese, a retired Conservative leader, hands out awards to his loyal followers, after which the speaker's podium remains empty for a moment. Andy gets up, walks firmly to the front and presents Meese as the new rival to George W. The crowd approves!

Their mission accomplished, they decide to go out in style; Mike rents a Gorilla suit in order to reinforce the message, after which their position becomes untenable.

Text: Yes Men

KNOW YOUR ENEMY

«Louise, Mike, and Andy beschliessen, am jährlichen Treffen der 'Heritage Foundation' (29 – 30 Apr. 2004) in Chicago (USA) teilzunehmen. Heritage ist der grösste private Think Tank in Washington DC (USA). Die Stiftung hat ein Budget von 25 Millionen Dollar, und bietet 'Anlaufstellen' für konservative Kongressmitglieder, die keine Zeit für eigene Hintergrundrecherchen haben. Heritage ist eine Art von grauer Eminenz des Kongresses, und beteiligt sich sehr aktiv an der US-Politik.

Und sie sind radikal dabei! Wie der vereinzelte Ultra-Anarchist, wollen sie den 'Staat zerschlagen' aber anders als Anarchisten sind sie reich, nicht so selten und erfolgreich. Sie organisieren sogar inszinierte Proteste für die Teilnehmer des Treffens, um die Stimmung anzuheizen für ihre Forderung nach der Lösung von 'Problemen' wie dem 'Sozialstaat' usw. Um sich (gratis) für die Konferenz anmelden zu können, haben sie einen rechtskonservativen 'Think-Tank' gegründet (12 Dollar für den Domain-Namen). Ebenfalls gratis haben sie einen Tisch reserviert, so dass sie nach ihrer Ankunft sofort einen freien Platz für ihre Dinge suchen: ein 30 Zentimeter langes Modell eines römischen Kriegsschiffes (30 Dollar) und einige verrückte, aber vollkommen auf Fakten basierende 'Positionspapiere'. (Ja, die Bush-Regierung denkt darüber nach, Ozeane von FCKW in die Atmosphäre zu blasen, um die Erderwärmung zu erleichtern).»

Erst während des Schlussdinners bietet sich die goldene Chance. Ed Meese, eine pensionierte konservative Parteigrösse, verteilt Auszeichnungen an seine loyale Gefolgschaft; danach bleibt das Podium für einen Moment leer. Andy springt auf, geht entschlossen nach vorne und stellt Meese als den neuen Herausforderer von George W. vor. Die Teilnehmer stimmen zu!
Ihre Mission ist beendet, daher beschliessen sie einen stilvollen Abgang; Mike mietet ein Gorillakostüm – danach wird ihre Position schnell unhaltbar. Text: Yes Men

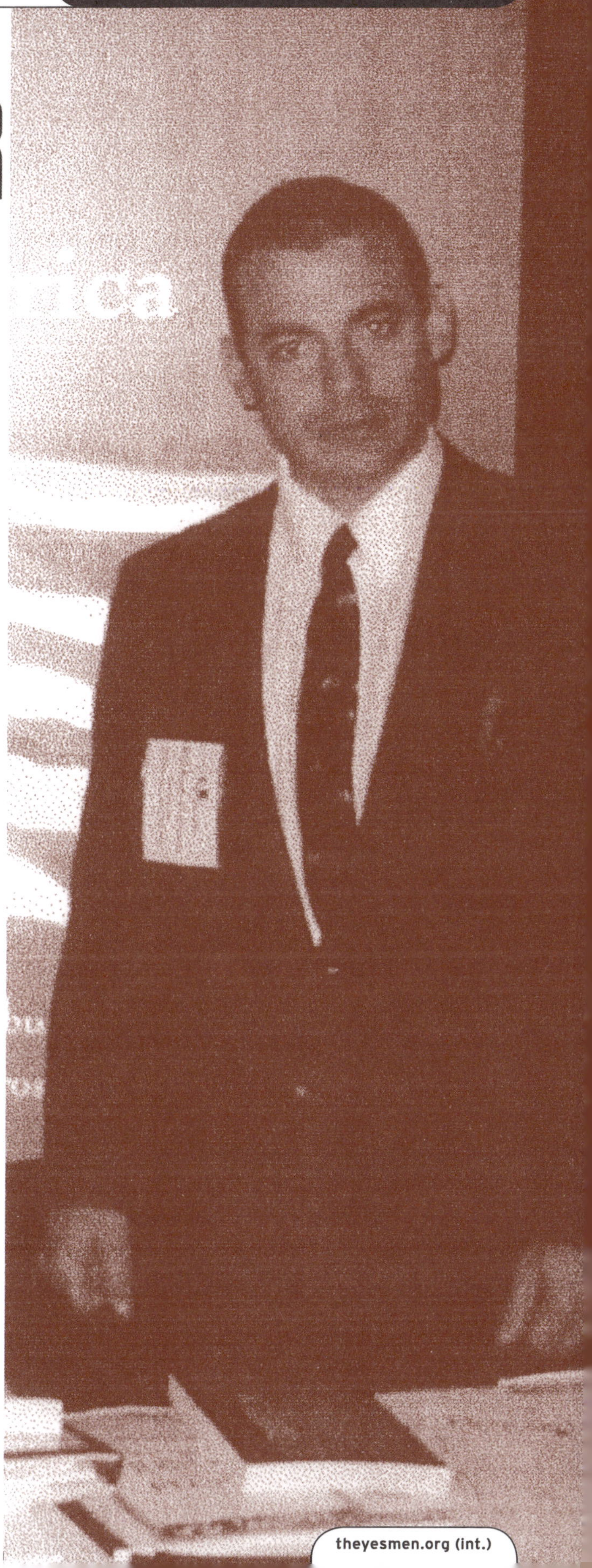

theyesmen.org (int.)

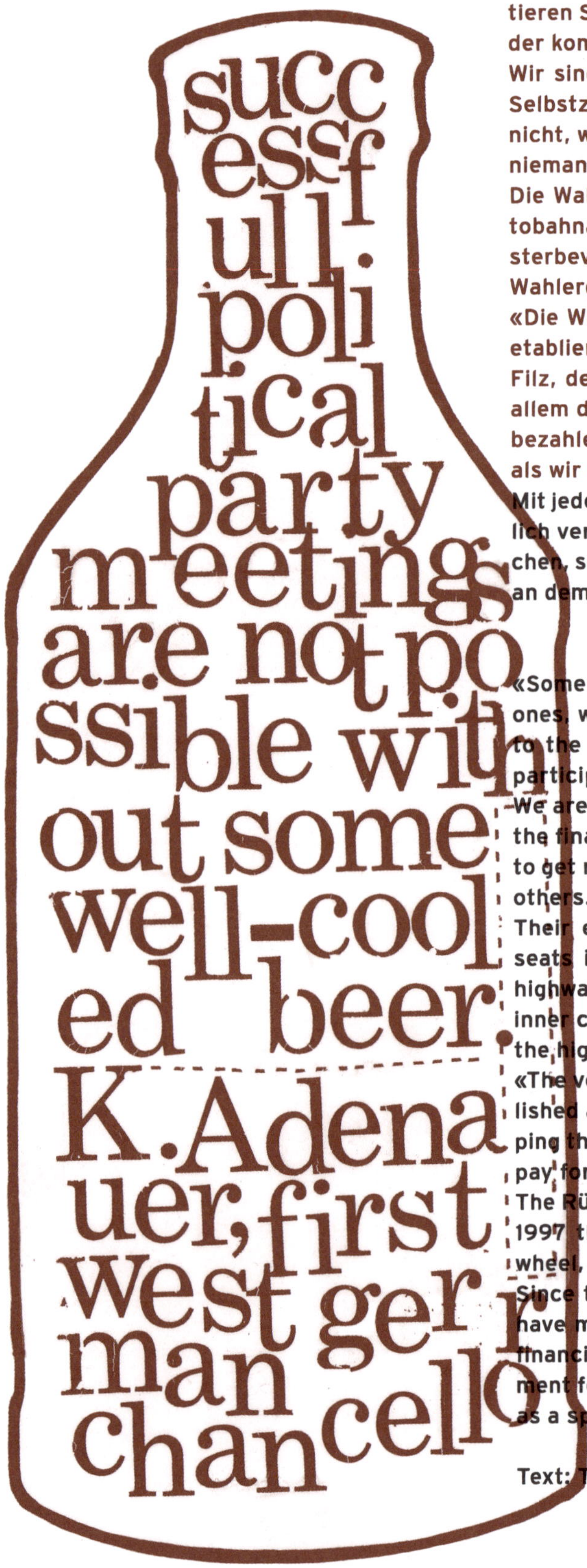

«Einige haben Mitglieder. Andere haben die Diktatur der Angepassten, wir haben das Diktat der Aktivisten. Wir diskutieren Sachen aus. Bei uns wird nicht abgestimmt, und jeder der kommt kann bei uns mitmachen.
Wir sind Politiker wider Willen. Wir sehen Politik nicht als Selbstzweck und betätigen uns in der Kommunalpolitik nicht, weil wir wiedergewählt werden wollen. Damit sind wir niemandem gegenüber zu etwas verpflichtet.»
Die Wahlkampfforderungen 1993: ein Müllauto und ein Autobahnanschluss pro Haus, Tempo 180 in der Stadt, Waldsterbeverbot, und der Bau des höchsten Gebäudes der Welt. Wahlergebnis: drei Sitze im Parlament.
«Die Wähler schickten uns los, um die alten, ritualisierten, etablierten, standardisierten Machtzusammenhänge, den Filz, der sie Stadt lähmte, zu entstaubten. Wir sagen, vor allem die junge Generation wird einmal die Zeche der Alten bezahlen, also versuchen wir nicht mehr Geld auszugeben, als wir einnehmen.
Mit jeder Legislaturperiode hat sich die Liste Rüssel wesentlich verändert. Die Fraktion hat sich 1997 dafür ausgesprochen, selbst das Ruder zu übernehmen. Seitdem arbeiten wir an dem Umbau der Stadt.» Text: Liste Rüssel

«Some have members. Others have a dictate of the adjusted ones, we have a dictate of the activists. We discuss things to the end, we don't put them to the vote. Anybody can participate.
We are politicians against our will. We don't see politics as the final end and we didn't become local politicians in order to get re-elected. That makes us free of obligations towards others.»
Their election demands in 1993, the year they got three seats in parliament included: one garbage truck and one highway exit for every house, speed limit 180 km/h in the inner city, prohibiting the dying of trees by law and building the highest building in the world.
«The voters wanted us to clean up the old, ritualised, established and standardised power relationships that were gripping the city. We think that the young generation will have to pay for our debts, so let's stop accumulating them.
The Rüssel Ticket has changed with every legislative period; 1997 the faction approved the taking over of the steering wheel, and the Rüssel took over governing responsibilities. Since then we have been working on changing our city. We have made it clear to the people that the city's broke. The financial crisis is our steady companion; it's not a good moment for becoming adored as a politician. People regard you as a spoilsport.»

Text: The Rüsselsheim Ballot Initiative

«Critical Shareholders don't ask how high their dividends are, but where they come from. They loudly demand more environmental protection, more social justice, and the maintenance of human rights in the annual general meetings of shareholders in about 30 German corporations.
More and more, small shareholders are joining the Critical Shareholders and are giving them their proxy rights. Some 1,500 people did it in the year 2000.
'We respect anyone who wishes to keep his or her Daimler or Siemens shares as an investment,' assures the executive board member of the Association of Critical Shareholders, Henry Mathews. 'But if you don't think that part of your dividend should be earned with weapons or nuclear technology, you can let the company managers know through us.'

Shareholders who wish to be represented by the Association and its member organizations only have to provide a power of attorney once a year. It covers the proxy rights in all companies in whose annual general meetings the Critical Shareholders are active.
'We do not charge any fees for this service,' assures Mathews, 'but our work is only possible if the shareholders donate a small portion of their dividends to us.'» The guideline is 0,15 Euro per share, but many people donate more.

Text: Critical Shareholders

«Die Kritischen Aktionäre fragen nicht nach der Höhe ihrer Dividenden, sondern woher diese kommen. Auf den Generalversammlungen von ungefähr 30 deutschen Konzernen fordern sie lautstark mehr Umweltschutz, soziale Gerechtigkeit und die Wahrung der Menschenrechte.
Immer mehr Kleinaktionäre treten den Kritischen bei und übertragen ihnen das Stimmrecht. Im Jahre 2000 waren es etwa 1500 Personen.
'Wir respektieren jeden, der seine Daimler- oder Siemens-Aktien als Investments behalten will,' sagt Henry Mathews, einer der KA-Vorstände. 'Aber wenn du denkst, dass ein Teil deiner Dividende nicht durch Waffen oder Nukleartechnologie erwirschaftet werden sollte, dann kannst du dies den Firmenmanagern durch uns mitteilen.'
Um von der Gruppe und ihren Partnerorganisationen vertreten zu werden genügt es, einmal jährlich eine Stimmvollmacht zu erteilen. Diese gilt für alle Generalversammlungen, in den die KA tätig sind.
'Wir verlangen keine Gebühren' versichert Mathews, 'aber unsere Arbeit ist nur möglich, wenn die Aktionäre uns einen Teil ihrer Dividenden spenden.'» Die Richtlinie sind 0,15 Euro per Aktie, aber viele Leute spenden mehr.

Text: Kritische Aktionäre

kritischeaktionaere.de (Germany)

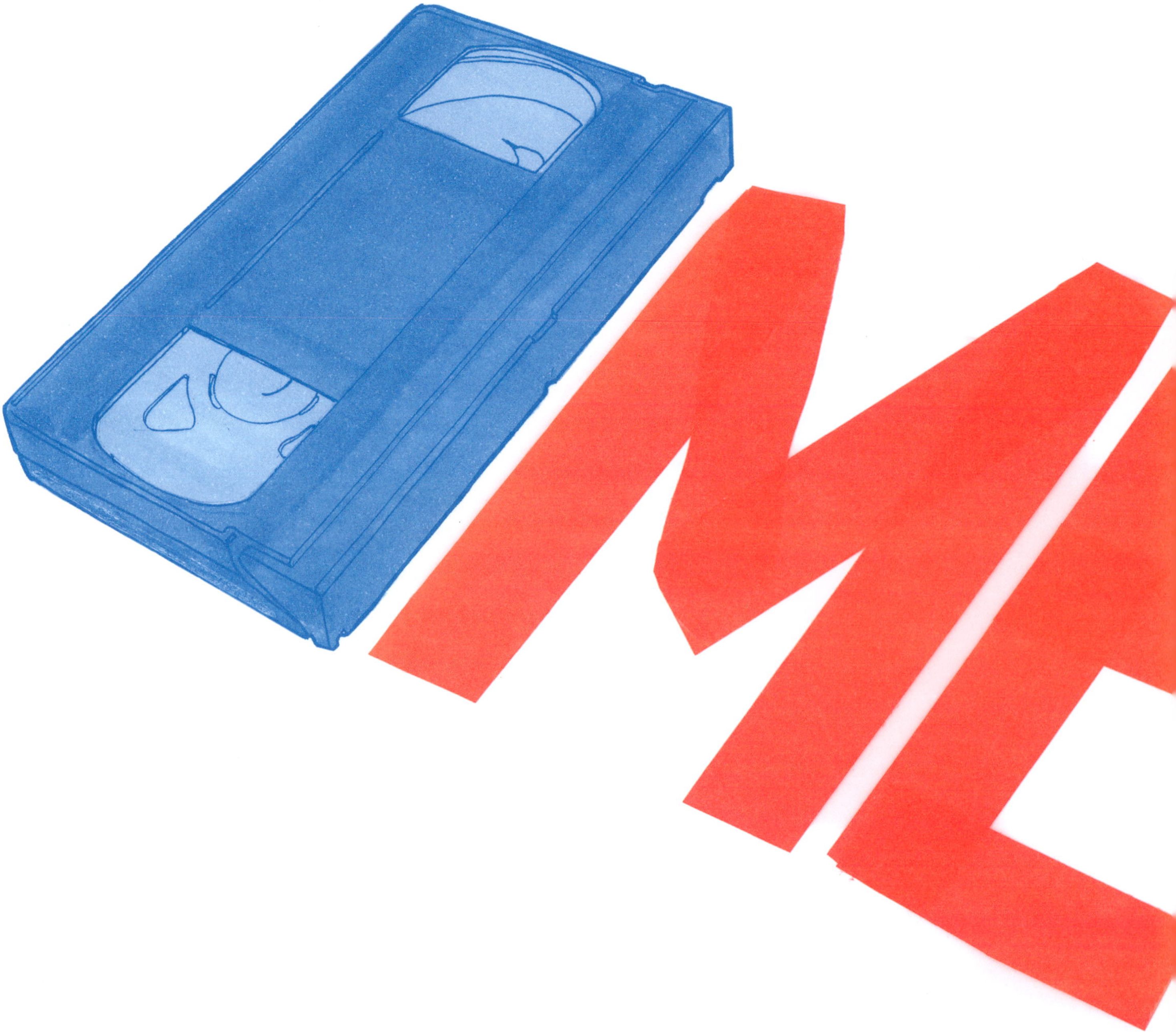
M

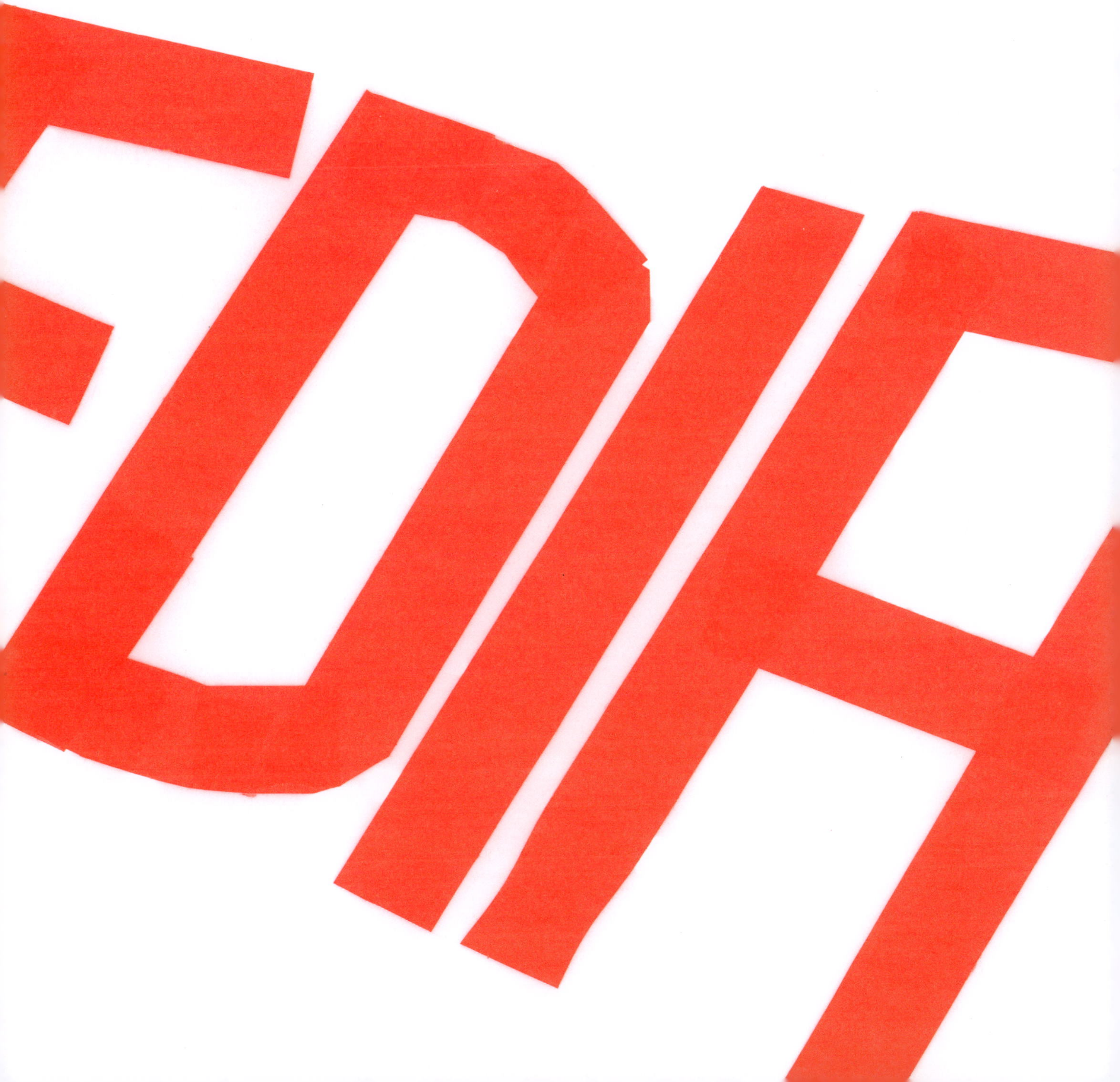

In May 2003 a giant consumer hoax came to its final showdown in an open field near Prague. Over the course of several weeks two Czech filmmakers directed and documented an all-out media campaign for a new hypermarket, the 'Czech Dream'. Watch «Cesky Sen» to see what happened when the alledged supermarket turned out to be a hollow facade in front of thousands of hopeful consumers. Im Mai 2003 erreichte eine gigantische Werbekampagne für einen neuen Hypermarkt ihren Höhepunkt auf einem offenen Feld bei Prag. Zwei Tschechische Filmemacher hatten die Kampagne für «Cesky Sen» (Tschechischer Traum) in Auftrag gegeben und ihren Verlauf über Wochen dokumentiert. Sehe ihren Film «Cesky Sen», um zu sehen was passiert wenn Tausende hoffnungsvoller Käufer eine leere Filmkulisse stürmen.

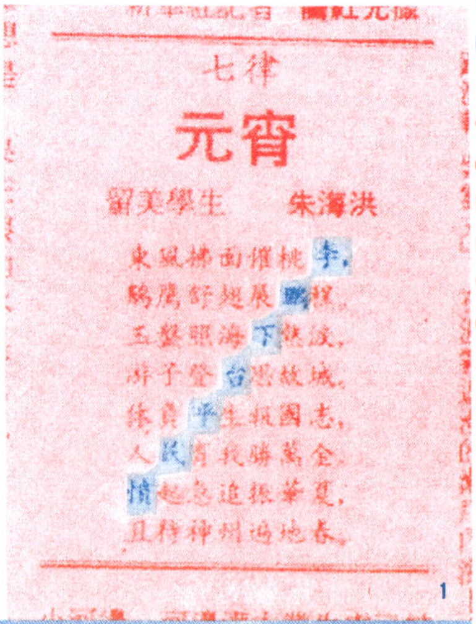

1

<1> A cunning media infiltration was executed in 1991 by an exiled Chinese student from Los Angeles (USA). He sent a homesick poem to the Chinese communist party's official newspaper, the People's Daily. The poem, praising life in China, made it into print; however, if you read the letters diagonally the following message appeared: «Li Peng must step down to appease the people's anger!» (double-sense poems are a Chinese tradition). The incident forced Li Peng himself to downplay it during a press conference.
<1> Ein Student im Exil benutzte List, um von L.A. aus die offizielle Parteizeitung Chinas, die 'Zeitung des Volkes', zu infiltrieren. Er schickte ein China preisendes Gedicht, das auch abgedruckt wurde. Liest man den Text diagonal, erscheint die Botschaft «Li Peng muss zurücktreten um den Volkszorn zu beschwichtigen!» (doppelsinnige Gedichte sind eine chinesische Tradition). Das Gedicht wurde auch von der Partei verstanden und Li Peng selbst sah sich genötigt, den Vorfall auf einer Pressekonferenz herunterzuspielen.

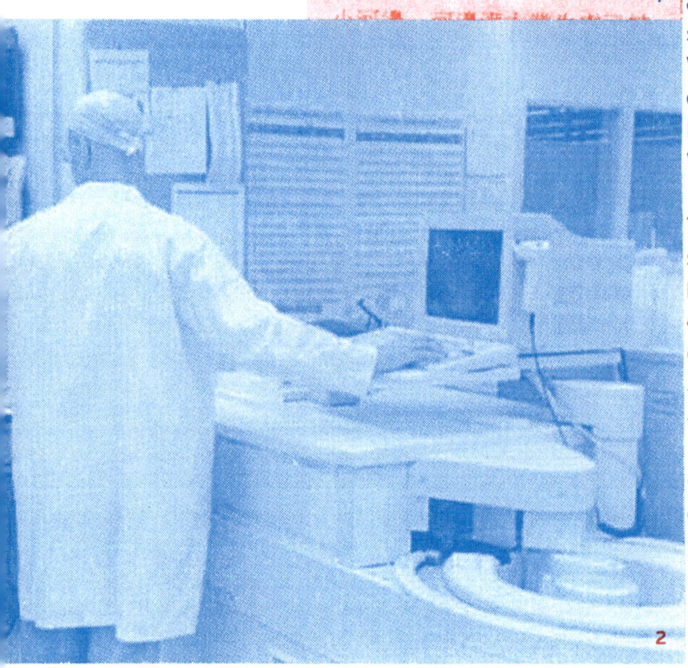
2

The Californian duo «South to the Future» do something similar, although in a less dramatic context; for years they have written nonsense articles for lifestyle mags such as «Soma». Das kalifornische Duo «South to the Future» macht etwas ähnliches, wenn auch im Kleinen; sie schreiben seit Jahren Nonsenseartikel für Lifestyle-Zeitschriften wie «Soma».

<3> Sometimes, when done well, even the mass media become part of a protest; whether it's their conviction or simple selling strategy – who knows. <3> Ob aus Kalkül oder aus Überzeugung, manchmal mutieren Massenmedien von selbst zu Protestierern.

<2,4> The master of media hoaxing is Joey Skaggs, who since the 1960s has managed again and again to fool newspapers and TV into believing such great nonsense as a brothel for dogs or a total cure for all of man's ailments from cockroach hormones. Lately, he has begun using the Internet as a rumor generator. In the elaborate «Stop BioPEEP» project a 'disloyal scientist' revealed a globespanning biotech conspiracy. A complex background story including e-mail correspondence, graphs, photographs of facilities, machinery and 'research stats' was displayed on a website, and fake protests staged in places such as the UN headquarters. His pranks sometimes start with classified ads and press releases, and almost always include the real setup of detailed scenarios, which reporters regularly take for real. <2,4> Der Meister der Medientäuschung ist Joey Skaggs, der es seit den 60er Jahren immer wieder schafft, Zeitungen und TV gefakte Geschichten anzudrehen. Eine Kostprobe? New Yorker Bordelle für Hunde oder ein russischer Wissenschaftler, der Krebsmedizin aus Kakerlakenmilch herstellt. Seine Täuschungen beginnen meist mit Kleinanzeigen und Pressemitteilungen, und enden mit der Vorbereitung detaillierter Szenarien die Reporter noch immer zu täuschen vermochten. In letzter Zeit ging er dazu über Gerüchte per Internet zu verbreiten. Der «Biopeep»-Fake wurde von einem 'abtrünnigen Wissenschaftler' ausgelöst, der eine Menge Details einer angeblichen Biotech-Verschwörung veröffentlichte. Für die Presse wurden sogar Proteste vor der New Yorker UN-Zentrale veranstaltet.

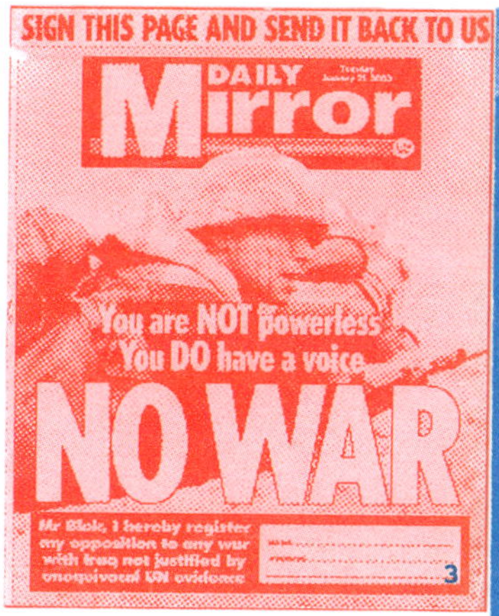
SIGN THIS PAGE AND SEND IT BACK TO US

DAILY Mirror

You are NOT powerless
You DO have a voice

NO WAR

Mr Blair, I hereby register my opposition to any war with Iraq not justified by unequivocal UN evidence

3

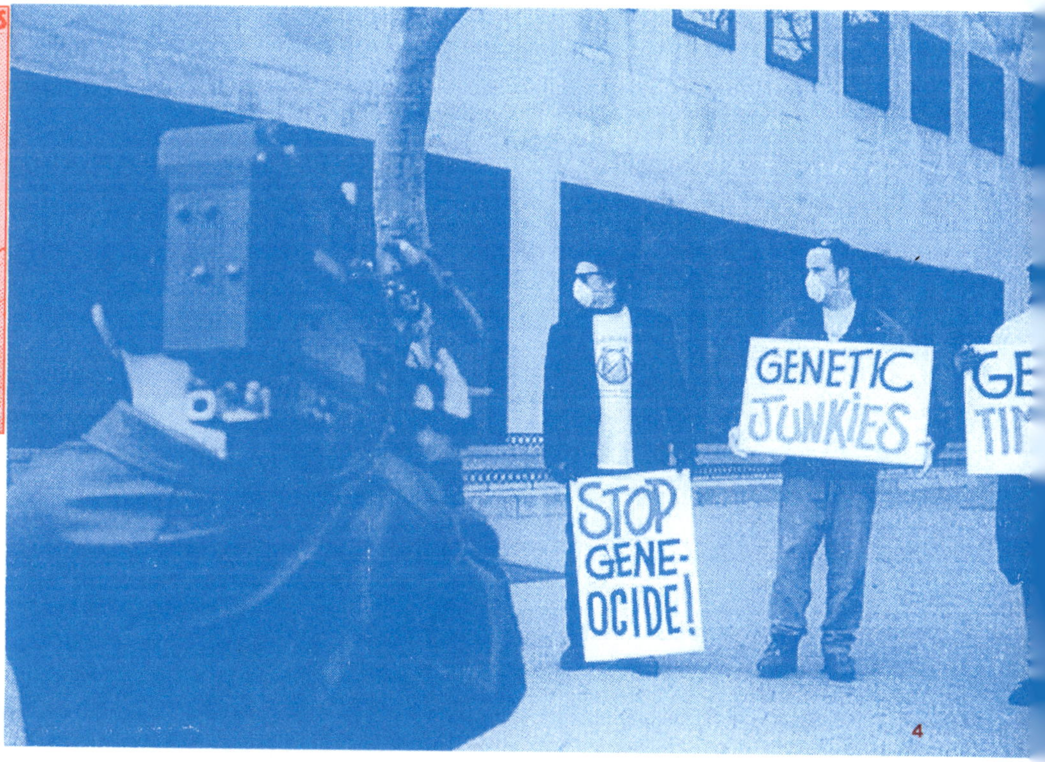

4

3 in: indymedia.org / 2,4 joeyskaggs.com, NYC (USA)

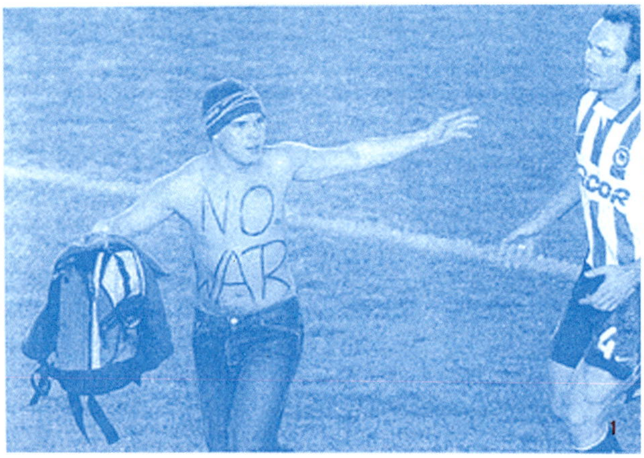

1

Choose any televised public event, strip naked and run! It's almost guaranteed that you'll be on TV the same night.
Such dir ein öffentliches Ereignis, das im TV übertragen wird, zieh dich nackt aus und lauf los! Am Abend wirst du wahrscheinlich im Fernsehen sein.

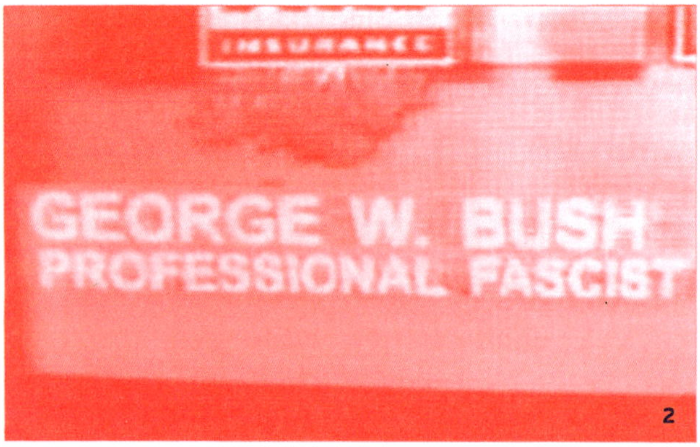

2

<2> An unknown worker at New Zealand's TV3 changed the weather forecast at the end of the evening news on July 5, 2003. According to the NZ Herald, his slogan «George W. Bush – Professional Fascist» reached about 360, 000 viewers. He still hasn't been identified.
<2> Ein unbekannter Fernsehtechniker des neuseelän dischen Senders TV3 änderte am 5. Juli 2003 den Ansagetext der Wettervorhersage. Laut der Zeitung NZ Herald erreichte sein Slogan «George W. Bush – Professioneler Faschist» ca. 360.000 Zuschauer. Er blieb bis heute unentdeckt.

<3> In October 1996 KSBY-TV, a local USA network, aired a story about a city program for arming homeless people. The «Arm The Homeless» program's goal was, supposedly, to help the helpless with guns – so-called «social equalizers». The story was started by a simple press release, which stated that ATH crews were running firearm safety training and distributing donated guns on the streets.
<3> Im Oktober 1996 brachte der lokale US-Sender KSBY-TV die Nachricht über ein neues soziales Hilfsprogramm: «Waffen für Obdachlose». Gespendete Waffen, oder «soziale Gleichmacher», sollten den Armen mehr Selbstwertgefühl und Sicherheit verschaffen. Auslöser der Nachricht war eine satirische Pressemitteilung.

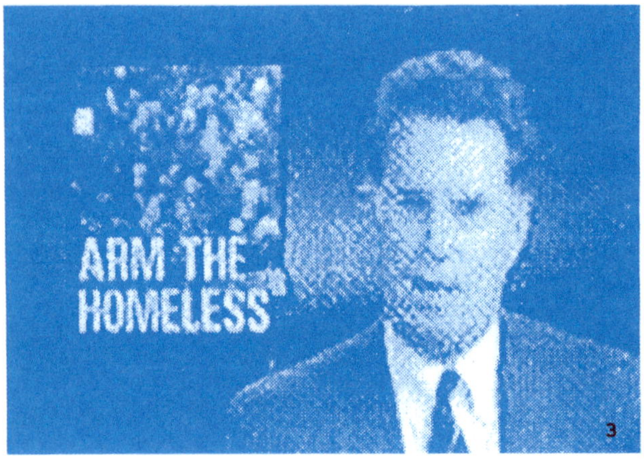

3

A hoax that became news history was a story about computer judges replacing the human ones; it ran across the USA.
Genauso entstand die Nachricht, dass Computer in naher Zukunft Richter ersetzen würden; sie ging wie ein Lauffeuer durch die USA.

DIY news: there are far too many video activist nets to list. Try starting your search through subtv.org and aclip.net.
Self-Made Nachrichten: es gibt bei weitem zu viele Video-Aktivistennetze um sie hier zu beschreiben. Fange die Suche über subtv.org und aclip.net an.

1 TV screenshot (Germany) / 2 in: guerrillanews.com (NZ) / 3 sniggle.net/ath.php (USA)

Fake WTO and DOW websites present the «Yes Men» with many unexpected speaking opportunities: Shortly before the G8 meeting in Genua on July 19, 2001 CNBC's European Market Wrap invited a fake «WTO spokesman» to participate in a TV discussion on global commerce along with both a renowned activist and an economic consultant.
Yes Man Andy (aka «Mr Hulatberi») obliged, making the invited activist boil with rage and the economic expert applaud as he spoke of privatizing education and of making justice a free-market commodity.
It is the affirmation the «Yes Men» receive from their unsuspecting counterparts that really reveals the absurdity of their hoax proposals.
Even the venerable BBC fell into their trap. On the 20th anniversary of a chemical accident that killed 15,000 people in Bhopal (India), the BBC went on air with a «Yes Man» impersonating a Dow Chemicals spokesman (the company responsible for the desaster but refusing to accept responsibility). Within minutes and towards a worldwide audience the fake spokesman acknowledged his company's guilt, announced the extradition of the responsible manager to India and the coming payment of damages to the victims' families.

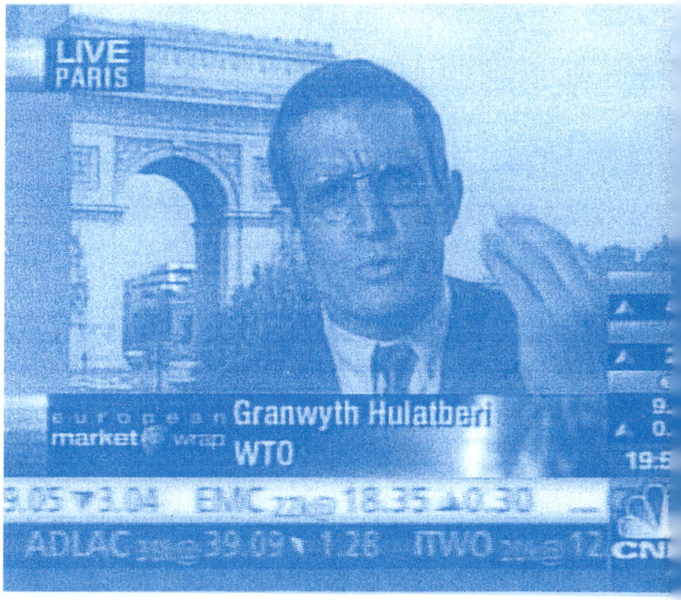

Gefälschte WTO- und DOW-Webseiten bringen den «Yes Men» zahlreiche Einladungen für öffentliche Auftritte ein, so auch im Fernsehen: kurz vor dem G8 Treffen in Genua, am 19. Juli 2001, buchte der Wirtschaftskanal des US-Senders CNBC einen vermeintlichen WTO-Sprecher für eine Diskussion zu Fragen der globalen Wirtschaft.
Während der ebenfalls eingeladene Aktivist vor Wut kochte und ein Wirtschaftsexperte Beifall zollte, erläuterte Yes Man Andy (aka «Mr Hulatberi») neue «WTO-Strategien» wie die vollständige Privatisierung von Bildung und Rechtsprechung.
Durch die Zustimmung ihrer ahnungslosen Gegenspieler offenbaren die «Yes Men» die Absurdität ihrer vermeintlich echten Vorschläge.
Sogar die ehrwürdige BBC fiel in ihre Falle und buchte zum 20. Jahrestag des Chemieunfalls in Bhopal (Indien) einen «Yes Man» als vermeintlichen Dow Chemicals Sprecher (der Konzern lehnt jede Verantwortung für das Desater welches über 15.000 Opfer forderte ab).
Vor einem weltweiten Publikum erklärte der falsche Firmensprecher den Konzern für schuldig, kündigte die Auslieferung des verantwortlichen Managers nach Indien und die Zahlung von Entschädigungen an.

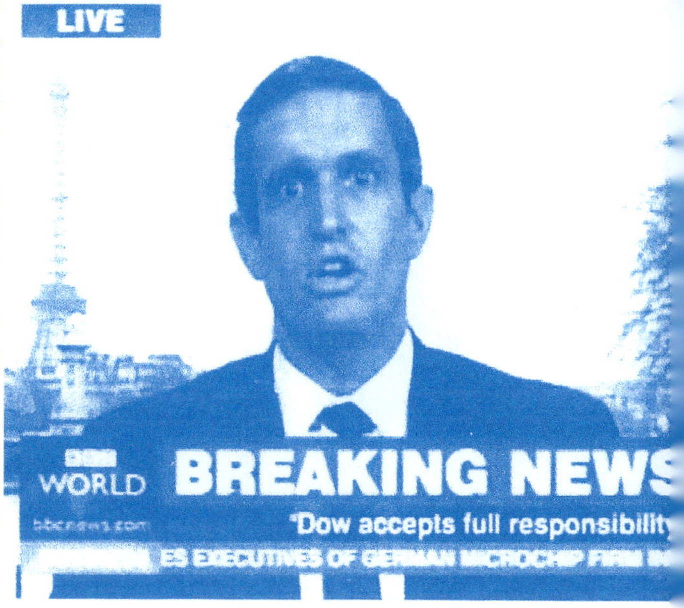

1996 leitete ®TMark $5.000 von einem New Yorker Ladenbesitzer an einen Programmierer im Silicon Valley weiter. Als Gegenleistung vertauschte dieser hunderte Computerspielfiguren der neuen SimCopter-Version gegen kusswütige Männer in Badehosen.

50.000 Exemplare des Spiels gelangten in die Läden, bevor der provokative Hack entdeckt wurde; der Programmierer, Jacques Servin, wurde entlassen.

«Ich war für die Gestaltung der Figuren mit einem KörperAnimationsprogramm zuständig,» sagte Servin, der schwul ist. Er schrieb den Spielcode um, so dass während des Spiels halbnackte Muskelmänner auftauchen, die man küssen muss sobald man ihnen begegnet; dies löst laute Schmatzgeräusche aus – wie auch das Küssen der weiblichen Spielfiguren. An Servins Geburtstag und am Freitag, den 13. generiert das Spiel besonders viele Liebesangreifer.

«Ich wollte schon immer ein Aktivist sein,» sagt Servin, «aber Aktivismus ist so abgehoben heutzutage. Denkt ihr, dass Firmenchefs in Galerien gehen und sagen 'Oh, wow – ich mache was falsch'? Symbole sind so viel stärker dort, wo sie nicht erwartet werden.» Text: ®TMark

®TMark stellt Subvertierungsprojekte ins Netz, an den man sich entweder finanziell oder durch Mitarbeit beteiligen kann; Projekte kann jeder vorschlagen. ®TMark versteht sich als eine Art von Mittelsmann für illegale Aktionen.

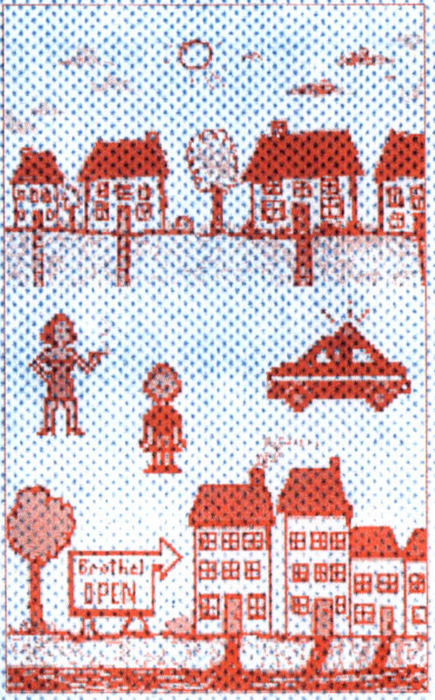

1

<1> Super Kid Fighter: die Kunst-Aktivisten Critical Art Ensemble haben ein Spiel für Jugendliche programmiert dessen Ziel es ist, die Schule zu schwänzen um ein offenes Bordell zu finden. Der Weg muss mit anarchistischer List und der Hilfe von zufälligen Bekanntschaften gefunden werden; Geld und Gewalt helfen nicht weiter. Vorsicht: Polizeistreifen und Aufsichtspersonen bringen dich zurück.

<1> Super Kid Fighter: the Art-Activists Critical Art Ensemble has created a game, that will teach anarchic cunning to the youth playing it. The computer game hero's goal is to skip school and to find the brothel, with the help of chance acquaintences and by avoiding police and supervisor patrols. Money or violence won't help you along.

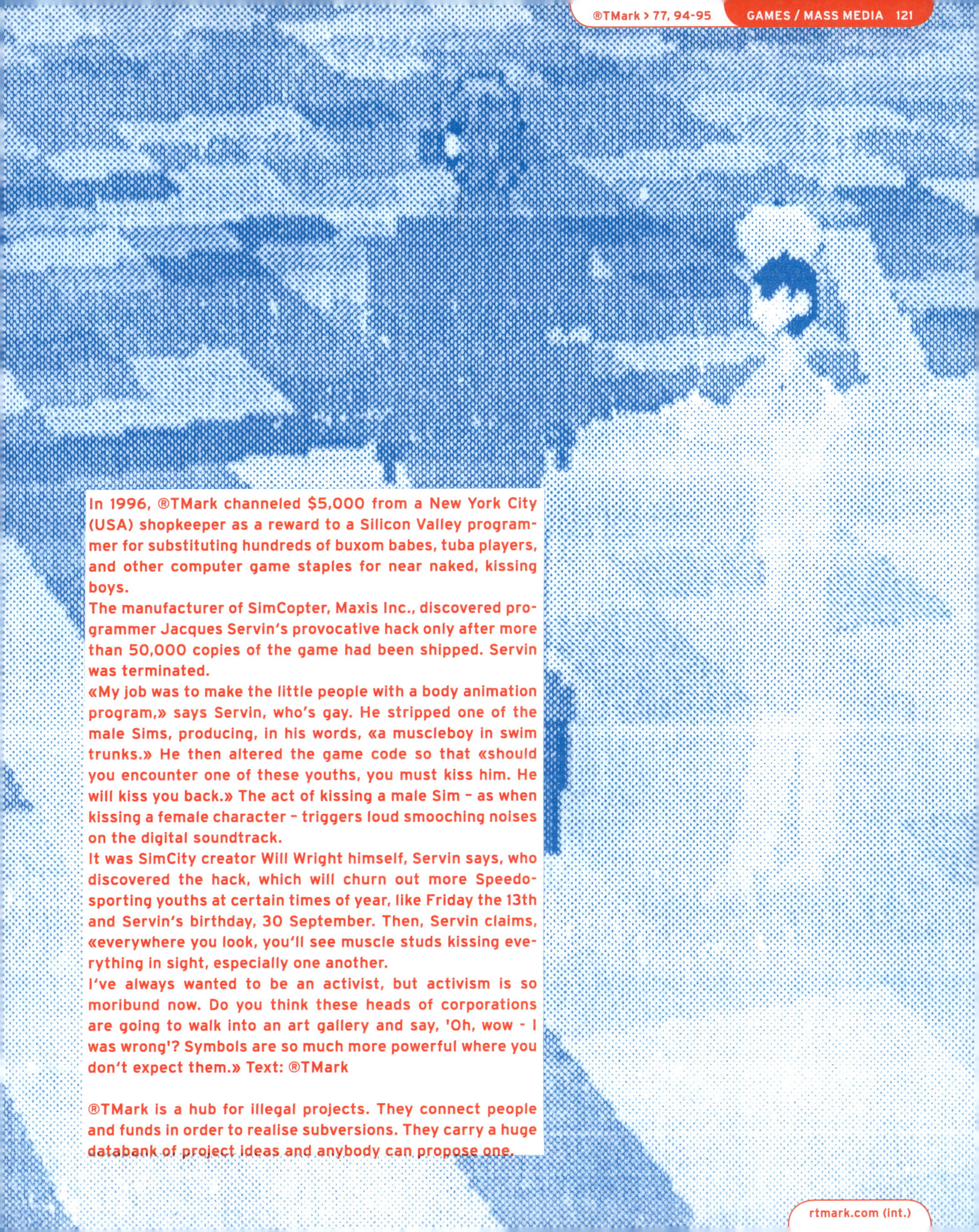

In 1996, ®TMark channeled $5,000 from a New York City (USA) shopkeeper as a reward to a Silicon Valley programmer for substituting hundreds of buxom babes, tuba players, and other computer game staples for near naked, kissing boys.
The manufacturer of SimCopter, Maxis Inc., discovered programmer Jacques Servin's provocative hack only after more than 50,000 copies of the game had been shipped. Servin was terminated.
«My job was to make the little people with a body animation program,» says Servin, who's gay. He stripped one of the male Sims, producing, in his words, «a muscleboy in swim trunks.» He then altered the game code so that «should you encounter one of these youths, you must kiss him. He will kiss you back.» The act of kissing a male Sim – as when kissing a female character – triggers loud smooching noises on the digital soundtrack.
It was SimCity creator Will Wright himself, Servin says, who discovered the hack, which will churn out more Speedo-sporting youths at certain times of year, like Friday the 13th and Servin's birthday, 30 September. Then, Servin claims, «everywhere you look, you'll see muscle studs kissing everything in sight, especially one another.
I've always wanted to be an activist, but activism is so moribund now. Do you think these heads of corporations are going to walk into an art gallery and say, 'Oh, wow - I was wrong'? Symbols are so much more powerful where you don't expect them.» Text: ®TMark

®TMark is a hub for illegal projects. They connect people and funds in order to realise subversions. They carry a huge databank of project ideas and anybody can propose one.

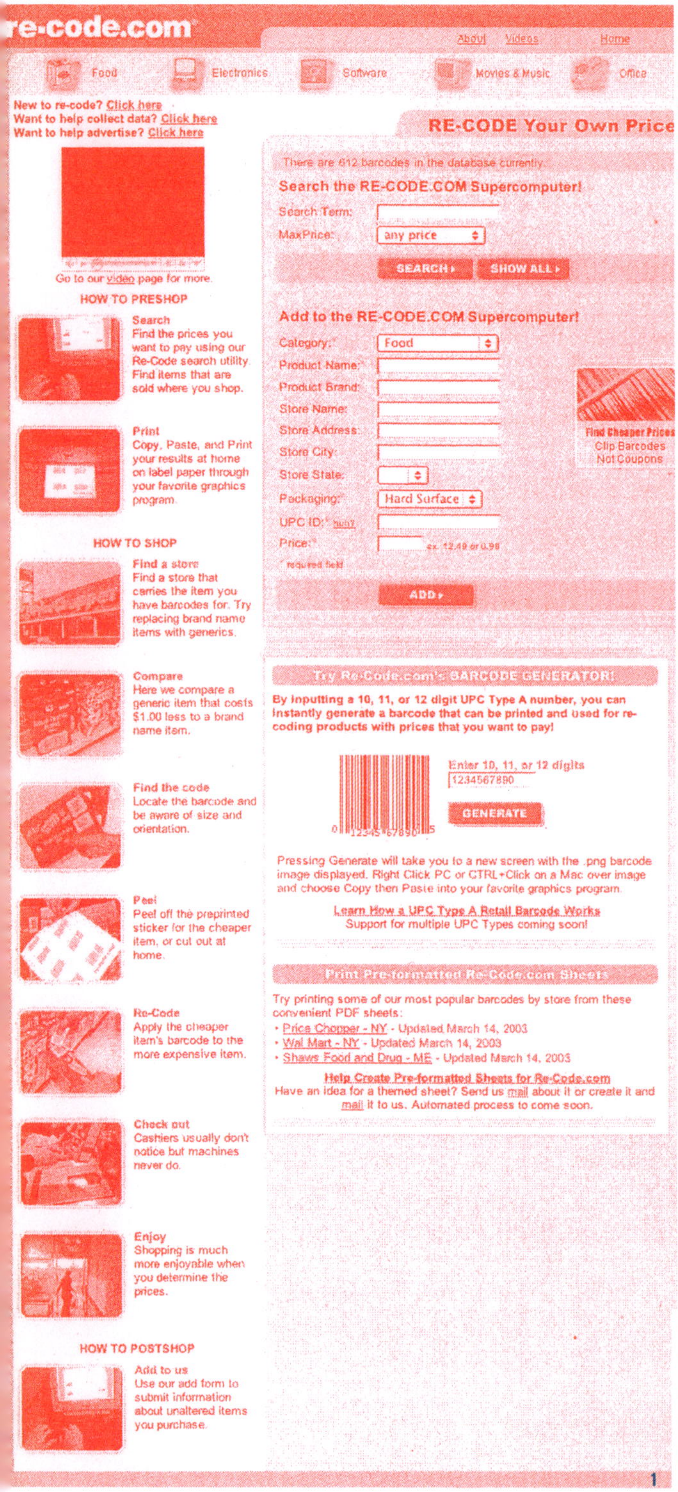

«Worldwide electronic insurrection» (FBI).

Some mark the beginning of internet activism by a FloodNet jamming attack on the Pentagon's and Mexican Government's websites, organised by various tech activist groups to support the Zapatista cause. FloodNet is a simple script that continously reloades a website, overloading weak servers or blocking access to other users in the process.

«Weltweiter elektronischer Aufstand» (FBI).

Der FloodNet-Angriff auf die Websites des Pentagon und der mexikanischen Regierung wird von vielen als die Geburtsstunde des Internet-Aktivismus angesehen. Floodnet ist ein einfaches Programm, das endlos eine angewählte Webseite aufruft. Fixieren Tausende der Programme eine Adresse, kann ein schwacher Server zusammenbrechen oder die Site wird für die Dauer der Aktion für weitere Benutzer blockiert.

Two stories of sites that made an impact:

Both voteauction.org and sellthevote.com aim at «Bringing Capitalism and Democracy Closer Together», and let bidders shop for disillusioned citizens' votes. Although strictly satirical they were banned as illegal voting frauds in some US states and finally taken off line under pressure from the authorities. Maybe the proposed scheme is too close to reality to be taken for a joke.
Re-code.com met the same fate. It was a site that offered the opportunity to generate and print bar codes with reduced prices. Intended as a satirical proposition for using commercial technology against itself, it was quickly killed off by corporate lawyers claiming trademark infringements.

Zwei Webseiten die von sich reden machten:

Voteauction.org und sellthevote.com wollten die Demokratie mit dem Kapitalismus in einer Art Ebay-Satire verbinden. Verbitterte Wähler konnten ihre Wahlstimmen per Auktion an Höchstbietende verkaufen. Gemeint als Kritik an der Einflussnahme von Konzernen auf die Politik, wurde die Seite in vielen US-Bundesstaaten sofort wegen Wahlbetrugs verboten, und schliesslich vom Netz genommen. Möglicherweise war die Idee zu realistisch.
Ähnliches passierte re-code.com, einem netzbasierten Generator, mit dem man Ean Codes produzieren und auf Produkte kleben konnte, um billiger einkaufen zu können. Re-Code wurde von Wirtschaftsanwälten mit dem Argument der Copyright-Verletzung aus dem Netz verbannt.

re-code.com & conglomco.org / voteauction.org & sellthevote.com - now offline (all: USA)

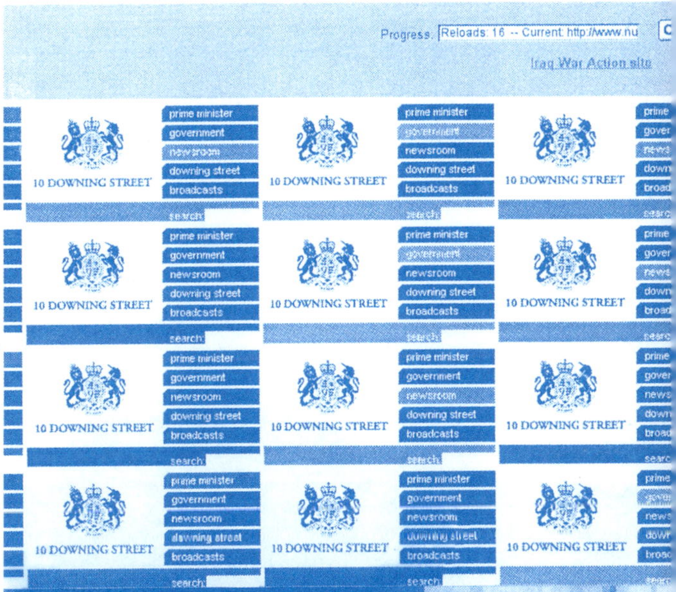

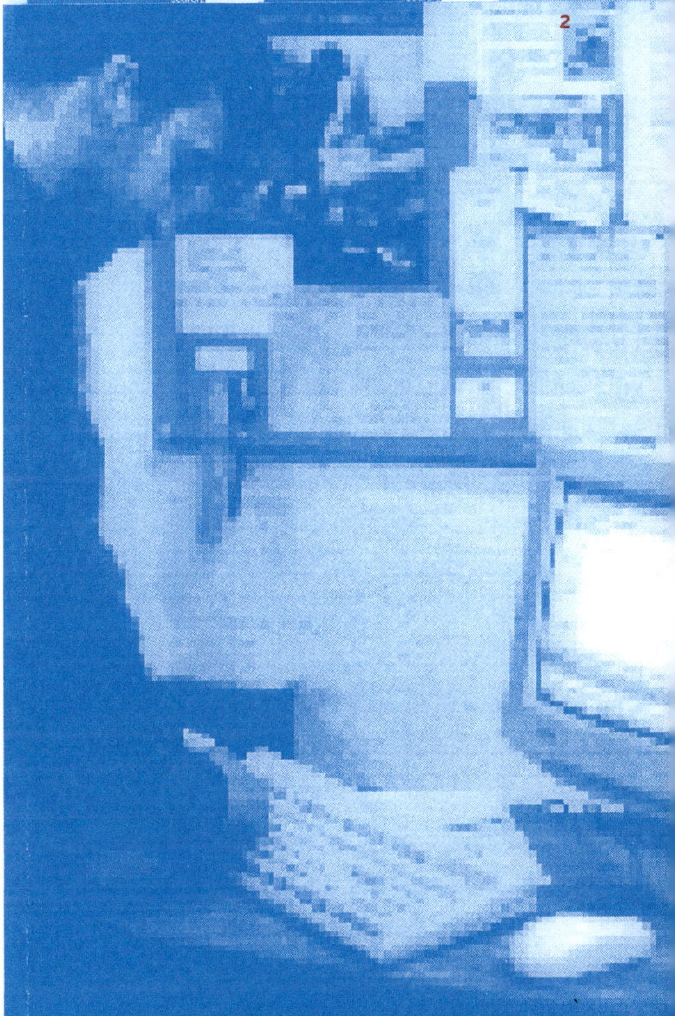

Iraq War Action Site: automatic reload scripts in an attempt to crash the British PM's website

Finally, there are those (still) rare but extreme law enforcement actions, such as the 2004 confiscation of independent providers' server hardware by British police and their 'extradition' to the FBI. Among other things, the disks contained data of several Indymedia chapters.

That same year a German internet police division conducted a series of random online 'checks' on thousands of private computers. Subsequently, blackmail e-mails were sent to the owners, threatening persecution for posession of 'pirated' music and software - a well- timed fake, as it turned out later.

Seltener sind direkte Eingriffe der Behörden, wie die Beschlagnahmung von Serverfestplatten unabhängiger Provider durch die britische Polizei und ihre 'Auslieferung' an das FBI im Herbst 2004; oder die gigantsche 'Stichprobenaktion' der deutschen Polizei, die im selben Jahr über das Netz Tausende privater Computer auf illegal heruntergeladene Programme und Musik durchstöberten, um hinterher den Besitzern eMails mit Strafandrohnungen zu schicken - ein gut getimter Fake, wie sich später herausstellte.

The internet offers a common ground for critical actions from outside, too, such as video and sound sampling (the cutting-up and rearranging of found materials). It's the creation of media collages: film pioneers include Craig Baldwin, Phil Pateris, Bruce Connor and the Emergency Broadcast Network; in music: Negativland, The KLF, The Tape Beatles or John Oswald. Such anarchistic techniques are regarded as piracy by the industry, the copyright watchdog.

Das Internet gibt aber auch anderen Projekten Raum, wie dem Musik- und Videosampling (collagieren gefundener Materialien). Pioniere des Collagefilms sind Craig Baldwin, Phil Pateris oder Bruce Connor, die wichtigsten Musikcollagisten Negativland, The KLF, The Tape Beatles oder John Oswald. Diese anarchistische Arbeitsweise sieht die Industrie, der Wachhund des Copyrights, natürlich als Piraterie an.

The net, much like real space, offers a vast variety of possibilities for protest and the activists. These can be divided in four directions: dissemination of tools and information (networks, blogs, mailing lists), activist's own websites, fake corporate or governmental pages and the occasional hack attack. Again, far too many to list. See the index for starters and keep in mind that URLs have a habit of often change or disappear.

Das Internet wird für unterschiedlichste Protestarten benutzt; man kann sie in vier grobe Richtungen unterteilen: Nachrichtenverbreitung und Organisation (durch Netzwerke, blogs, mailing lists), Webseiten der Gruppen und Aktivisten, gefälschte 'offizielle' Homepages und die vereinzelte Hackerattacke.

images: 1 thing.net (USA) / 2 electrohippies - fraw.org.uk (UK)

PRO

MARKE

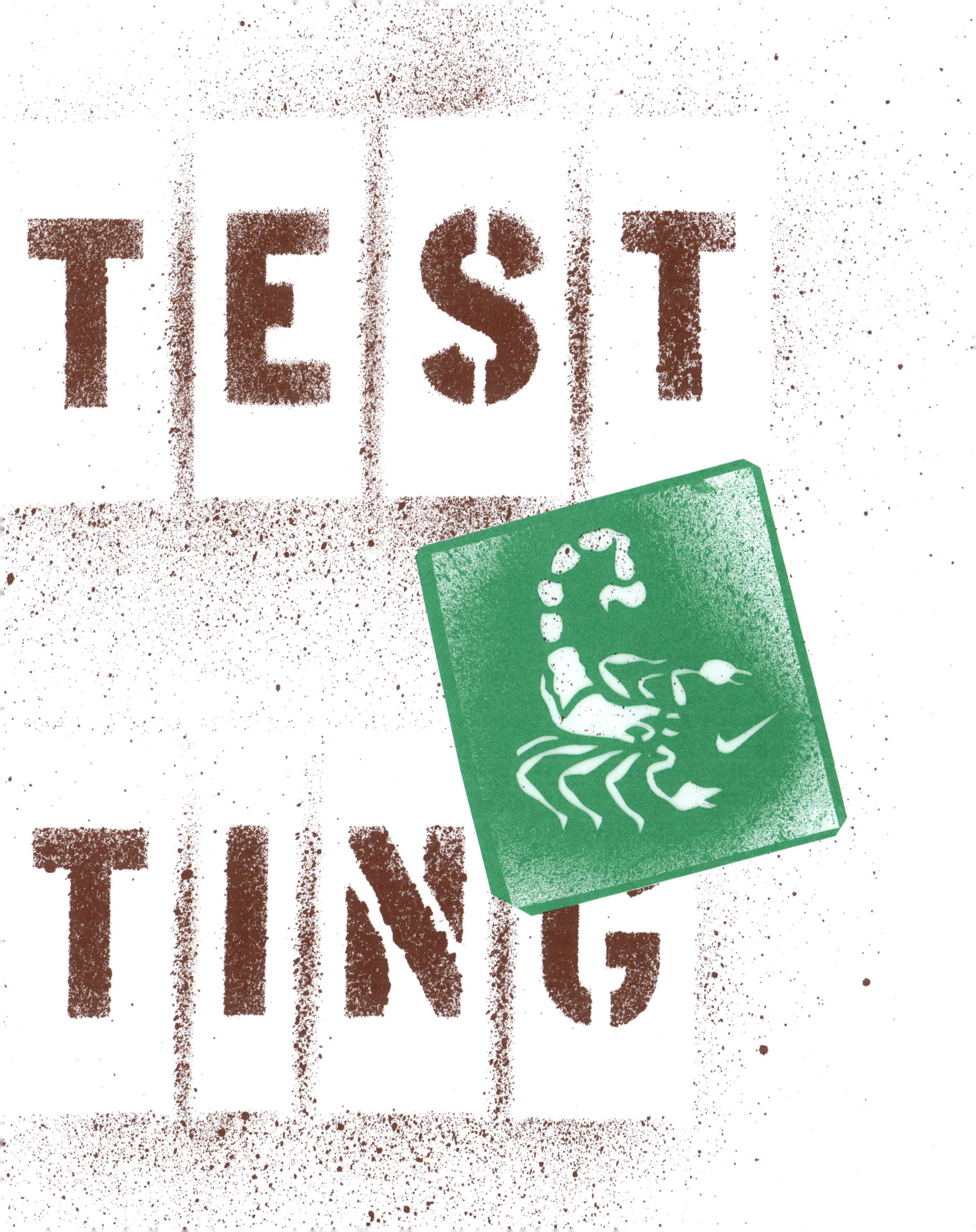
TEST
TING

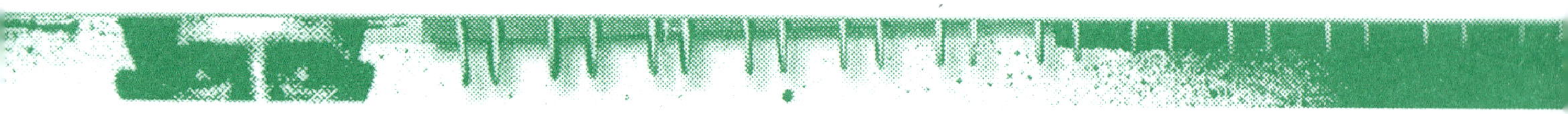

Commercial cool-hunters are never far away from places where new cultural currents, styles and ways of expression evolve. They depend on these in order to sell their clients the essential 'edge' that's supposed to take them one step ahead of the competition.

THE ORGANIZATION

HISTORY / MISSION
SERVICES
CLIENTS
PRESS

IDENTITY

PROJECTS

ROYAL ELASTICS
EPITAPH
THE STREET NETWORK
BLACK EYED PEAS
NISSAN
DC SHOES
FLYPAPER
ONL
NEIL FINN
HAWAIIAN PUNCH
FLEETWOOD MAC
MUSIC MISC
NON-PROFIT
NEW JERSEY TURNPIKE

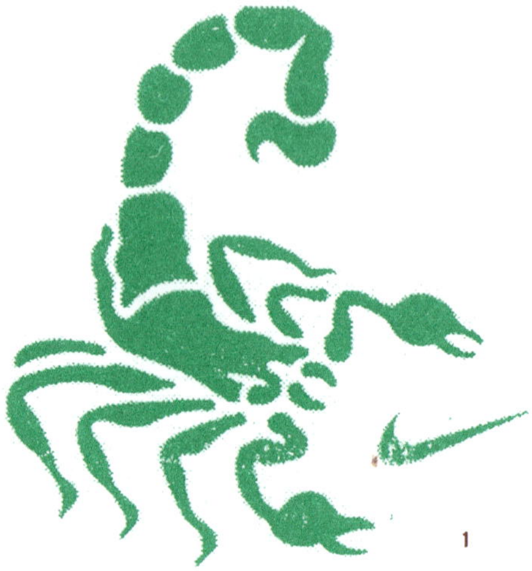

1

<1> An international stencil ad campaign
<2> The counter-campaign

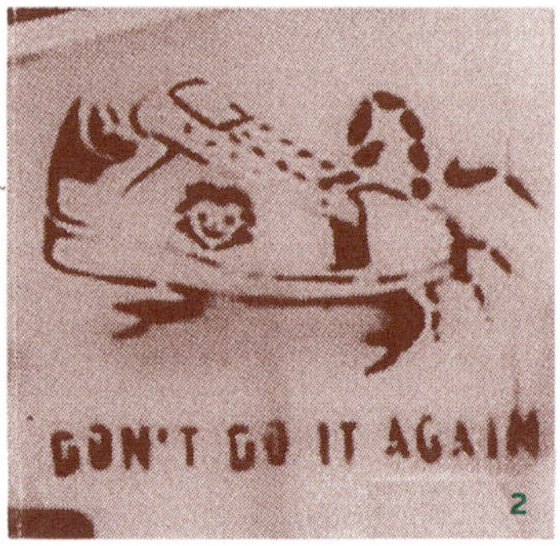

2

Nowadays the commercial strategists' prize catch is the 'hard-to-reach trendsetter', be it the inner-city teenager, dressed from head to toe in branded sportswear or the cynical, self-confident youth as depicted in iPod ads; even the no-global, anti-brand 'activist'. Waiting for every one of them are specially tailored marketing strategies that try to keep in step with youth culture.

Since both protest tactics and marketing strategies aim at attracting attention, it was just a matter of time until marketing took over the former, copying first the visible 'protest aesthetic', later creating its own 'protest' spectacle.
In doing so PR firms succeed in getting free publicity using their targets' networks and visual codes.

Kommerzielle Coolness-Scouts sind immer dort zu finden, wo neue kulturelle Strömungen, Stile und Ausdrucksmittel entstehen. Sie benutzen diese, um ihren Klienten den 'notwendigen Vorsprung vor der Konkurrenz' zu verkaufen.

Die Lieblings-Zielgruppe der kommerziellen Strategen sind 'schwer erreichbare Trendsetter', egal ob es sich um den von Kopf bis Fuss in Markenartikel eingekleideten 'Ghetto-kid' handelt, den zynisch-selbstbewussten Jugendlichen aus der iPod-Werbung oder den No Global 'Aktivisten'. Auf jeden wird eine Marketingstrategie zugeschnitten, die ständig mit der Jugendkultur Schritt halten muss.

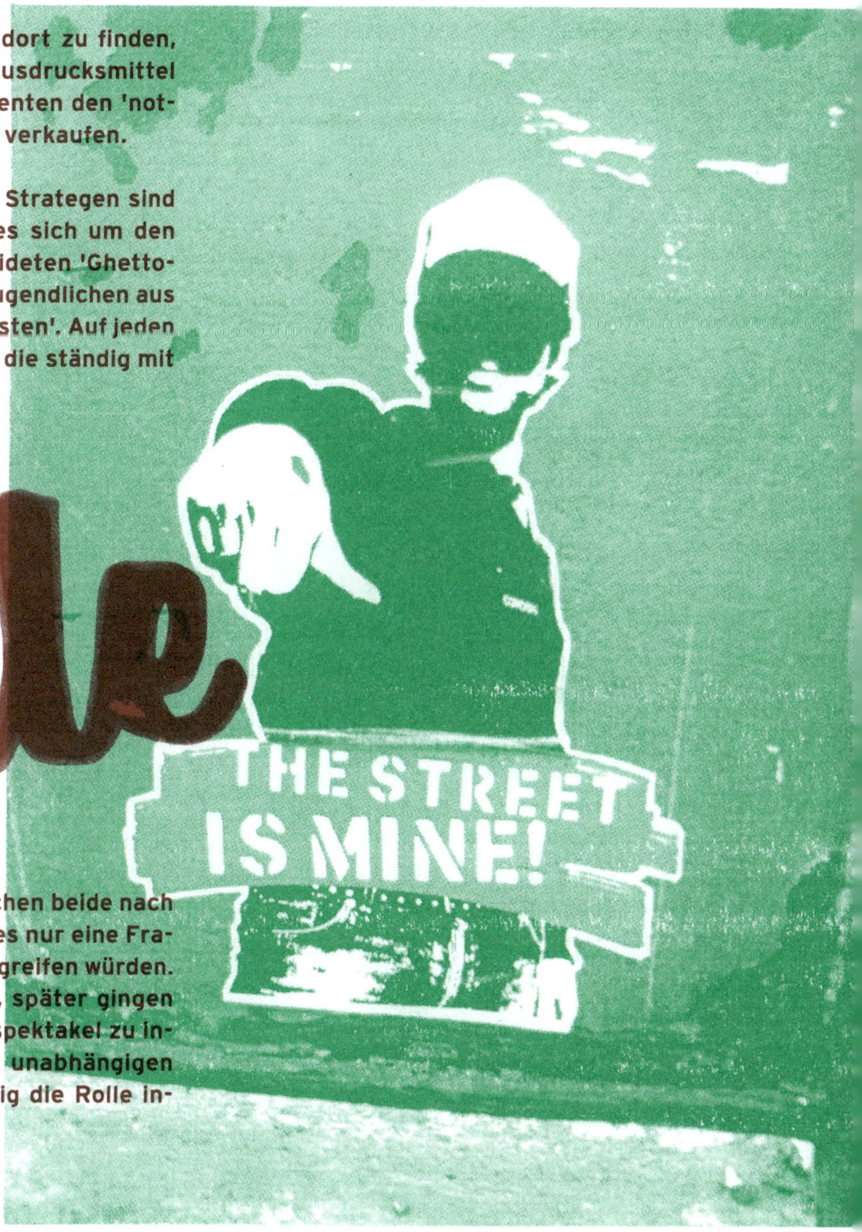

Protesttaktiken und Marketingstrategien suchen beide nach Wegen, um bemerkt zu werden; deshalb war es nur eine Frage der Zeit, wann Vermarkter den Protest aufgreifen würden. Anfangs kopierten sie nur 'Protestästhetik', später gingen Kampagnen dazu über, ihr eigenes 'Protest'spektakel zu inszenieren. Die Diskussionen darüber in den unabhängigen Internet-Netzwerken übernahmen unfreiwillig die Rolle indirekter PR.

Street postering campaign

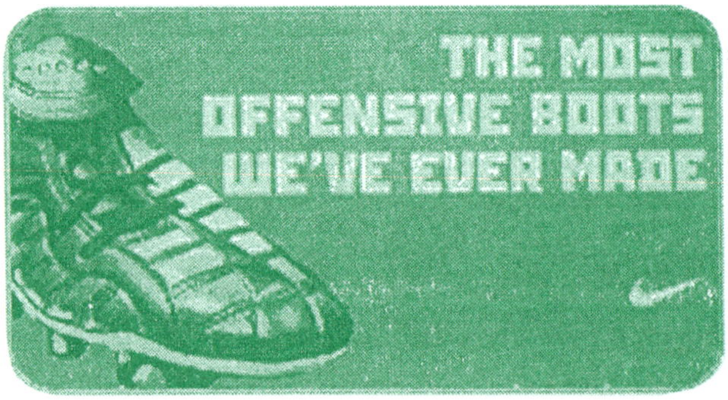

1

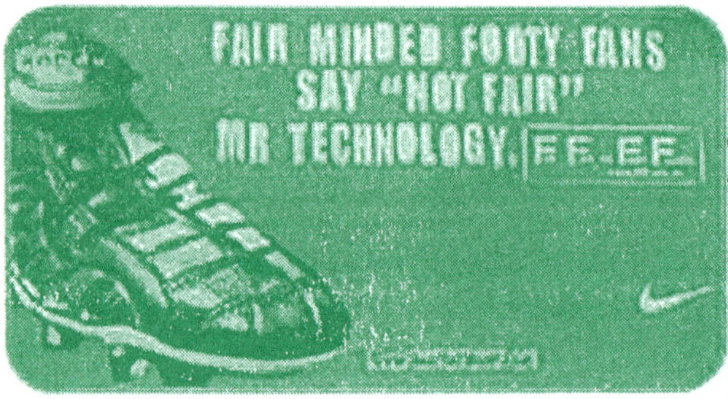

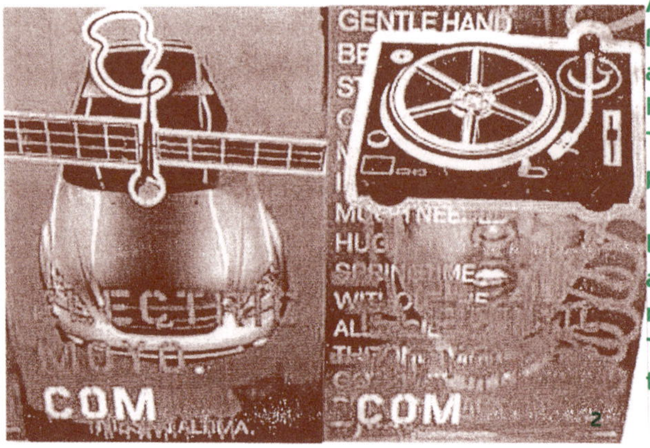

Judging from the amount of attention that the «Jonah Peretti story» got through indy mailing lists and blogs, it must have been invaluable PR for a new Nike product. Jonah ordered a pair of personalised «ID» sneakers, but instead of having his name on them, he asked Nike to print 'sweatshop' instead.
The company refused his repeated e-mail requests, unaware of the fact that Peretti was posting all correspondence in a net blog. The story snowballed, in the end even mainstream TV got the news. But all the while Nike was flooded with requests for sneakers with all sorts of messages.

Die Aufmerksamkeit, die der «Jonah Peretti-Affäre» geschenkt wurde, war Gratiswerbung für ein neues Nike Produkt. Jonah bestellte für seine neuen personalisierten Nike «ID» Schuhe den Schriftzug 'sweatshop'.
Die Firma lehnte die Umsetzung ab und eine e-Mail Diskussion begann zwischen Jonah und Nike. Peretti stellte die Korrespondenz während sie sich entwickelte ins Netz.
Die Geschichte wurde zu einer Lawine quer durch die meisten Independent-Nachrichtensites... und Nike überschwemmte eine Welle von Bestellungen für Schuhe mit verschiedensten Schriftzügen.

After this experience Nike decided to take it to the next level. They launched a new billboard campaign in Australia, and had it defaced by a group called «Fans Fight for Fairer Football» (who staged public 'protests' in the streets, too). The whole thing was a scheme created by a PR agency, the protesters were paid extras. <1>

But the company had learned its lesson from the Peretti affair. They paid a columnist of the indie news network antimedia.net to reveal every detail of the campaign.
Their plan worked perfectly: the 'revealing' article became the most popular mail forwarded around many networks.

1 in: antimedia.net/nikesweatshop / 2 blkmrkt.com, Culver City (USA)

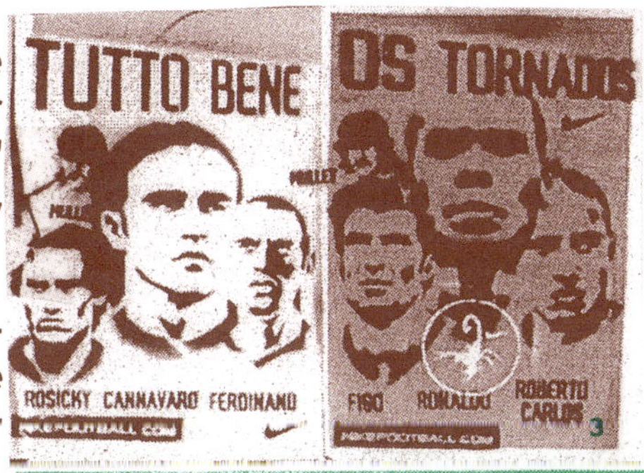

Parasite stencil on ad campaign

Nach dieser Erfahrung startete Nike die nächste Runde, eine Plakatkampagne in Australien, die von den «Fans Fight for Fairer Football» überklebt wurde (auch 'Strassenproteste' fanden statt). Die Gruppe bestand aus bezahlten Statisten, organisiert von einer PR-Agentur. <1>

Damit der Ball auch global ins rollen kam, bezahlte Nike einen Kolumnisten des Indynetzwerks antimedia.net, der die gesamte Kampagne offenlegen sollte. Sein 'Enthüllungsbericht' war monatelang im Internet im Umlauf.

<2,3> In order to appeal to its target market Nike commissioned a stencil-aesthetics camapign, including the illegal spraying of scorpion images in major cities. BLK/MRKT, an agency specialised in copying underground styles was the author of the stencil; they also fabricated this seemingly overpainted 'street-art' car ad (the URL redirects you automatically to the Nissan, USA web site).

<2,3> Auch illegale Aktionen gehören zum Repertoire, wie die in Grosstädten gesprühten 'Nike-Skorpione', Teil einer Schablonenästhetik-Kampagne.

Die Skorpione erfand die auf Undergroundmarketing spezialisierte Agentur BLK/MRKT, die auch diese 'Street Art' Plakate illegal kleben liess. Die url leitet automatisch um auf die Webseite von Nissan/USA.

<4> Die Jeansmarke Cordon liess diese Plakate in Berliner U-Bahnstationen kleben, besonders in solchen die von Strassenkünstlern und Sprühern bevorzugt werden.

<4> The jeans maker Cordon plastered these billboards in Berlin; what looks like it's been ripped apart is a photo. The campaign included illegally posted bills and stickers.

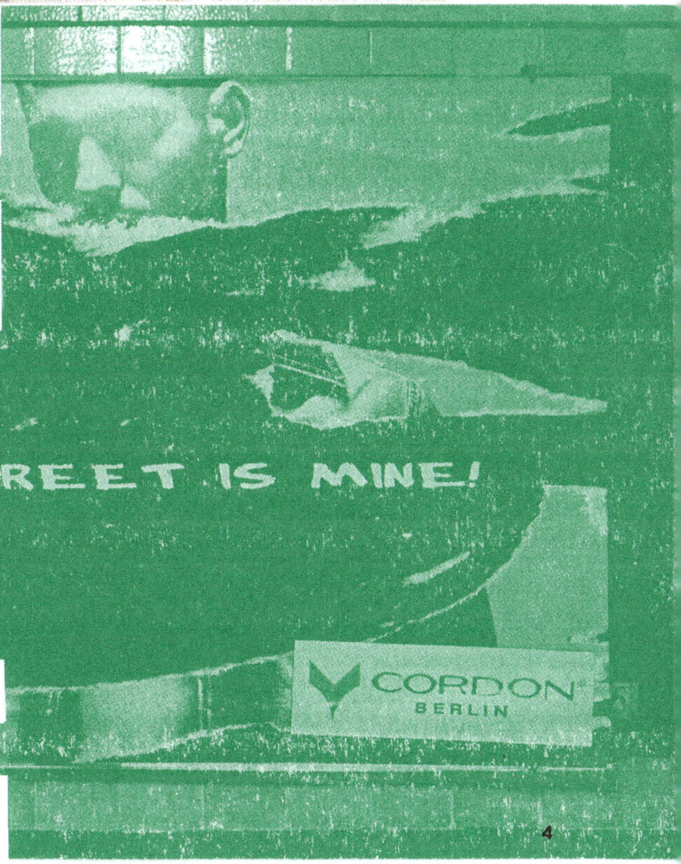

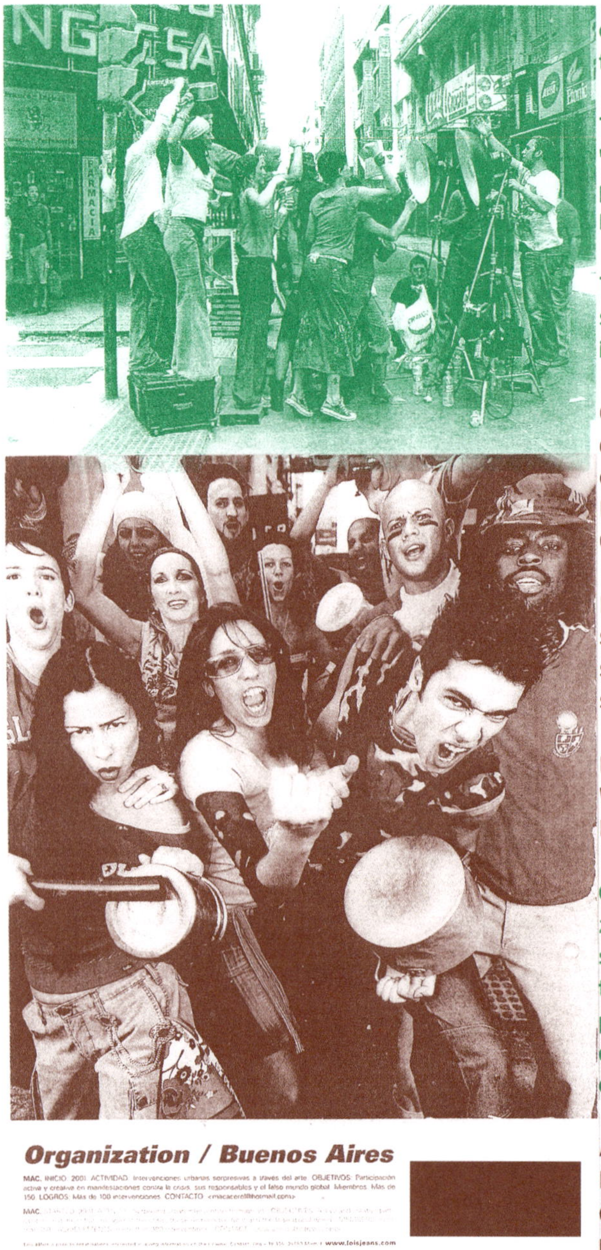

Whether its a new-age girl riding on a giant turtle into the sunrise, breathing deeply the fresh sea breeze (the 'freedom-wear' fashion line of a French tobacco company), or Diesel's nonsense-protestor fashion victims, there seems to be no limit to superficial selling.

The moment a company decides to create or refresh its 'street credibility', protest actions and ideals which are a part of life and society become reduced to selling aids, just like any other cultural facet might.

The Quatermaster label does it through a series of 'workshops' for street artists (Artstorm), where illegal art turns into fashion advertising.

Ob ein New-Age-Mädchen glücklich auf einer Schildkröte durch klare Wellen und saubere Luft dem Sonnenaufgang entgegenschwebt ('Freiheitsmode' von Gauloises), oder Diesel-Modeopfer für «Mehr Blumen» demonstrieren, der Oberflächlichkeit scheinen keine Grenzen gesetzt.

In dem Moment, wenn Firmen ihre 'Strassenkredibilität' erschaffen oder auffrischen möchten, verkommt Protest und seine Ideen – wie auch andere Facetten des kulturellen und sozialen Lebens – zu einfachen Verkaufshilfen.

Das Label Quatermaster macht es durch ihre «Artstorm» Workshops, in denen Strassenkünstler statt illegaler Bilder Modeanzeigen und Magazinseiten gestalten.

Others, like Lois jeans publish 'socially-orienteted' magazines. In Lois's own «ORG/A Different Mag», it's hard to tell staged fashion shoots from real street photography. In it, the company appeares to be just an ad client, occurences, places, issues and fashion become a mix; and some existing groups sell themselves as manequins. Social protest goes catwalk.

Andere geben 'sozial orientierte' Magazine heraus. In der Lois-Produktion «ORG/Ein Anderes Mag» vermischen sich gestellte Shootings mit Strassenbildern, und die Kleidungsmarke erscheint eher als Anzeigenkunde denn als Herausgeber. Geschehen, Orte, Themen und Mode werden zu einem Lifestylemix, in dem auch existierende Gruppen die Rolle von Mannequins annehmen: Protest auf dem Laufsteg.

When PR goes wild even serious issues become corporate spin. For years Shell Petroleum has been fighting to save its reputation, but when new reports of repressions against African eco-activists appear in the media around 1999, Shell decided to acquire a 'clean' image once and for all.

In a regular series of print ads in international magazines, Shell Petroleum claims to have changed, working together with activists, even «encouraging» these groups to monitor its progress - because, «Time and again at Shell we're discovering the rewards of respecting the environment when doing business».

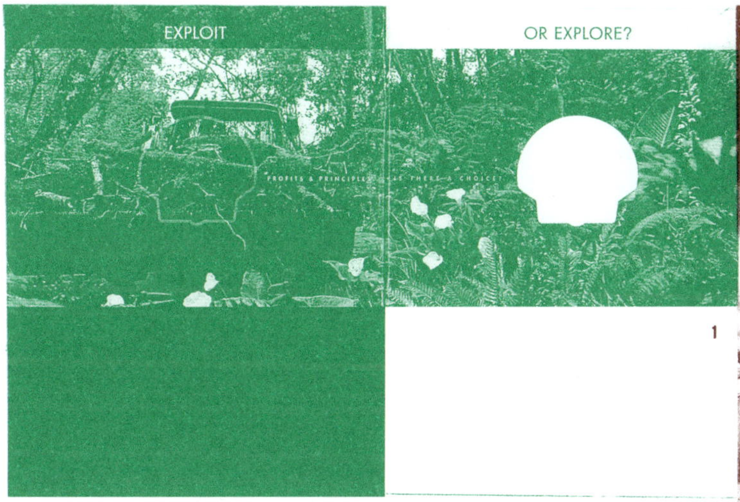

1

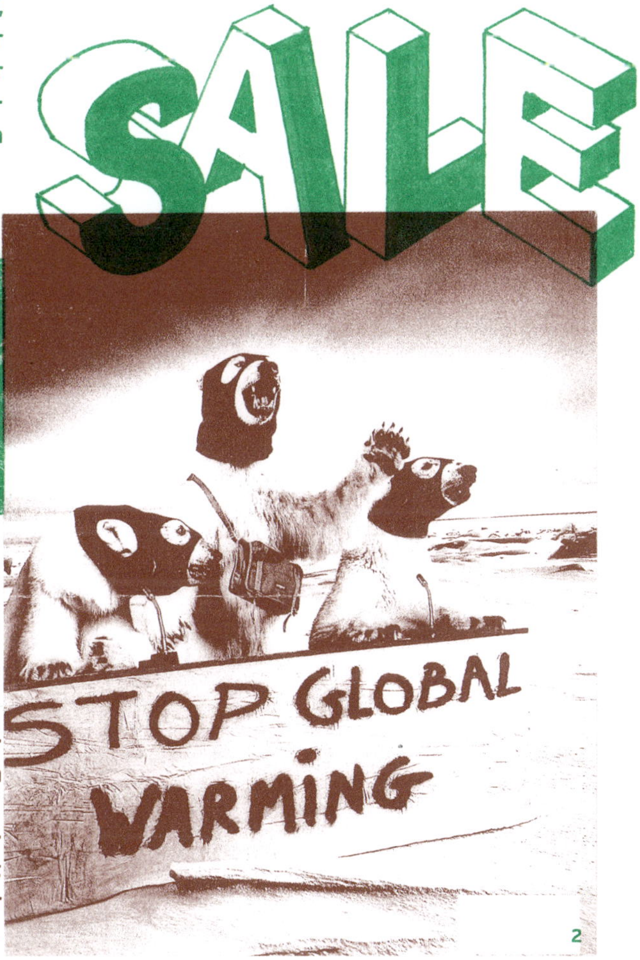

2

Wenn PR durchdreht, werden auch ernste Themen zu kommerzieller Propaganda. 1999 beschloss Shell, sein Image ein für alle Mal zu säubern.
Im Laufe des Jahres erschienen regelmässig Anzeigen in internationalen Printmedien, in denen Shell sich als geläutert darstellte, mit Umweltaktivisten zusammenarbeite, sie sogar «ermutige», die Fortschritte des Konzerns zu überwachen.

«Immer wieder entdecken wir bei Shell die dankbare Aufgabe, die Umwelt zu respektieren, während wir unseren Geschäften nachgehen», so die Subline.

«The Bivings Group specializes in internet lobbying. Its website contains an article entitled 'Viral Marketing: How to Infect the World' and it explains how 'there are some campaigns where it would be undesirable or even disastrous to let the audience know that your organization is directly involved... it's simply not an intelligent PR move. Perhaps the greatest advantage of viral marketing is that your message is placed into a context where it is more likely to be considered seriously.'

In the November 29, 2003, issue of Nature magazine, two researchers from the University of California, Berkeley published a paper that claimed that native maize in Mexico had been contaminated, across vast distances, by genetically modified pollen. The findings were a disaster for the biotech companies lobbying for embargoes on GM crops to be lifted.

You'v

The same day that the report was published, posts began to appear on the listserver AgBioWorld, a biotechnology forum used by more than 3,000 scientists. These messages accused the paper's authors of being biased; some claimed, falsely, that the paper had not been reviewed, that the authors were 'first and foremost activists' and that the research was influenced by environmentalists. The defamatory emails continued in the days following the paper's publication, insinuating that the authors had been paid to arrive at their findings. The messages stimulated hundreds of others, some of which repeated or embellished the accusations they had made.
The pressure on Nature magazine was so severe that its editor did something that the magazine had never done previously in its 133-year history: they published a retraction, and published two opposing papers.

mail.

The parties involved with undermining the original research were successful, and it started with nothing more than emails from two people. One person had defamed anti-GM researchers years before, sending her messages from a server with the identification number of a Bivings branch.
The other person had a history of posting scores of messages accusing groups such as Greenpeace of terrorism. Her messages always promote The Center For Food and Agricultural Research, which exists only as a website, which happens to be registered to the 'director of associations' at Bivings Woodell.

'Sometimes,' Bivings boasts, 'we win awards. Sometimes only the client knows the precise role we played.' Sometimes real people have no idea that they are being managed by fake ones.»

Source: commondreams.org

e got

«Someone emails you what looks like a parody of a popular television commercial. You watch, laugh, and forward it, assuming it is the work of a mischievous, tech-savvy activist. There's a good chance, however, that the spoof was made by the very brand it appears to bash, otherwise known as a 'subviral' campaign.

'They're designed to look amateurish, to leave recipients with the impression that the advert has a cult following,' says Matthew Smith, director of viral marketing agency The Viral Factory, which masterminds subviral campaigns. 'If people are going to spoof it, you might as well spoof it yourself. It's a very good way of getting cheap publicity.'

The typical approach is to walk into an internet cafe and email it to viral sites such as Lycos' Viral Chart and Punch Baby where it will be downloaded and distributed by hundreds of attachment-hungry emailers.
But you can also pay to have it seeded on communities of 'connected opinion-formers' registered to receive and distribute the latest virals.»

Source: theviralfactory.com

A now defunct firm, Elsnor Consulting, went even further by proposing to form collaborations between activist groups and corporations. Among others, their mission statement claimed:
«Corporations have more power to 'do good' than even our government and are expected to use that power wisely. (...)
A new era of goodness exists and companies seen as being on the side of the people will prevail. (...)
Activists need new, more effective forms of communication to elevate their causes. Word of Mouth is increasingly important to brands, PROTEST MARKETING will generate significant word of mouth in both the activist community and the consumer community.»

They proposed a politically charged, radical program that would support activist groups «aligned with the values of your company.»

FACE IT – IT'S A FREE MARKET WORLD ISN'T IT...

Their «hugely impactful WIN/WIN program» included:

* Selection of causes based on the true nature, principles, mission of the company; causes that the company already contributes to.

* Alignment with activists within those areas of interest.

* Development of custom program, facilitation of relationships, program tracking, results measurement.»

According to client demand, Elsnor Consulting programs could be scaled to «local, regional, national or international dimensions.»

Source: Mission Statement, Elsnor Consulting

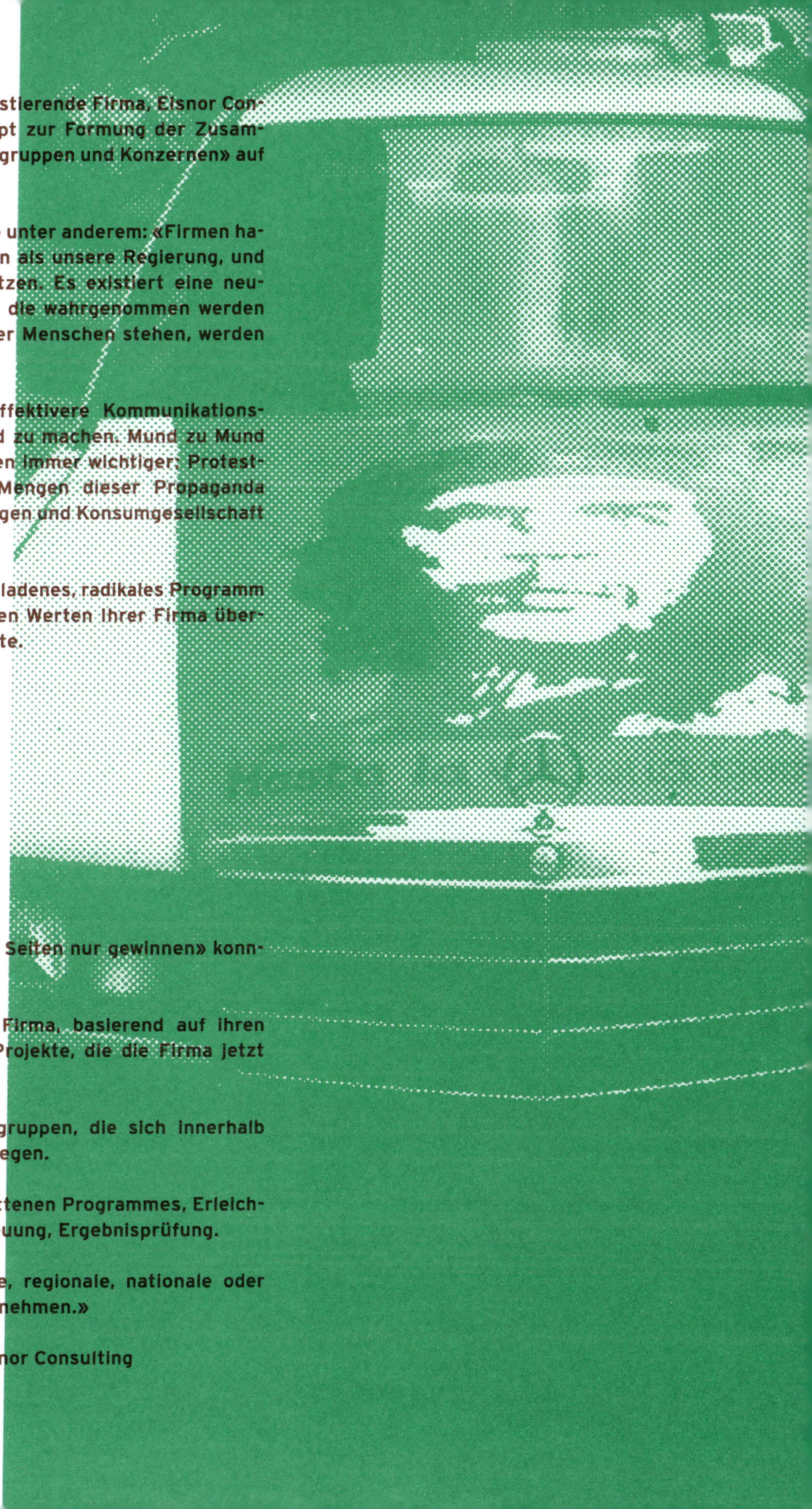

Eine inzwischen nicht mehr existierende Firma, Elsnor Consulting, versuchte ein «Konzept zur Formung der Zusammenarbeit zwischen Aktivistengruppen und Konzernen» auf den Markt zu bringen.

Ihr Positionspapier behauptete unter anderem: «Firmen haben mehr Macht, 'gutes' zu tun als unsere Regierung, und sollten diese Macht weise nutzen. Es existiert eine neuer Ära des Guten und Firmen, die wahrgenommen werden als solche, die auf der Seite der Menschen stehen, werden überleben.

Aktivisten benötigen neue, effektivere Kommunikationsformen, um ihre Sache geltend zu machen. Mund zu Mund Propaganda wird für die Marken immer wichtiger; Protestmarketing wird bedeutende Mengen dieser Propaganda unter die Aktivistengruppierungen und Konsumgesellschaft bringen.»

Sie schlugen ein politisch aufgeladenes, radikales Programm vor, das «Aktivisten, die mit den Werten ihrer Firma übereinstimmen unterstützen» sollte.

Ihr Programm, «bei dem beide Seiten nur gewinnen» konnten, beinhaltete:

* Auswahl der Anliegen der Firma, basierend auf ihren Absichten, ihre Mission und Projekte, die die Firma jetzt schon unterstützt.

* Ausrichtung mit Aktivistengruppen, die sich innerhalb dieser Interessenbereiche bewegen.

* Entwicklung eines zugeschnittenen Programmes, Erleichterung der Beziehungen, Betreuung, Ergebnisprüfung.

Die Programme können lokale, regionale, nationale oder internationale Dimensionen annehmen.»

Quelle: Mission Statement, Elsnor Consulting

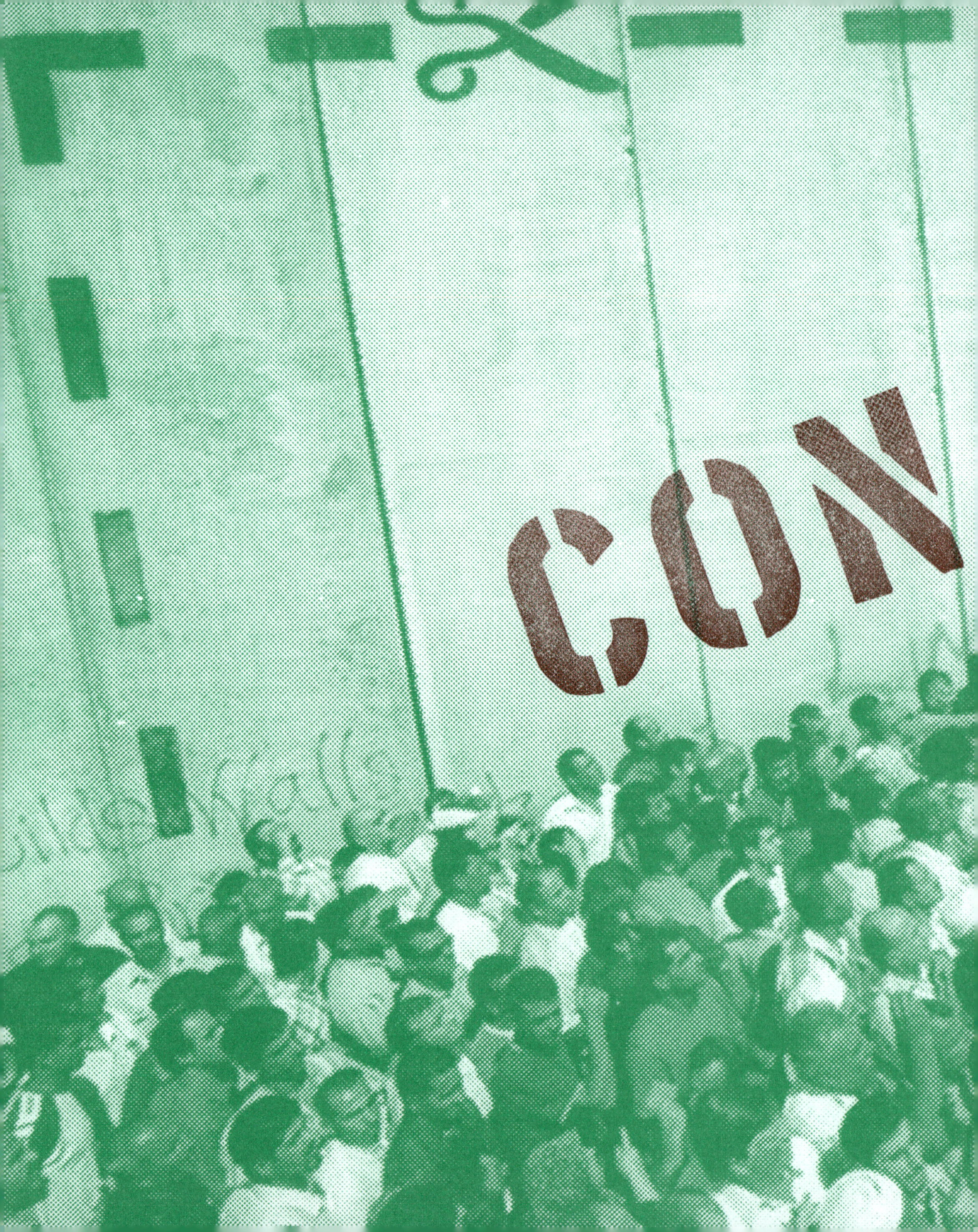
CON

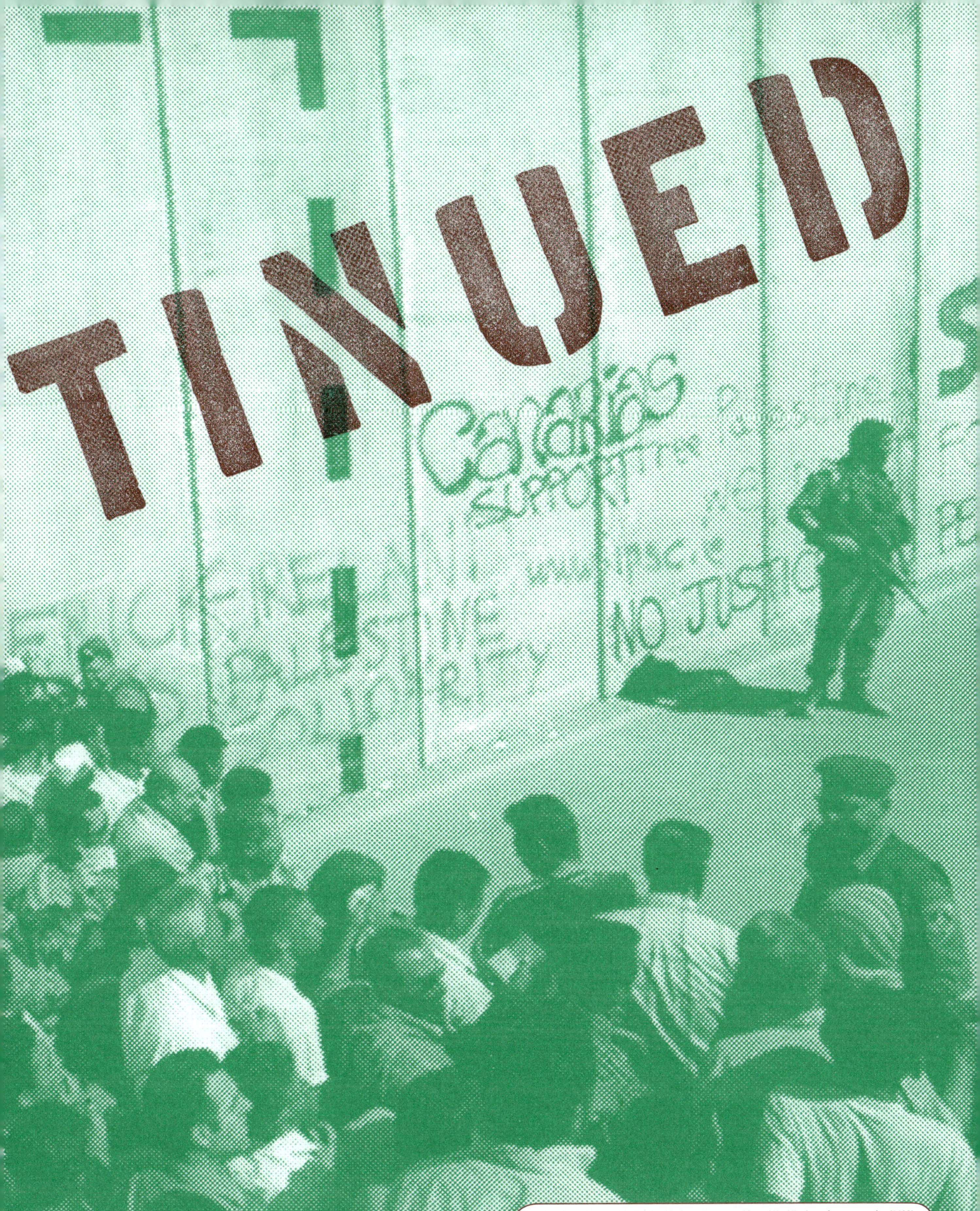

Banksy (Israeli-Palestinian Seperation Wall), banksy.co.uk, (UK)

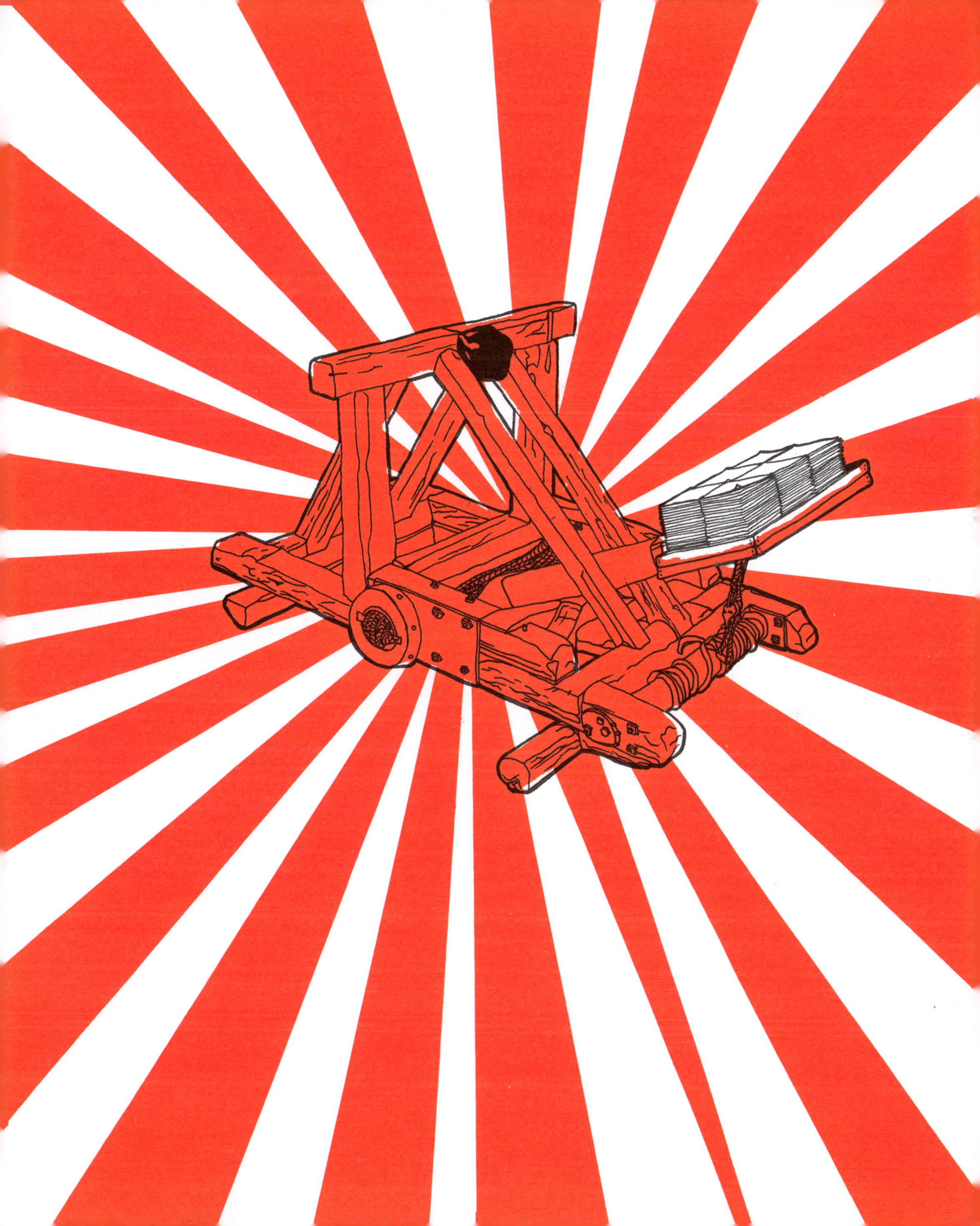

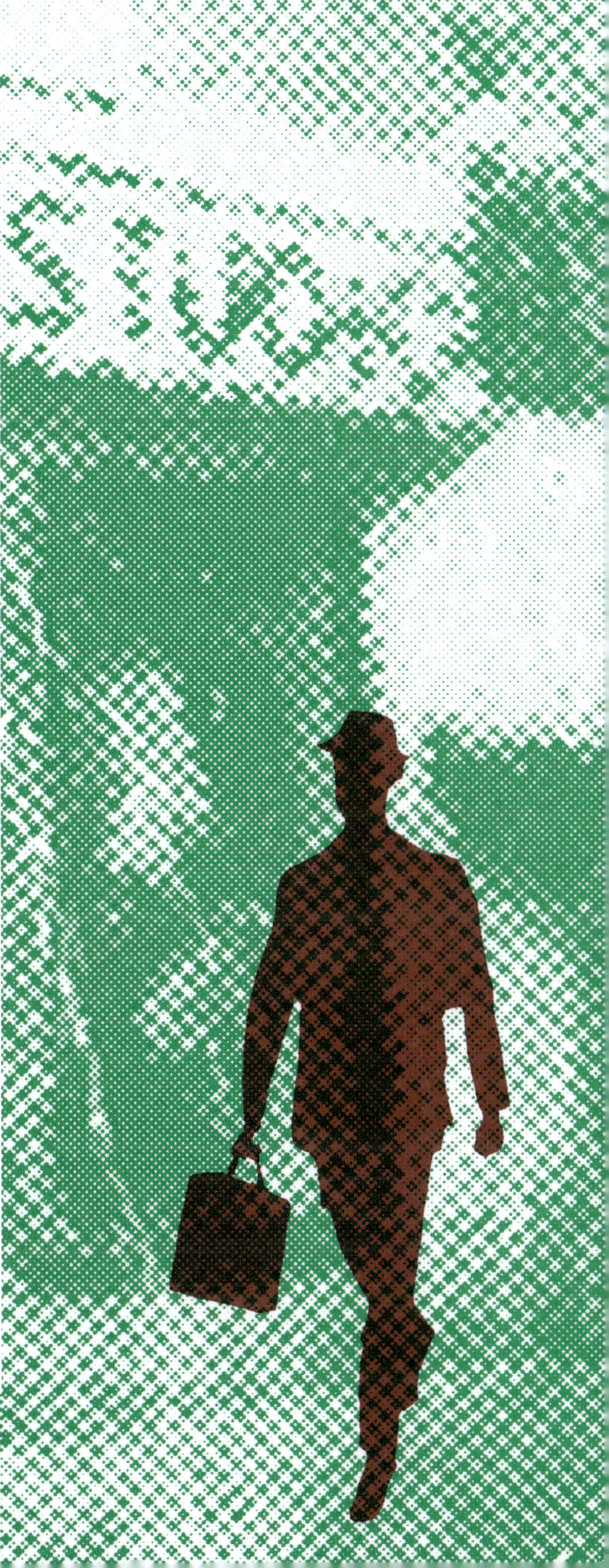

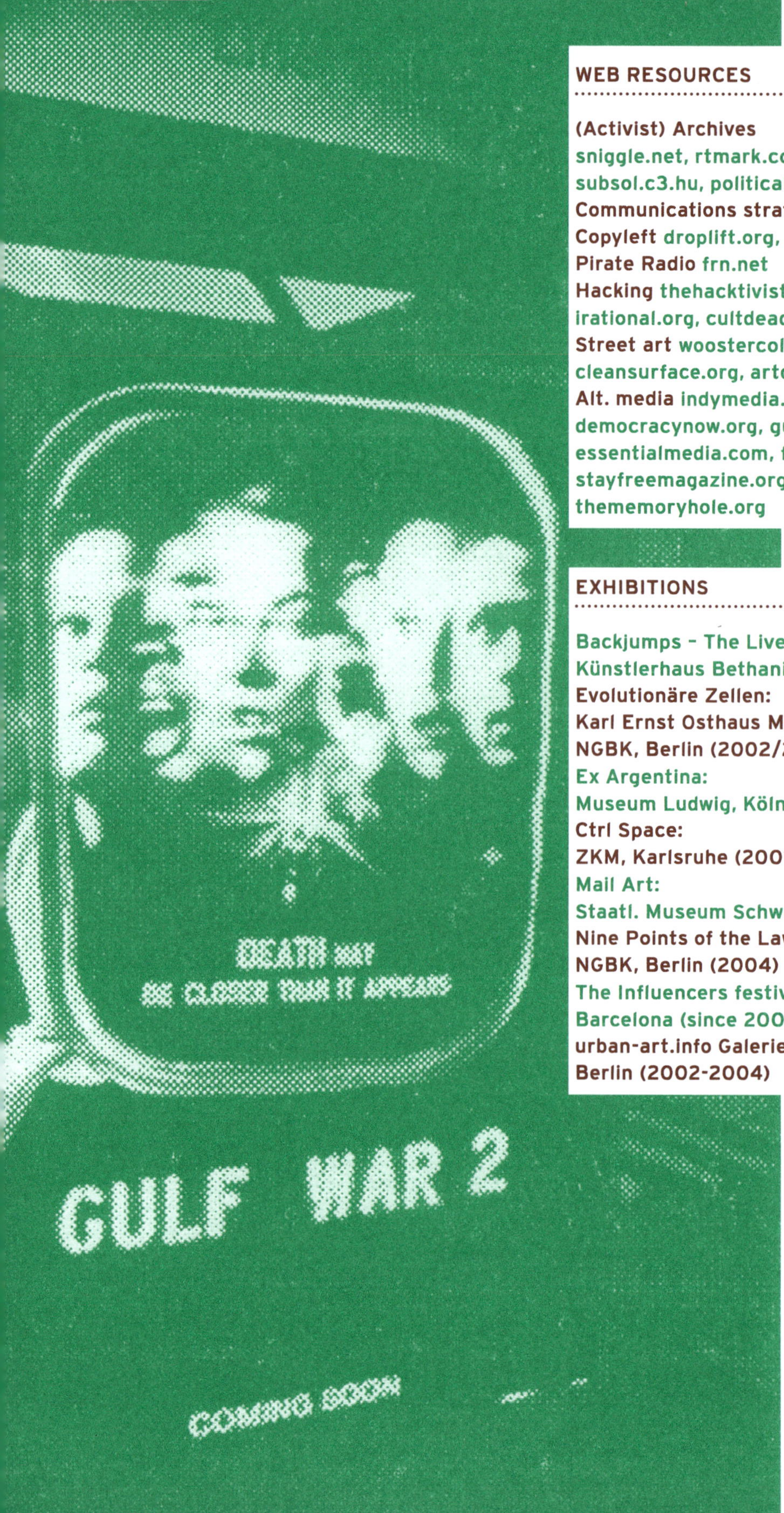

WEB RESOURCES

(Activist) Archives
sniggle.net, rtmark.com, contrast.org, subsol.c3.hu, politicalgraphics.org
Communications strategies memefest.org
Copyleft droplift.org, plagiarist.org, detritus.net
Pirate Radio frn.net
Hacking thehacktivist.com, thing.net, irational.org, cultdeadcow.com
Street art woostercollective.com, cleansurface.org, artcrimes.com, ekosystem.org
Alt. media indymedia.org, disinfopedia.org, democracynow.org, guerrillanews.com, essentialmedia.com, frontwheeldrive.com, stayfreemagazine.org, whitedot.org, thememoryhole.org

EXHIBITIONS

Backjumps – The Live Issue:
Künstlerhaus Bethanien, Berlin (2003)
Evolutionäre Zellen:
Karl Ernst Osthaus Mueum, Hagen
NGBK, Berlin (2002/2005)
Ex Argentina:
Museum Ludwig, Köln (2004)
Ctrl Space:
ZKM, Karlsruhe (2001)
Mail Art:
Staatl. Museum Schwerin (1992)
Nine Points of the Law:
NGBK, Berlin (2004)
The Influencers festival, theinfluencers.org
Barcelona (since 2004)
urban-art.info Galerie
Berlin (2002-2004)

CDC > 45 / geocities.com/billboardcorrections (USA)

ESSAYS

Bureau of Public Secrets:
On Wielding the Subversive Scalpel (1970)
A User's Guide to Détournement (1970)
Craig Baldwin:
Ways and Means for Jamming Culture
in: othercinema.com
Critical Art Ensemble:
Electronic Civil Disobedience (1995)
David Cox:
Notes on Culture Jamming, in: nettime.org
Gareth Branwyn:
Jamming the Media, in: Black Hole (1992)
Geert Lovink:
Strategies for Media Activism (1997)
Geert Lovink, David Garcia:
The ABC of Tactical Media (1997)
Hakim Bey:
Poetic Terrorism
in: Temporary Autonomous Zone (1985/91)
Mark Dery:
CultureJamming
in: Open Magazine Pamphlet Series #25 (1993)
Peter Ackermann, Jack Duvall:
Otpor – a Case Study, in: A Force More Powerful /
A Century of Nonviolent Conflict (2001)
Stephen Downes:
Hacking Memes, in: First Monday, vol.4 (10/98)
Tom Holert (ed.):
Imageneering, in: Jahresring #47 (2000)
Umberto Eco:
Für eine semiologische Guerrilla
in: Über Gott und die Welt (1967)
Wiliam Burroughs:
The Electronic Revolution (1970)

BOOKS

Augusto Boal:
Theatre of the Oppressed (1979)
Legislative Theatre (1998)
Autonome Afrika-Gruppe, Luther Blissett,
Sonja Brünzels:
Handbuch der Kommunikationsguerrilla (2001)
Bill Drummond & Jimmy Cauty (aka The KLF):
The Manual (1998)
Granier & Schütze:
Corazzu, Wandbilder in Sardinien (1979)
Guy Debord:
The Society of the Spectacle (1967)
Hakim Bey:
The Information War (1995)
Kalle Lasn:
Culture Jam (2001)
Manfred Spies:
Denkanschläge (1980)
Naomi Klein:
No Logo (2000)
Robbie Conal:
Art Attack (1992)
Saul Alinsky:
Rules for Radicals (1971)
The Biotic Baking Brigade:
The BBB Cookbook (2004)

IMAGE CREDITS BY PAGE (IMAGE)

All images not listed here courtesy of the featured artists. For credits please see page legends. Copyrights may apply.

14(2): Rob Cockerham
19(2): Marine Detroux
24-25: Jürgen Grosse, urban-art.info
28-31 (backgr.): Peter Kenner
46(2): David Gross
50: Tim Cole, snappytim.com
60, 72-74: London RTS (photographers unknown)
75(3): Scott Beale/Laughing Squid
80-81 (backgr.): EPIC.org
88: Yomango (COPYLEFT)
89(1): Las Agencias (COPYLEFT)
89(2): Pieter Hugo
102-103: Rev. Billy (photographer unknown)
107: Matthias Lüdecke
10-11, 18, 19(1), 23(3), 51, 52, 54, 97(4), 113, 118(1), 126(1), 127, 129(3,4), 135, 138-139: Ake Rudolf
15(2), 16, 20, 36(1,2), 42(1), 46(1), 58(2), 62, 92(1,2): Photographers unknown

CREDITS

Concept, research, content editing, graphic design & illustrations:
Ake Rudolf
print-graphics.de

Pre-press: Ake Rudolf
Production: Christopher D Salyers
Artwork scans: Repro Ringel, Berlin

Library of Congress Control Number: 2007930511

Printed and bound in Hong Kong through Asia Pacific Offset

10 9 8 7 6 5 4 3 2 1 First Edition

Mark Batty Publisher
36 W 37th St, Penthouse
New York, NY 10018

www.markbattypublisher.com

ISBN: 0-9790486-9-9
ISBN-13: 978-0-9790486-9-2

Distributed outside North America by:
Thames & Hudson Ltd
181A High Holborn
London WC1V 7QX
United Kingdom
Tel: 00 44 20 7845 5000
Fax: 00 44 20 7845 5055
www.thameshudson.co.uk